Teaching Languages to Young Learners

CAMBRIDGE LANGUAGE TEACHING LIBRARY

A series covering central issues in language teaching and learning, by authors who have expert knowledge in their field.

In this series:

Affect in Language Learning *edited by Jane Arnold*

Approaches and Methods in Language Teaching *by Jack C. Richards and Theodore S. Rodgers*

Beyond Training *by Jack C. Richards*

Classroom Decision-Making *edited by Michael Breen and Andrew Littlejohn*

Collaborative Action Research for English Language Teachers *by Anne Burns*

Collaborative Language Learning and Teaching *edited by David Nunan*

Communicative Language Teaching *by William Littlewood*

Designing Tasks for the Communicative Classroom *by David Nunan*

Developing Reading Skills *by Françoise Grellet*

Developments in English for Specific Purposes *by Tony Dudley-Evans and Maggie Jo St. John*

Discourse Analysis for Language Teachers *by Michael McCarthy*

Discourse and Language Education *by Evelyn Hatch*

English for Academic Purposes *by R.R. Jordan*

English for Specific Purposes *by Tom Hutchinson and Alan Waters*

Establishing Self-Access *by David Gardner and Lindsay Miller*

Foreign and Second Language Learning *by William Littlewood*

Language Learning in Intercultural Perspective *edited by Michael Byram and Michael Fleming*

The Language Teaching Matrix *by Jack C. Richards*

Language Test Construction and Evaluation *by J. Charles Alderson, Caroline Clapham, and Dianne Wall*

Learner-centredness as Language Education *by Ian Tudor*

Managing Curricular Innovation *by Numa Markee*

Materials Development in Language Teaching *edited by Brian Tomlinson*

Psychology for Language Teachers *by Marion Williams and Robert L. Burden*

Research Methods in Language Learning *by David Nunan*

Second Language Teacher Education *edited by Jack C. Richards and David Nunan*

Society and the Language Classroom *edited by Hywel Coleman*

Teacher Learning in Language Teaching *edited by Donald Freeman and Jack C. Richards*

Teaching the Spoken Language *by Gillian Brown and George Yule*

Understanding Research in Second Language Learning *by James Dean Brown*

Vocabulary: Description, Acquisition and Pedagogy *edited by Norbert Schmitt and Michael McCarthy*

Vocabulary, Semantics, and Language Education *by Evelyn Hatch and Cheryl Brown*

Voices from the Language Classroom *edited by Kathleen M. Bailey and David Nunan*

Teaching Languages to Young Learners

Lynne Cameron

CAMBRIDGE
UNIVERSITY PRESS

PUBLISHED BY THE PRESS SYNDICATE OF THE UNIVERSITY OF CAMBRIDGE
The Pitt Building, Trumpington Street, Cambridge CB2 1RP, United Kingdom

CAMBRIDGE UNIVERSITY PRESS
The Edinburgh Building, Cambridge CB2 2RU, UK
40 West 20th Street, New York, NY 10011–4211, USA
10 Stamford Road, Oakleigh, VIC 3166, Australia
Ruiz de Alarcón 13, 28014 Madrid, Spain

http://www.cambridge.org

First published 2001

Printed in the United Kingdom at the University Press, Cambridge

Typeset in Sabon 10/12 pt   CE

A catalogue record for this book is available from the British Library

ISBN 0 521 77325 3 Hardback
ISBN 0 521 77434 9 Paperback

For Nick and Neil

Contents

Preface   *page* xi
Acknowledgements   xvi

1   **Children learning a foreign language**   1
1.1   Taking a learning-centred perspective   1
1.2   Piaget   2
1.3   Vygotsky   5
1.4   Bruner   8
1.5   From learning to language learning   11
1.6   Advantages to starting young with foreign languages   16
1.7   The foreign language: describing the indivisible   17
1.8   Summary of key learning principles   19

2   **Learning language through tasks and activities**   21
2.1   The task as an environment for learning   21
2.2   Task demands   22
2.3   Task support   25
2.4   Balancing demands and support   26
2.5   The importance of language learning goals   28
2.6   Defining 'task' for young learner classrooms   29
2.7   Stages in a classroom task   31
2.8   Hani's Weekend: Possible preparation and follow-up
      activities   32
2.9   Task-as-plan and task-in-action   35

3   **Learning the spoken language**   36
3.1   Learning the spoken language: guiding principles   36
3.2   Discourse and discourse events   37
3.3   Meaning first   38
3.4   Analysis of a task-in-action   42
3.5   Discourse skills development in childhood   51

Contents

3.6	Effective support for children's foreign language discourse skills	58
3.7	Short activities for learning the spoken language	60
3.8	Supporting the spoken language with written language	66
3.9	Using dialogues	68
3.10	Summary	70
4	**Learning words**	**72**
4.1	Introduction	72
4.2	Vocabulary development in children's language learning	73
4.3	Organisation of words in a language	81
4.4	Learning and teaching vocabulary	83
4.5	Children's vocabulary learning strategies	92
4.6	Summary	94
5	**Learning grammar**	**96**
5.1	A place for grammar?	96
5.2	Different meanings of 'grammar'	98
5.3	Development of the internal grammar	101
5.4	A learning-centred approach to teaching grammar: background	105
5.5	Principles for learning-centred grammar teaching	110
5.6	Teaching techniques for supporting grammar learning	111
5.7	Summary	121
6	**Learning literacy skills**	**123**
6.1	Introduction	123
6.2	Literacy skills in English	124
6.3	Factors affecting learning to read in English as a foreign language	134
6.4	Starting to read and write in English as a foreign language	139
6.5	Continuing to learn to read	150
6.6	Developing reading and writing as discourse skills	154
6.7	Summary and conclusion	157
7	**Learning through stories**	**159**
7.1	Stories and themes as holistic approaches to language teaching and learning	159
7.2	The discourse organisation of stories	160
7.3	Language use in stories	163
7.4	Quality in stories	166
7.5	Choosing stories to promote language learning	167

7.6	Ways of using a story	169
7.7	Developing tasks around a story	175
7.8	Summary	179
8	**Theme-based teaching and learning**	**180**
8.1	Issues around theme-based teaching	180
8.2	Theme-based teaching of a foreign language	181
8.3	Planning theme-based teaching	184
8.4	Learning language through theme-based teaching	191
8.5	Increasing target language use in theme-based teaching	195
8.6	Summary	197
9	**Language choice and language learning**	**199**
9.1	Introduction	199
9.2	Patterns of first language use in foreign language classrooms	200
9.3	Dynamics of language choice and use	205
9.4	Taking responsibility, making choices	209
9.5	Summary	213
10	**Assessment and language learning**	**214**
10.1	Issues in assessing children's language learning	214
10.2	Principles for assessing children's language learning	218
10.3	Key concepts in assessment	222
10.4	Teacher assessment of language learning	228
10.5	Self-assessment and learner autonomy	233
10.6	Use of assessment information	238
10.7	Messages from assessment	240
11	**Issues around teaching children a foreign language**	**241**
11.1	Review of ideas	241
11.2	The need for research	242
11.3	The need to develop pedagogy	243
11.4	Teaching foreign languages to children	246
	References	247
	Index	256

Preface

This is a book about teaching that puts learning in the centre of the frame. Teaching and learning are not two sides of the same coin, but are essentially different activities, although they both take place in the public arena of the classroom. This book aims to help readers to make teaching more effective, by attending to learning and the inner mental world of the learner, and by then understanding how classroom activities and teacher decisions can create, or limit, children's opportunities for learning.

Teaching foreign languages to young children, which in this book will mean those between five and twelve years of age, has been happening for a long time; in many African and Asian countries, primary children have long been taught French or English as preparation for their use as a medium of instruction. In Europe and South America, the last ten years have seen an explosion of English classes, both in state systems and in private language schools. While the recent surge of interest has led to the publication of methodology books (e.g. Brewster *et al.* 1992; Dunn 1984; Halliwell 1992; Moon 2000; Phillips 1994; Scott and Ytreberg 1990), an accompanying debate about theoretical and research issues has been largely absent (but see Rixon 1999, some chapters of Kennedy and Jarvis 1991, and Brumfit, Moon and Tongue 1991). This book aims to provide teachers, and trainers of teachers, of foreign languages to young learners with a useful and workable theoretical framework and set of principles in which they can embed and develop their practice. In that it can be said to be initiating a much needed process of developing an applied linguistics for teaching foreign languages to young learners.

The professionalism of teachers of young learners requires an underpinning of theoretical knowledge that can help counteract prevalent misunderstandings of the job. These misunderstandings are not just annoying but they may contribute, I believe, to a continuing devaluation of teaching languages at primary level. Theorising the teaching of young learners has an important role to play in complexifying oversimplifications about working with children and thereby increasing the quality of foreign language education.

Misunderstandings about teaching young learners (1): *teaching children is straightforward*

In many societies, teaching children is seen as an extension of mothering rather than as an intellectual enterprise. Teachers at primary level are then often given less training, lower status, and lower pay, than their colleagues in the same educational system who teach teenagers or adults.

Children do have a less complicated view of the world than older children and adults, but this fact does not imply that teaching children is simple or straightforward. On the contrary, the teacher of children needs to be highly skilled to reach into children's worlds and lead them to develop their understandings towards more formal, more extensive and differently organised concepts. Primary teachers need to understand how children make sense of the world and how they learn; they need skills of analysing learning tasks and of using language to teach new ideas to groups and classes of children.

Teaching languages to children needs all the skills of the good primary teacher in managing children and keeping them on task, plus a knowledge of the language, of language teaching, and of language learning.

Misunderstandings about teaching young learners (2): *children only need to learn simple language*

It is also misleading to think that children will only learn simple language, such as colours and numbers, nursery rhymes and songs, and talking about themselves. Of course, if that is all they are taught, that will be all that they can learn. But children can always do more than we think they can; they have huge learning potential, and the foreign language classroom does them a disservice if we do not exploit that potential. Teachers often tell me that they worry about their 'slow learners'. When I talk to the children and watch lessons, I do see some children struggling with written English, but more often I see *'fast'* learners who already know most of the vocabulary in their text books and are keen to use their English to talk about international topics like football, pop music and clothes. Many children around the world, including those who live in isolated communities, become part of a global community of English language users when they watch television and use computers. Children need more than 'simple' language in the sense that only 'simple' topics are covered. Children are interested, or can be interested, in topics that are complicated (like dinosaurs and evolution), difficult (like how computers work), and abstract (like why people pollute their own environment or commit crimes). This is one reason why, in this book, I avoid taking a so-called 'child-centred' approach, and adopt instead a *learning-centred* approach, hoping to avoid patronising children by assuming limits to their interests.

There is a second way in which children need more than 'simple' language, and that is in terms of language structures. It is becoming clearer and clearer that first language development builds from a lexical base, and that grammar emerges from lexical and communicative development. Children use supposedly 'difficult' structures in their first languages as part of their lexical repertoires. In foreign language teaching, some syllabuses for primary children look rather like watered-down secondary syllabuses, which present children with just a few of the structures typically found early on at secondary level, such as the Present Continuous tense for describing current actions, Simple Present for describing habitual action, and prepositions. In this way, adding on primary level language teaching in a school system merely stretches out what has been done before over a longer period of time. It may be more fruitful to consider the possibility of primary level language teaching providing children with a broad discourse and lexical syllabus, that then changes focus as they move into later stages. If children learn a foreign language from the age of 5 or 6 until they leave school at about 16 years old, there is time to be imaginative with the syllabus and methodology, changing as the child changes and grows. This prospect should be of interest and concern to secondary sectors too; as language learning begins at younger and younger ages, children will arrive in secondary classrooms with much higher and more diverse levels of the foreign language than teachers will have been accustomed to.

The organisation of the book

The book starts with a review of learning theories and language learning research that offer insights in how to think about young children learning a foreign language (FL). A central principle for teaching young learners is that children should be supported in constructing *meaning* for every activity and language use in the FL classroom, and that understanding is essential for effective learning. From this, the second chapter focuses on tasks and activities, and the language learning opportunities they create. It develops a set of principles and a framework that teachers can use to analyse language teaching tasks and activities from a learning perspective. Chapter 3 attends to the language that is the content of teaching, and starts from the premise that young learners will work mostly with the spoken language. Vocabulary and discourse are taken as offering the most meaningful ways into a foreign language, and children's use of these in the foreign language are discussed through analysis of classroom data from Norway. Different types of spoken language practice activities are described.

Chapter 4 takes vocabulary as a starting point and links vocabulary development in the foreign language to children's conceptual development. Grammar is the topic of Chapter 5; the place of grammar in young learner classrooms is discussed in terms of children's emergent understandings of the FL system and how activities can support this without confusing children by going beyond their cognitive capabilities at different ages.

Chapter 6 deals with literacy in the foreign language, with a particular focus on the early stages of learning to read. This is a complex area with little research evidence available, and suggestions for practice are made based on current thinking in L1 (first language) reading and theoretical analysis of cross-linguistic factors.

Chapters 7 and 8 consider the discourse-level approaches of stories and theme-based learning. They apply the ideas of earlier chapters, bringing them together to explore how these approaches can best help language learning. In Chapter 9, the sometimes controversial topic of the use of the mother tongue and target language in the FL classroom is tackled from a learning-centred viewpoint. By looking at the functions of language use, I suggest how teachers might switch between languages with the deliberate aim of supporting language development.

Chapter 10 identifies issues in the assessment of FL learning by children, and deals in some depth with classroom-based assessment. The final chapter returns to the big issues in teaching young learners, some of which have knock-on impact on language teaching more generally. I set out an agenda for curriculum design, for research into early language learning, and for further theory development, hoping that this will help develop this new and exciting field further.

A note on *which* language is the foreign language is needed. My own foreign language teaching experience is restricted to English, as will be obvious from the data and examples used in the book. Much of the book will be applicable to the teaching of other languages to children, and where this is the case, I talk more generally in terms of 'the foreign language'. In some sections that involve language-specific analysis, the discussions will apply only to English: for example, in Chapter 6 where literacy in English is explored. I apologise for being unable to offer alternatives to English at these points and trust that those interested in the teaching of languages other than English will carry out analyses of these languages to fill the gap. The differences between English and other languages that emerge in this process will be important for the development of language teaching.

Teachers of young learners may, I suspect, have more fun, as well as more frustration, than teachers of older learners. Throughout my life in education I have found that working with children continually surprises and offers new perspectives, even on the most profound or theoretical ideas. I hope that theorising and developing the teaching of young learners may likewise challenge and offer new ways of thinking to longer-established areas of applied linguistics and language teaching.

Acknowledgements

I would like to thank all those teachers in Malaysia, Norway, Malta, the Sultanate of Oman, and many other countries, who have shared their classrooms and ideas with me over the years. Their commitment and enthusiasm has motivated me to write this book.

I would like to acknowledge the debt I owe to colleagues at the University of Leeds, particularly Jennifer Jarvis; I have learnt much from working with her on young learners' courses. She highlighted for me the importance of Margaret Donaldson's work on children's views on intention and purpose that are developed in Chapter 1. The ideas in Chapter 2 on task support and demands benefited greatly from working with Jayne Moon and others. Thanks also to Mickey Bonin at Cambridge University Press for his support and perceptive advice.

The publishers and I are grateful to the following copyright owners for permission to reproduce copyright material: Ministry of Education, the Sultanate of Oman for *Hani's Weekend* in Chapter 2; NFS Forlaget (Norway) and WSOY (Finland) for the animal pictures in Chapter 3; Penguin Books for the pictures and text from *Dinosaurs* by Michael Foreman in Chapter 7; Pearson Education for the figure from *Teaching Primary Children English* by S. Halliwell; Cambridge University Press for *Cambridge English For Schools* by Andrew Littlejohn and Diane Hicks; *Playway to English* by Günter Gerngross and Herbert Puchta.

1 Children learning a foreign language

1.1 Taking a learning-centred perspective

What is different about teaching a foreign language to children, in contrast to teaching adults or adolescents? Some differences are immediately obvious: children are often more enthusiastic and lively as learners. They want to please the teacher rather than their peer group. They will have a go at an activity even when they don't quite understand why or how. However, they also lose interest more quickly and are less able to keep themselves motivated on tasks they find difficult. Children do not find it as easy to use language to talk about language; in other words, they do not have the same access as older learners to metalanguage that teachers can use to explain about grammar or discourse. Children often seem less embarrassed than adults at talking in a new language, and their lack of inhibition seems to help them get a more native-like accent. But these are generalisations which hide the detail of different children, and of the skills involved in teaching them. We need to unpack the generalisations to find out what lies underneath as characteristic of children as language learners. We will find that important differences do arise from the linguistic, psychological and social development of the learners, and that, as a result, we need to adjust the way we think about the language we teach and the classroom activities we use. Although conventional language teaching terms like 'grammar' and 'listening' are used in connection with the young learner classroom, understanding of what these mean *to the children who are learning them* may need to differ from how they are understood in mainstream language teaching.

In the learning-centred perspective taken in this book, knowledge about children's learning is seen as central to effective teaching. Successful lessons and activities are those that are tuned to the learning needs of pupils, rather than to the demands of the next text-book unit, or to the interests of the teacher. I distinguish a *learning*-centred perspective from '*learner*-centred' teaching. Learner-centred teaching places the child at the centre of teacher thinking and curriculum planning. While this is a great improvement on placing the subject or the curriculum at the centre, I have found that it is not enough. In centring on the child, we risk losing sight of what it is we are trying to do in schools, and of the enormous potential that lies beyond the child.

Imagine a child standing at the edge of a new country that represents new ideas and all that can be learnt; ahead of the child are paths through valleys and forests, mountains to be climbed and cities to be explored. The child, however, may not be aware of the vast possibilities on offer, and, being a child, may either be content with the first stream or field s/he comes across, or may rush from one new place to the next without stopping to really explore any. If a teacher's concern is centred on the child, there is a temptation to stay in that first place or to follow the child. I have seen too many classrooms where learners are enjoying themselves on intellectually undemanding tasks but failing to learn as much as they might. The time available in busy school timetables for language teaching is too short to waste on activities that are fun but do not maximise learning. The teacher has to do what the child may not be able to do: to keep in sight the longer view, and move the child towards increasingly demanding challenges, so that no learning potential is wasted. A learning-centred perspective on teaching will, I believe, help us to do that more effectively.

In this chapter I give an overview of theory and research relevant to children's language learning. The field of teaching young learners, particularly in teaching English, has expanded enormously in the last 10 years but is only just beginning to be researched. We need therefore to draw on work from beyond language classrooms: in child development, in learning theory, in first language development, and in the development of a second language in bilingual contexts. Implications for teaching young learners are taken from each of these and used to establish guiding principles and a theoretical framework to be developed in the rest of the book. I begin with the work of two of the major theorists in developmental psychology, Piaget and Vygotsky, highlighting key ideas from their work that can inform how we think of the child as a language learner.

1.2 Piaget

1.2.1 The child as active learner

Piaget's concern was with how young children function in the world that surrounds them, and how this influences their mental development. The child is seen as continually interacting with the world around her/him, solving problems that are presented by the environment. It is through taking action to solve problems that learning occurs. For example, a very young child might encounter the problem of how to get food from her bowl into her mouth. In solving the problem, with a spoon or with fingers, the child learns the muscle control and direction-finding needed to feed herself. The knowledge that results from such action is not imitated or in-born, but is *actively constructed* by the child.

What happens early on with concrete objects, continues to happen in the mind, as problems are confronted internally, and action taken to solve them or think them through. In this way, *thought is seen as deriving from action*; action is internalised, or carried out mentally in the imagination, and in this way thinking develops. Piaget gives a much less important role to language in cognitive development than does Vygotsky. It is action, rather than the development of the first language which, for Piaget, is fundamental to cognitive development.

Piagetian psychology differentiates two ways in which development can take place as a result of activity: *assimilation* and *accommodation*. Assimilation happens when action takes place without any change to the child; accommodation involves the child adjusting to features of the environment in some way. Returning to the example of feeding, let's imagine what might happen when a child, who has learnt to use a spoon, is presented with a fork to eat with. She may first use the fork in just the same way as the spoon was used; this is assimilation of the new tool to existing skills and knowledge. When the child realises that the prongs of the fork offer new eating opportunities – spiking food rather than just 'spooning' it – accommodation occurs; the child's actions and knowledge adapt to the new possibility and something new is created. These two adaptive processes, although essentially different, happen together. Assimilation and accommodation are initially adaptive processes of behaviour, but they become processes of thinking. Accommodation is an important idea that has been taken into second language learning under the label 'restructuring', used to refer to the re-organisation of mental representations of a language (McLaughlin 1992). We will encounter it again when we consider the development of grammar.

From a Piagetian viewpoint, a child's thinking develops as gradual growth of knowledge and intellectual skills towards a final stage of formal, logical thinking. However, gradual growth is punctuated with certain fundamental changes, which cause the child to pass through a series of stages. At each stage, the child is capable of some types of thinking but still incapable of others. In particular, the Piagetian end-point of development – thinking that can manipulate formal abstract categories using rules of logic – is held to be unavailable to children before they reach 11 years of age or more.

The experimental studies used to support Piaget's theories have been criticised for not being sufficiently child-friendly, and for underestimating what children are capable of. In a series of ingenious experiments, Margaret Donaldson and her colleagues have convincingly shown that when appropriate language, objects and tasks are used, very young children are capable of many of the ways of thinking that Piaget held too advanced for them, including formal, logical thought (Donaldson 1978). These results undermine some of Piaget's theoretical views, particularly the notion of discrete stages and the idea that children cannot do certain things if they have not yet 'reached' that stage. An example of how stage theory can lead to restricting children's learning occurred in the UK in the late 1970s and early 1980s. Before children were allowed to start writing sentences, they had to complete sets of 'writing readiness' activities that worked on part-skills. In spending so long on writing patterns and bits of letter shapes, they were missing out on the more holistic experiences that also help children understand the purposes of writing as communication.

An important dimension of children's lives that Piaget neglects is the *social*; it is the child on his or her own in the world that concerns him, rather than the child in communication with adults and other children. As we will see, Vygotsky's ideas give a much greater priority to social interaction.

1.2.2 Implications of Piagetian theory for language learning

The child as sense-maker

We can take from Piaget the very important idea of the child as an active learner and thinker, constructing his or her own knowledge from working with objects or ideas. Donaldson's work emphasises that

> (the child) *actively tries to make sense of the world* . . . asks questions, . . . wants to know . . . Also from a very early stage, the child has *purposes and intentions*: he wants *to do*. (Donaldson 1978: 86, my emphasis)

Children also seek out intentions and purposes in what they see other people doing, bringing their knowledge and experience to their attempts to make sense of other people's actions and language. Realising that children are active '*sense-makers*', but that their sense-making is limited by their experience, is a key to understanding how they respond to tasks and activities in the language classroom that we will use throughout this book.

The world as offering opportunities for learning

If we take Piaget's idea that children adapt through experiences with objects in their environment, and turn it around, we can see how that environment provides the setting for development through the opportunities it offers the child for action. Transferring this idea metaphorically to the abstract world of learning and ideas, we can think of the classroom and classroom activities as creating and offering opportunities to learners for learning. This view coincides with 'ecological' thinking that sees events and activities as offering *affordances* or opportunities for use and interaction that depend on who is involved (Gibson 1979): for example, to a human being, a tree 'affords' shelter from the rain or firewood, to a bird, the same tree 'affords' a nest site or buds to eat.

1.3 Vygotsky

1.3.1 The child as social

Vygotsky's views of development differ from Piaget's in the importance he gives to language and to other people in the child's world. Although Vygotsky's theory is currently most noted for his central focus on the social, and modern developments are often labelled 'sociocultural theory', he did not neglect the individual or individual cognitive development. The development of the child's first language in the second year of life is held to generate a fundamental shift in cognitive development. Language provides the child with a new tool, opens up new opportunities for doing things and for organising information through the use of words as symbols. Young children can often be heard talking to themselves and organising themselves as they carry out tasks or play, in what is called private speech. As children get older they speak less and less aloud, and differentiate between social speech for others and 'inner speech', which continues to play an important role in regulating and controlling behaviour (Wertsch 1985). Adults sometimes resort to speaking aloud when faced with a tricky task, like finding the way to an unfamiliar place, verbalising to help themselves think and recall: *Turn left then right at the roundabout . . .*

In considering the early speech of infants and its development into language, Vygotsky (1962) distinguishes the outward talk and what is happening in the child's mind. The infant begins with using single words, but these words convey whole messages: when a child says *juice*, s/he may mean *I want some more juice* or *my juice has spilt*. As the child's language develops, the whole undivided thought message can be broken down into smaller units and expressed by putting together words that are now units of talk.

Underlying Vygotskyan theory is the central observation that

5

development and learning take place in a social context, i.e. in a world full of other people, who interact with the child from birth onwards. Whereas for Piaget the child is an active learner alone in a world of objects, for Vygotsky the child is an active learner in a world full of other people. Those people play important roles in helping children to learn, bringing objects and ideas to their attention, talking while playing and about playing, reading stories, asking questions. In a whole range of ways, adults *mediate* the world for children and make it accessible to them. The ability to learn through instruction and mediation is characteristic of human intelligence. With the help of adults, children can do and understand much more than they can on their own. To illustrate this idea, let's return to the example of the baby learning to feed herself with a spoon. At some point in learning to use a spoon to eat with, the baby may be able to get the spoon in the food and can put a spoonful of food in her mouth, but cannot quite manage the middle step of filling the spoon with food. A helpful adult may assist the baby with the difficult part by putting his hand over the baby's and guiding it in filling the spoon. In this way, adult and child together achieve what the baby was unable to do by herself, and the baby receives some useful training in turning the spoon at the angle needed to get hold of the food. Before long the baby will master this step and can be left to do the whole feeding process by herself. The adult could have helped the baby in many different ways, including just doing it all to save time and mess! The kind of spoon-filling help, targeted at what the baby can nearly but not quite do herself, is seen as particularly useful in promoting development; filling the spoon with food was an action in the baby's *zone of proximal development* (or ZPD). We can note before we leave this example that parents are often very 'tuned-in' to their own children and know exactly what help is needed next, and that skilful teachers also manage to do this in a class of thirty or more different ZPDs.

Vygotsky used the idea of the ZPD to give a new meaning to 'intelligence'. Rather than measuring intelligence by what a child can do alone, Vygotsky suggested that intelligence was better measured by what a child can do with skilled help. Different children at the same point in development will make different uses of the same help from an adult. Take as an example seven or eight year olds learning to do arithmetic and perhaps meeting subtraction problems for the first time. For some pupils, a demonstration by the teacher using counting bricks may be all they need to grasp the idea and do other sums of the same type. Others will be able to do the same sum again but not be able to generalise to other sums. In foreign language learning, we might imagine children listening to the teacher model a new question: *Do you like swimming?* and being encouraged to ask similar questions. One child may be able to use other phrases he has learnt previously and say *Do you like drinking orange juice?* whereas another may be able to repeat *Do you like swimming?* and yet another would have trouble repeating it accurately. In each case, the ZPD, or what the child can do with the help of the adult is different; this, Vygotsky suggested, is a more useful measure of intelligence or ability.

Learning to do things and learning to think are both helped by interacting with an adult. Vygotsky saw the child as first doing things in a social context, with other people and language helping in various ways, and gradually shifting away from reliance on others to independent action and thinking. This shift from thinking aloud and talking through what is being done, to thinking inside the head, is called *internalisation*. Wertsch (1985) emphasises that internalisation for Vygotsky was not just a transfer but also a transformation; being able to think about something is qualitatively different from being able to do it. In the internalising process, the *interpersonal*, joint talk and joint activity, later becomes *intrapersonal*, mental action by one individual.

1.3.2 Implications of Vygotskyan theory for language learning

Words and meanings

The importance of the *word* as unit has been downplayed by those who have developed Vygotsky's theories (e.g. Lantolf 2000). However, I believe that words do have a special significance for children learning a new language. The word is a recognisable linguistic unit for children in their first language and so they will notice words in the new language. Often too we teach children words in the new language by showing them objects that they can see and touch, and that have single word labels in the first language. From their earliest lessons, children are encouraged to think of the new language as a set of words, although of course this may not be the only way they think of it.

The importance of the word as unit is underscored by recent research into word frequency and use undertaken by corpus linguists, and the discovery that much of our knowledge of our first language can be accounted for by the information we build up over time about statistical probabilities of which words are used with which other words.

The zone of proximal development

Many of Vygotsky's ideas will help in constructing a theoretical framework for teaching foreign languages to children. In deciding what a teacher can do to support learning, we can use the idea that the adult tries to mediate *what next it is the child can learn*; this has applications in both lesson planning and in how teachers talk to pupils minute by minute. In the next chapter I develop a framework for analysing classroom tasks that incorporates the notion of the ZPD. We can look at stages in tasks for how well they help a child to move in language skills from the interpersonal to the intrapersonal.

Learning as internalisation

The concept of internalisation will be used in later chapters to under-stand learning processes in the foreign language. The new language is first used meaningfully by teacher and pupils, and later it is transformed and internalised to become part of the individual child's language skills or knowledge

1.4 Bruner

1.4.1 Scaffolding and routines

For Bruner, language is the most important tool for cognitive growth, and he has investigated how adults use language to mediate the world for children and help them to solve problems (Bruner 1983, 1990). Talk that supports a child in carrying out an activity, as a kind of verbal version of the fine-tuned help given in the baby feeding example above, has been labelled *scaffolding* (Wood, Bruner and Ross 1976). In experi-ments with American mothers and children, parents who scaffolded tasks effectively for children did the following:

- they made the children interested in the task;
- they simplified the task, often by breaking it down into smaller steps;
- they kept the child on track towards completing the task by reminding the child of what the goal was;
- they pointed out what was important to do or showed the child other ways of doing parts of the tasks;
- they controlled the child's frustration during the task;
- they demonstrated an idealised version of the task.

Moreover, good scaffolding was tuned to the needs of the child and adjusted as the child became more competent. Scaffolding has been transferred to the classroom and teacher–pupil talk. Wood (1998) suggests that teachers can scaffold children's learning in various ways:

Table 1.1

Teachers can help children to	By
attend to what is relevant	suggesting
	praising the significant
	providing focusing activities
adopt useful strategies	encouraging rehearsal
	being explicit about organisation
remember the whole task and goals	reminding
	modelling
	providing part–whole activities

(from Wood 1998)

Each of these teaching strategies can be applied to language teaching. The notion of *helping children attend to what is important* will recur in various topics, and echoes discussions in English language teaching about 'noticing' (e.g. Schmidt 1990). In directing attention and in remembering the whole task and goals on behalf of the learner, the teacher is doing what children are not yet able to do for themselves. When they focus on some part of a task or the language they want to use, children may not be able to keep in mind the larger task or communicative aim because of limits to their attentional capacity. Between them, teacher and pupils manage the whole task, but the way in which the parts and aspects are divided up varies with age and experience. The teacher does most of the managing of joint engagement on a task.

Bruner has provided a further useful idea for language teaching in his notions of *formats and routines*. These are features of events that allow scaffolding to take place, and combine the security of the familiar with the excitement of the new. Bruner's most useful example of a routine is of parents reading stories to their children from babyhood onwards (see also Garton and Pratt 1998). I will develop it at some length, both because it clarifies the important idea of routines, and also because it will be used in later discussions of the role of stories in language classrooms.

In situations where parents read bedtime stories to their children (Bruner researched middle-class American families), the routine that is followed at the same time each day goes something like this: the child sits on the parent's lap with a large picture story book, and parent and child turn the pages together. As the child gets older, the type of book changes and the roles of adult and child change, but the basic format remains. When action and language use are analysed, another layer of routine emerges. With very young children, adults do most of the talking, describing the characters and objects in the pictures and involving the child with instructions, tag questions and talk about salient images, such as *Look at the clown. He's got a big nose, hasn't he?* The child can be further involved by being asked to point to known pictures: *Where's the clown? and where's his big nose?* As the child learns to talk, so the child's verbal involvement increases as she or he joins in naming pictures and events. Over any short period of time, the language used by the parent includes a lot of repetition, and uses finely tuned language that the child, helped by the pictures, can make sense of. The book-reading event is scaffolded by the adult to let the child participate at the level he or she is capable of. The repeated language allows the child to predict what is coming and thus to join in, verbally or non-verbally.

At a later stage, when the five or six year old child is beginning to read, the format may be much the same, with the routine and language more advanced. At this stage, the parent may read the story aloud as well as ask questions about the pictures. The child may finish sentences, recalling how the story ends from memory of previous reading events. Later still, the child may read the story to the parent.

Notice how novelty and change are incorporated alongside the familiar security of the routine, and how the child can participate at an increasingly more demanding level as the parent reduces the scaffolding. Again, language use is predictable within the routine, but there is a 'space' within which the child can take over and do the language her/himself. This *space for growth* ideally matches the child's zone of proximal development. Bruner suggests that these routines and their adjustment provide an important site for language and cognitive development.

1.4.2 Routines in the language classroom

Transferring to the language classroom, we can see how classroom routines, which happen every day, may provide opportunities for language development. One immediate example would be in classroom management, such as giving out paper and scissors for making activities. As a routine, this would always take basically the same form: for example, the teacher talking to the whole class, organising distribution, perhaps using children as monitors; the scissors might be kept in a box, the paper in a cupboard. The language used would suit the task and the pupils' level; so early stage learners might hear, *George, please give out the scissors. Margaret, please give out the paper.* The context and the familiarity of the event provide an opportunity for pupils to predict meaning and intention, but the routine also offers a way to add variation and novelty that can involve more complex language: *Sam, please ask everybody if they want white paper or black paper*, or *Give out a pair of scissors to each group*. As the language becomes more complex, the support to meaning that comes from the routine and the situation helps the children to continue to understand. The increased complexity of language provides a space for language growth; if the new language is within a child's ZPD, she or he will make sense of it and start the process of internalising it.

Routines then can provide opportunities for meaningful language development; they allow the child to actively make sense of new language from familiar experience and provide a space for language growth. Routines will open up many possibilities for developing language skills.

1.5 From learning to language learning

1.5.1 First, second and foreign languages

The first sections of this chapter have reviewed important theories of learning that yield valuable tools for theorising the teaching of languages to young learners. They have been largely concerned with the learning of children in general rather than the learning of language. In the second half of the chapter, I review theory and research that are relevant to the learning of foreign languages by children.

To help us understand the nature of language learning, we can draw on studies of first language acquisition and from North American research into second language development in children. However, the language learning that is studied in these contexts is different in important ways from the learning of a foreign language. When we make use of theory and empirical research from these other situations, we need always to do so with care, extracting what is transferable, and if possible, carrying out research to check that it does transfer.

The central characteristics of *foreign language learning* lie in the *amount and type of exposure* to the language: there will be very little experience of the language outside the classroom, and encounters with the language will be through several hours of teaching in a school week. In the case of a global language like English, however, even very young children will encounter the language in use on video, TV, computers and film. What they might not be exposed to is 'street' use, i.e. people using the language for everyday life purposes all around them, as might happen in a second language immersion context such as learning French or English in Canada, or an additional language context, such as children of Pakistani heritage in England. In foreign language teaching, there is an onus on the teacher to provide exposure to the language and to provide opportunities for learning through classroom activities.

The cultural 'foreign-ness' of countries in which the language is a national language, e.g. Australia, USA or UK for English; France or Canada for French, may be brought into the learning of the language, or it may be considered irrelevant because the motivation for teaching the language is to use it as a lingua franca between non-native speakers.

1.5.3 Learning the first language

It was thought until quite recently that by the age of 5, first language acquisition was largely complete. We have come to understand that this is not the case. Formal literacy skills are still in the early stages of development at five and six years of age, even though the beginnings of literacy can be traced back to experiences in infancy, such as listening to stories. Some structures in spoken language are acquired late because of their connection with the written language. In English, relative clauses are one example of this: Perera (1984) reports that children of 11 years tend not to use relative clauses beginning with *whose*, or preposition + relative pronoun e.g. *in which*. She suggests that this is because such structures occur mainly in written text and so children have little experience of them in their early years. Children also have problems using words that express logical relations between ideas, like cause and effect. The full use of co-ordinators, including *but* and *yet*, is still to be developed after the age of 11 years, and clauses introduced with *although* or *unless* can cause problems even for 15 year olds. The meanings of these linking terms are logically complicated and correct use requires the child to have developed both logical understanding and the language in which to express it. If young first language children find such aspects of English difficult then there seems little reason for including them on syllabuses for child learners of English as a foreign language, and the same would be true for similar aspects of other languages.

Discourse skills in the first language continue to develop throughout the early school years. At 7 years of age, children are still acquiring the skills needed for extended discourse. In telling narratives, for example, children are still learning how to create thematic structure through language, and are still developing the full range of uses of pronouns and determiners (Karmiloff-Smith 1986; Snow 1996). Given the importance attached in the methodology literature to using stories in foreign language teaching (e.g. Wright 1997), teachers need to remember that children may still be finding it difficult to use pronouns correctly in their first language to control reference to characters across a sequence of events and plot actions, and not to demand unreasonable skills in the foreign language.

Important work from the USA is showing that first language proficiency does not develop as a single, global phenomenon, but that different domains of language use develop differently (Snow 1996). In a project to investigate the language development of children aged 14–32 months, language was measured across the linguistic domains of phonology, morphology, lexis, syntax, conversation and discourse, and have been shown to be largely independent. Extended discourse seems to develop differently from conversation. Furthermore, a connection has been found between children's early experiences with language use in their families, and their language development in various domains. In families where narratives are told around the dinner table, on topics such as what happened to parents at work or siblings at school, children develop narrative and discourse skills faster; children whose families use a wide vocabulary develop faster in the lexical domain.

One implication for teachers of foreign languages to young children is that children will come into foreign language learning at the earliest stages bringing with them differently developed skills and learning abilities in their first language. By the age of five, individual differences in language domains will be established and so, for example, some children will find it easier to learn vocabulary than others, or children with more developed conversational skills may transfer these to the new language more easily than others. From the same language lesson, it is likely that different children will learn different things, depending partly on what they find easier to learn. In Vygotskyan terms, it seems likely that a second or foreign language ZPD may not be global, but that different aspects of language will have different ZPDs.

1.5.2 Learning a second language

Age and second language learning

It has long been hypothesised that children learn a second language better than adults, and this is often used to support the early introduction of foreign language teaching. The Critical Period Hypothesis is the name given to the idea that young children can learn a second language particularly effectively before puberty because their brains are still able to use the mechanisms that assisted first language acquisition. The Critical Period Hypothesis holds that older learners will learn language differently after this stage and, particularly for accent, can never achieve the same levels of proficiency. While some empirical studies offer support for the Critical Period Hypothesis, other studies provide evidence that there is no such cut-off point for language learning. Lightbown and Spada (1999) present some of the evidence for and against the Critical Period Hypothesis, and remind us to attend to the different needs, motivations and contexts of different groups of learners. They suggest that where native-like proficiency in a second language is the goal, then learning benefits from an early start, but when the goal is communicative ability in a foreign language, the benefits of an early start are much less clear.

Further support for making this key distinction comes from a recent study into brain activity during language processing (Kim *et al.* 1997). This study discovered that the brain activity patterns of early bilinguals, who learn two languages at the same time from infancy, differ from those of learners who begin learning a language after about 7 or 8 years of age; different parts of the brain are used for language recall and activation. Foreign language learning of the sort we are concerned with is thus an essentially different mental activity from early simultaneous bilingualism and from L1 acquisition.

The influence of the first language on the second

The 'Competition Model' of linguistic performance is a theory that explains how first language learning may affect subsequent second or foreign language development (Bates and MacWhinney 1989). In this model, different languages have different ways of carrying meaning, and the particular ways in which a language encodes meaning act as 'cues' to interpreting the meaning of what is said. For example, word order in English is a very reliable and helpful cue that helps listeners identify Subject and Object, i.e. who is acting and on what. In a sentence like *the cat ate the snake*, the cat and the snake do not have endings that show which is the 'eater' (the agent or Subject of the verb) and which is the eaten (acted-on or Object). It is their position in the sentence, or the word order, that reveals this; we can tell that *the cat* is the Subject and does the eating because it comes before the verb, while *the snake*, which comes after the verb, has to be the Object. Other languages, such as Italian, do not have restrictions on word order in sentences, and so the order of the words does not offer as much information about meaning as in English; word order is a stronger cue in English than in Italian (Liu *et al.* 1992). All levels of language can provide cues, including lexis, morphology (word endings or prefixes) and phonology (the sound system of a language). Sometimes one source of information reinforces another, and sometimes they conflict, or are in competition, in which case the most reliable cue wins out. Studies carried out across different languages have led to the important conclusion that children become sensitive to the reliability of cues in their first language from early infancy (Bates *et al.* 1984). As babies, they learn to pay attention to particular cues which hold useful information for meaning. Later, if faced with trying to understand a second language, they will transfer these first language strategies to make sense of L2 sentences, trying to find information in familiar places. Where two languages make use of very different types of cues, the transfer of strategies from L1 to L2 may not be very fruitful. Learners may need to be helped to notice and pay attention to the salient cues of the new language. In the case of English, word order is most salient, but so too are word endings that show tense (e.g. *walk – ed*) and plurality (*shop – s*) (Slobin 1985).

Age and first language

The cue effect is compounded by an effect of age. In studies of immersion language learning, younger children (7–8 years) seem to pay more attention to sound and prosody (the 'music' of an utterance), whereas older children (12–14 years) are more attentive to cues of word order (Harley *et al.* 1995). Children are generally less able to give selective and prolonged attention to features of learning tasks than adults, and are more easily diverted and distracted by other pupils. When faced with talk in the new language, they try to understand it in terms of the grammar and salient cues of their first language and also pay particular attention to items of L2 vocabulary that they are familiar with (Harley 1994; Schmidt 1990). These findings will not surprise experienced primary teachers, but they give further empirical support to the idea that teachers can help learners by focusing their attention on useful sources of information in the new language, as also suggested by Bruner's scaffolding studies (section 1.4 above). Which cues need explicit attention will vary with the first language of the learners. How to help pupils do this will be considered in more detail in later chapters, but here I present *directing attention* as a key principle with many applications in the young learner classroom.

The competition model of understanding a second language, and empirical findings that support the view that first language experience influences second language use, remind us that in learning a foreign language, students are learning both *the whole and the parts*. In this case, the 'parts' are tiny aspects of grammar or phonology that are crucial in reaching a 'whole' interpretation.

Influence of teaching on second language learning

There is mounting evidence from foreign language learning contexts of the influence of teaching method on what is learnt. The range of language experiences that children get in their foreign language lessons is likely to influence how their language develops; for example, if lessons provide opportunities to participate in question and answer type talk then they will be good at that but not necessarily at other, more extended, types of talk. Mitchell and Martin (1997) document the different teaching styles and beliefs of teachers of French to 11 year old children (English L1), and show how this seems to result in children producing certain types of language rather than others. Weinert (1994) details how 11–13 year old learners of German (English L1) reproduce in their talk the language types used by their teachers.

Further research is needed into the extent of this teaching effect on language learning, and at what levels of specificity it operates (see also Chapter 5). Current knowledge reinforces an intuitively obvious notion: foreign language learners who depend on their teachers and texts for most of their exposure and input, will not, if this is restricted in type, develop across the full range of the foreign language. A particular aspect of this concerns extended discourse, i.e. talking at length, and later, writing at length. If, as seems to be the case from the first language research reported above, conversational skills develop independently of extended discourse skills, then we cannot assume that teaching children conversational language will lead to them being able to speak *at length* in the foreign language, but rather must work on the principle that if we want children to tell stories or recount events, they need to have experience of how this is done in the foreign language. *Modelling* of language use by teachers, already seen as an important step in scaffolding (section 1.4), needs further to be genre-specific.

1.6 Advantages to starting young with foreign languages

Many advantages are claimed for starting to learn a foreign language in the primary years; more evidence is needed to judge how far claims turn into reality. Experience in the UK twenty years ago found that language learning in primary schools was not as positive as expected, although in retrospect this seems likely to be due to how it was implemented and, in particular, to the lack of attention that planners paid to what would happen at secondary level, when FL teachers were faced with mixed classes of beginners and more advanced learners. The social, cultural and political issues around policies of teaching foreign languages early are complex and influence teaching and learning at classroom level. Comparative studies of different socio-political contexts would be useful in investigating these influences and their impact.

Published data on the outcomes of early language learning come from the North American experience with immersion teaching, where native speakers of English are placed in French-speaking nursery and infant schools, and vice versa (Harley and Swain 1994; Lightbown and Spada 1994; Harley *et al.* 1995). In these contexts, children who have an early start develop and maintain advantages in some, but not all, areas of language skills. Listening comprehension benefits most, with overall better outcomes for an earlier start; pronunciation also benefits in the longer term, but this is restricted to learning language in naturalistic contexts, and will not necessarily apply to school-based learning. Younger children learn the grammar of the L2 more slowly than older learners, so that although they start earlier with language learning they make slower progress, and overall gains are not straightforwardly linked to the time spent learning (Harley *et al.* 1995). Learning a second language through immersion differs from learning a foreign language as a subject lesson several times a week; immersion pupils study school subjects through the second language and thus have more exposure and more experience with the language. However, it is unlikely that the difference in quantity of language learning experience will affect the balance of benefits; in foreign language learning too, receptive skills are likely to remain ahead of productive skills, and grammatical knowledge, which is linked not just to language development but to cognitive development, is likely to develop more slowly for younger children.

1.7 The foreign language: describing the indivisible

In this section, I present a first dissection of the whole that is 'language' into the parts that comprise the content of teaching. In applied linguistics over the last decades, it has been common to divide language into 'the Four Skills': Listening, Speaking, Reading and Writing, and then to add Grammar, Vocabulary and Phonology to them. This division is not as logical as it may seem and has been challenged (Widdowson 1998). Some syllabuses also deal in Topics, Functions and Notions, describing language in terms of how it is used in communication rather than seeing it as a linguistic system or a set of skills.

Because children who start learning a foreign language very young may encounter nothing but the spoken language for several years, the customary division into the four skills seems somewhat inappropriate, and an alternative division of language has been attempted.

The first cut into the holism of language learning separates literacy skills from the rest, on the basis that learning to read and write in a foreign language presents distinct learning tasks that require teaching. I will argue that teachers need to plan and support literacy skills development informed by specific knowledge and understanding of literacy issues, although of course the learner will, and should, experience literacy development as integrated within spoken language development.

Having separated out literacy skills development from of the totality of the foreign language, what then remains is much wider than Speaking and Listening as perceived in secondary or adult language teaching. For young learners, spoken language is the medium through which the new language is encountered, understood, practised and learnt. Rather than oral skills being simply one aspect of learning language, the spoken form in the young learner classroom acts as the prime source and site of language learning. New language is largely introduced orally, understood orally and aurally, practised and automatised orally. My solution to the problem of how to divide up oral language learning comes from thinking about how children seek out meanings for themselves in language, and to focus on *words* and on *interaction*. For Vygotsky, words label concepts and are an entry point into thinking and networks of meaning. In language teaching terms, the development of words, their meanings and the links between them will be covered under the term Vocabulary.

Interaction will be labelled as Discourse skills, and in Chapter 3, will be further divided to reflect the distinction between conversational exchanges and longer stretches of talk that Snow's work in first language development has identified. Instead of thinking about children as 'doing Listening and Speaking', we will think about how they learn to interact in the foreign language. Classroom activities can also be seen and analysed as discourse in their own right.

Grammar will be seen as emerging from the space between words and discourse in children's language learning, and as being important in constructing and interpreting meaning accurately. The development of phonology is not considered separately in this book, since children seem to develop native-like accents without specific training through exposure to good models; it will, however, link into the development of spelling and rhyme (Chapter 6).

The organisational scheme for language is summarised in Figure 1.1. The carving up of language learning in this way seems to reflect reasonably well the real experience of young learners, and the structure of some, at least, of the course books written for them.

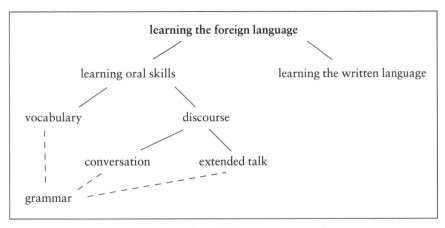

Figure 1.1 Dividing up 'language' for child foreign language learning

This division is, though, and can only ever be, an artificial breaking up of what grows through an 'organic' process in a child's mind. This is one reason why it is not always possible to predict what will be learnt from what is taught, and why attending to the *opportunities* offered by activities will be important.

1.8 Summary of key learning principles

The chapter concludes with a summary of the principles that have emerged as most important in thinking about young children learning a foreign language. Each of these will be used throughout the rest of the book as we consider concrete examples of what students are asked to do in lessons.

Children actively try to construct meaning

Children actively try to 'make sense', i.e. to find and construct a meaning and purpose for what adults say to them and ask them to do. They can only make sense in terms of their world knowledge, which is limited and partial. Teachers thus need to examine classroom activities from the child's point of view in order to assess whether pupils will understand what to do or will be able to make sense of new language.

Children need space for language growth

In both language and cognitive development, the ZPD or immediate potential of the child is of central importance for effective learning. Routines and scaffolding are two types of language-using strategies that seem to be especially helpful in making space for children's growth.

Language in use carries cues to meaning that may not be noticed

Children need skilled help in noticing and attending to aspects of the foreign language that carry meaning. Since they cannot benefit much from formal grammar, other ways of doing this have to be found.

Development can be seen as internalising from social interaction

Language can grow as the child takes over control of language used initially with other children and adults.

Children's foreign language learning depends on what they experience

There are important links between what and how children are taught, and what they learn. Within the ZPD, the broader and richer the language experience that is provided for children, the more they are likely to learn. Foreign language lessons often provide all or most of a child's experience of the language in use; if we want children to develop certain language skills, we need to ensure they have experiences in lessons that will build those skills.

The activities that happen in classrooms create a kind of 'environment' for learning and, as such, offer different kinds of opportunities for language learning. Part of teaching skill is to identify the particular opportunities of a task or activity, and then to develop them into learning experiences for the children. In the next chapter, the idea of identifying the language learning opportunities offered by classroom tasks is developed further.

2 Learning language through tasks and activities

2.1 The task as an environment for learning

In this chapter I set up a framework for analysing tasks from a learning perspective that takes account of young learners' social and cognitive development. Classroom tasks and activities are seen as the 'environment' or 'ecosystem' (van Geert 1995) in which the growth of skills in the foreign language takes place. The idea of 'task' will need to be adapted slightly from the way it is used in current 'task-based' approaches to language teaching, and will be given a (post-)Vygotskyan slant.

Our starting point in this chapter is children as (mentally) active learners, who will try to find a meaning and purpose for activities that are presented to them. Young learners work hard to make sense of what teachers ask them to do, and come to tasks with their own understandings of the purposes and expectations of adults. Studies of young children starting school have shown how much difference there often is between language use and activities at home and at school, but also how quickly children work out what is expected of them and how to fit into the new patterns of interaction (e.g. Tizard and Hughes 1984). We can predict that children will bring these abilities to their language lessons, and that this urge to find meaning and purpose can be a very helpful language learning tool for teachers to exploit. Unfortunately, even the most motivated child can have problems making sense of some of the activities in which they are asked to participate in their language lessons; the combined effect of the activity-type and new language can render everything just too mysterious. Teachers may not notice pupils' confusion because the children are anxious to please and may act *as if* they understand. For example, they may pick out and repeat key words from the teacher's language, giving an illusion of understanding, or they may persevere with a writing or matching task without really understanding what they are doing. Here again, we see the importance of a learning perspective that will go beyond a superficial evaluation of classroom activity, and give teachers tools for really checking on how much pupils are understanding and learning.

We begin by analysing the environment created by an activity in terms of *demands on learners* (in section 2.2) and *support for learning* (in section 2.3). In section 2.4 we see how learning opportunities can be deliberately constructed by adjusting the balance between demands and

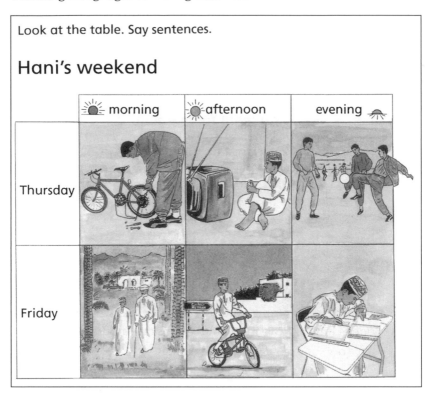

Look at the table. Say sentences.

Hani's weekend

*Figure 2.1 Hani's Weekend: an activity from 'Our World through English',
Activities Book 6E (B), p.18, for 11 year olds (Sultanate of Oman)*

support, and how, if teachers have clear language learning goals, this
can be done more effectively (section 2.5). Sections 2.6 and 2.7. set up a
task framework for young learner classrooms, first defining 'task', and
then showing how staging a task can help learning. In section 2.8, we
return to the classroom activity that starts the chapter, applying the task
framework to see how learning opportunities might be enhanced.

2.2 Task demands

I will use an activity to illustrate the first key points of the task
framework, returning in section 2.6 to define 'task' more precisely. The
activity in Figure 2.1 is taken from a course written for 11 year olds in
the Sultanate of Oman, who come to this book after learning English
for 3 years. The set of course materials, from which this particular
activity has been taken, has been carefully thought-out and structured
for the target audience. In its context of use, the activity is intended as

practice material, to supplement activities in the *Pupils' Book*, and to be used in conjunction with a *Teacher's Book*. I have removed the activity from its context in order to analyse its structure and its demands, and the support provided to meet those demands.

The basis for this speaking activity is a grid with 2 rows and 3 columns. This type of graphic is frequently found in foreign language materials as a prompt to speaking or writing practice. The rows represent the days of the weekend (the Islamic weekend is Thursday and Friday), and the columns show three times in the day: morning, after-noon and evening. Pupils are required to make up sentences using vocabulary and grammar they have already learnt, and the particular objective is to practise structures like *on Thursday afternoon* with the past tense, which has been focused on in preceding activities. Each box in the grid is supposed to prompt one sentence of the form:

Hani watched television on Thursday afternoon.

The original is nicely coloured and care has been taken to use activities familiar to pupils. For the moment, we will ignore the issue of how the teacher might use the course book in the lesson to get pupils started on this activity, and focus just on the *demands* placed on pupils when they try to make sense of the information given in the grid and use it to produce accurate sentences in English. We will also leave aside, for the time being, the question of whether this is an oral skills task or a grammar task (or both), and take a limited view of the goal of the task as the oral production of sentences, in order to take a learner's perspective on the text and visuals.

The grid must be 'read' in a particular way: times of day follow from left to right across the columns, and the days of the week go from top to bottom. As adults, we know this convention and use it automatically; children may not know the conventions so well, and graphical informa-tion may not be accessed as easily by children. In fact, the pupils for whom this was designed read and write their first language, Arabic, from right to left. So, in using the grid, they have to know, and remember to use, the 'English' convention of working from left to right across the page.

The pictures show boys involved in various activities; the title *'Hani's weekend'* suggests that Hani is the central character and he can be seen in each picture, although sometimes he is wearing his white *dishdasha* and sometimes a green track suit. A pupil must understand this in order for the grid and the task to make sense.

In each picture Hani is doing something, so that a further demand on the pupil is to *recognise* the action from the picture, and then *find the English words* for that action, e.g. *mend his bike*. The words must be *produced* in the past tense form: e.g. *watched*, even though there is nothing in the title or the grid to show that these things were done at some point in the past, rather than being planned for the future. The sentences are to be spoken aloud, so that a further demand beyond finding vocabulary and grammar is to *pronounce* words and find appropriate stress and intonation.

These demands on the pupil can be divided into two types of demand: cognitive and language, and are summarised below. *Cognitive demands* are those related to concepts, and to understanding of the world and other people. *Language demands* are those related to using the foreign language, and to uses of mother tongue in connection with learning the foreign language.

cognitive demands	~ understand the way the grid works to show times of actions ~ work left to right across columns and top to bottom from one row to next ~ understand that Hani appears in each picture ~ understand that the pictures show past actions ~ recognise the key action in each picture
language demands	~ find the vocabulary to describe each action ~ find the past tense ending for each verb ~ put the words together in the right order ~ pronounce the words ~ give correct stress and intonation to words and sentence ~ understand teacher's instructions and explanation, and feedback

There may be other demands on the pupils beyond the language and the cognitive. If they are required to do the activity in pairs, then each pupil needs to listen to his or her partner, paying attention to the particular box on the grid being talked about; this would be an *interactional* demand. *Metalinguistic* demands would require pupils to understand or use English to talk about the language, e.g. if pupils were instructed 'use the past tense of the verbs'. *Involvement* refers to the demand on the child to keep engaged with the task for as long as it takes to complete it; involvement demands will vary with how interesting the task is to the child. With younger children, especially, we need to remember that classroom tasks will present *physical* demands, sitting still long enough to do the task or using the fine-motor skills required to manipulate a pencil to write, draw or tick boxes. The box below shows a list of types of demands that a task may place on learners:

Table 2.1 *Types of task demand*

TASK DEMANDS

- **Cognitive**

demands vary with the degree of contextualisation of language; difficulty of concepts that are needed to do the task (e.g. use of graphics, colours, telling the time).

- **Language**

demands vary with whether the language is spoken or written, understanding or production, extended talk or conversation; with vocabulary and grammar needed; with the genre; with the amount of L1 and L2.

- **Interactional**

demands vary with the type of interaction required, e.g. pair work; with the participants in talk – adult / peers; with the nature of the interaction, e.g. question + answer.

- **Metalinguistic**

demands may include the use of technical terms about language in production or comprehension e.g. in instructions, in feedback.

- **Involvement**

demands vary with the ease or difficulty the learner has in engaging with the task, e.g. length of task stages; links to child's interest and concerns; novelty, humour, suspense.

- **Physical**

demands vary with how long the child must sit still for; with actions needed; with fine motor skills needed e.g. to write or draw.

The analysis of the demands that a task places on pupils is a key way to assess its suitability and its learning potential. It is, however, only one side of the equation; we also need to look at how the child is *supported* in achieving the goals of the task.

2.3 Task support

The grid in Figure 2.1 has been provided to support the learners' production of language. It offers support in two ways. Firstly, the pictures provide support for meaning, contextualising the language to be used. Secondly, the structure of the grid supports concepts, by using a graphical way of representing times of day and avoiding the need to do this through language. Graphics can often concretise quite abstract ideas without requiring the use of language, and can support understanding of ideas for second language learners (Tang 1992). The use of the rising, full and setting suns in the top row can give added support to recall of the meaning of *morning*, *afternoon* and *evening*. The task includes language support through the use of words and phrases already encountered in earlier lessons. Explanation and modelling of the task by the teacher will provide further support to pupils. They may also be supported by working in pairs and listening to their partners. We can categorise the types of support for learning in the same way as types of demand. When we think in terms of support, we try to use what the children can already do to help them master new skills and knowledge, or we try to match tasks to children's natural abilities and inclinations. Examples are given in Table 2.2.

2.4 Balancing demands and support

Clearly, whether learners can do the task, and whether they learn anything by doing it, depends not just on the demands or on the support, but on *the dynamic relationship between demands and support*. We can here recall the idea of the zone of proximal development, or space for growth, that children need for their language and cognitive development. If the demands are too high, learners will find the task too difficult; they are likely to 'switch off' and not finish the task, or to finish it as well as they can, using what they know to complete the task but not using the language intended. In either case, learning goals are not achieved. Perhaps, most dangerously of all for future learning, children may *appear* to the teacher to have completed the task, but may not have understood it or learnt from it. The teacher may then try to build on the unlearnt language in future lessons, and for a time may appear to succeed. Pupils' problems can remain hidden, particularly in contexts where the teacher leads and controls classroom activity very strongly, until revealed by some crisis, such as end of year examinations. While the desire of young children to please adults and participate as much as they can is one of the very positive sides of teaching young learners, we need to be aware that it can also hide a multitude of problems.

If a task provides too much support, then learners will not be 'stretched'. A very common example of too much support is the teacher's

Table 2.2 *Types of task support*

Task Support

- **Cognitive**

support can come from the contextualisation of language; from the use of concepts already developed; from familiar formats of graphics or activity; from familiar topics and content.

- **Language**

support can come from re-use of language already mastered; from moving from easier domain to more difficult, e.g. spoken to written; from using known vocabulary and grammar to help with the new; from use of L1 to support L2 development.

- **Interactional**

support can come from the type of interaction, e.g. pair work; from helpful co-participants; from the use of familiar routines.

- **Metalinguistic**

support can come from familiar technical terms to talk about new language; clear explanations.

- **Involvement**

support can come from content and activity that is easy for the learner to engage with, e.g. links to child's interest and concerns; from mixing physical movement and calm, seated activities.

- **Physical**

variation in sitting and moving; use of familiar actions; match to level of fine motor skills development, e.g. to write or draw.

---

use of the first language to explain the meaning of a reading text; this provides so much support to understanding that the learners do not need to think about the foreign language or to use more than just single words (see Chapter 9). In trying to strike a balance between demands and support, we can apply what cognitive scientists call 'the Goldilocks principle': a task that is going to help the learner learn more language is one that is *demanding but not too demanding*, that provides *support but not too much support*. The *difference between demands and support* creates the space for growth and produces opportunities for learning.

An analogy may help capture this idea. Imagine that you are working out in a gym and lifting weights. Your aim is to increase the size of weights you can lift, or the number of times you lift a weight. Either increase is an advance in fitness and can represent language learning. Now, the way to get fitter is not to try to pick up a weight that is very much heavier than the one you can lift at the moment, nor is it to use a weight much lighter. If the weight is too heavy (or task demands too great or support not enough), you will just fail to lift it altogether or, if you do manage to lift it, may well cause injury. If the weight is too light (demands too low or support too great), you will be able to lift the weight (complete the task) very easily, but it won't increase your fitness. What *will* promote increased fitness (or learning) is to work with a weight that is just a little bit heavier than your usual weight, so that muscles can adapt to the increase, and then, through practice, the new weight will become your new current limit. The process can then be repeated with a slightly heavier weight still. Over time, you will become able to lift much heavier weights, but at no time will the strain have been too great! Language learning for an individual can be seen similarly as a repeated process of stretching resources slightly beyond the current limit into the ZPD or space for growth, consolidating new skills, and then moving on to the next challenge.

2.5 The importance of language learning goals

How then can teachers achieve the most useful balance of demands and support when they plan lessons and adapt tasks from course books? If *language learning* is made the focus of this issue, the question then becomes, 'How can teachers ensure that the balance of demands and support produces language learning?' The answer we will pursue is that the teacher, in planning, must set clear and appropriate *language learning goals*.

As a bald statement, this may sound rather obvious. After all, surely language learning is a goal for all language teaching? At a general level, this may be so, but it does not always seem to be the case for individual lessons and tasks. Moreover, goals that result in learning need to be tailored to particular learners. The course book or syllabus may dictate what is to be *taught*, but what is to be *learnt* can only be planned by a teacher who knows the pupils, and can make the book or syllabus work for them. Learning goals are objectives or intended learning for particular learners working on particular tasks, made specific from the general learning aims of book or syllabus.

In setting clear and specific language learning goals, teachers are *scaffolding* the task for children. Further scaffolding can involve breaking down tasks into manageable steps, each with its own sub-goals. The teacher takes responsibility for the whole task while learners work on each step at a time. Careful design of sub-goals should help ensure success and achievement at each step, and of the task as a whole. Young learners face many years of classroom lessons and it is important that they feel, and are, successful from the start. Too many demands early on will make them anxious and fearful of the foreign language; too few demands will make language learning seem boring. Careful selection and grading of goals is one of the key tools available to teachers to build success into learning.

In primary language classrooms there is a further force that may shift teaching away from learning, and that is the borrowing of materials and activities from general primary practice. This transfer of methodology happens rather often at primary level, partly because of the methodological vacuum in teaching young learners, and partly because primary practice has some genuinely good techniques and ideas that clearly work well with children. My point is not that such transfer is wrong, but that, when ideas are transferred, they need to be adapted for the new aim of language learning. Thinking through the demands, support and learning opportunities of activities may help in this adaptation. Prime examples of techniques transferred from primary education would be theme-based learning and the use of songs and rhymes. Theme-based learning will be further discussed in Chapter 9, and rhymes will be shown to be useful in early literacy (Chapter 6).

2.6 Defining 'task' for young learner classrooms

My aim in this section is to produce a list of defining features of *task* for use in teaching foreign languages to children. I am not interested in an abstract concept of task but in a unit of activity that can be used for lesson planning and evaluation, and which will also work as a unit of analysis in research by teachers or by researchers coming into classrooms (Cameron 1997). I begin by seeing how the ways in which the term 'task' is commonly used in language teaching can contribute to re-defining for teaching children.

One way in which the construct 'task' entered language teaching was through work with adults, who needed to use the second language outside the classroom (Breen 1984; Nunan 1989, 1993). For these learners, there was sometimes a marked contrast between the kinds of activities they did in classrooms and the kind of activities they needed English for in their lives outside the classroom, and tasks were adopted as a unit that would try to bring the classroom and 'real' life closer together. The goals and outcomes of tasks were to relate to the real needs of learners, such as reading bus timetables or buying cinema tickets. Some writers argued that materials used should be real and authentic too, while others suggested that authenticity of texts was too difficult as a requirement but that authenticity of activities, or of interaction of learner and text, was more desirable (Breen 1984, Widdowson 1990). The latest versions of 'task-based learning' (TBL) locate real-ness in outcome, with learners working together to do things like 'solve a problem, do a puzzle, play a game or share and compare experiences' (Willis 1996). A young learner version of a task-based syllabus was tried out in the Bangalore project twenty years ago (Prabhu 1987), with children working on maths, geography or other problems through English.

In all these developments, the essential aspect of a 'task' is that learners were focused on the meaning of content rather than on form, i.e. the learners' goals and task outcomes are not explicitly language-focused. Recently there has been something of a return to form as needing attention too (Ellis 1994; Kowal and Swain 1994). We will explore this in more detail in Chapter 5 when we look at grammar, but it is of relevance here to note that the most meaning-focused of all language learning contexts, immersion, is where problems with lack of attention to form have been discovered (Lightbown and Spada 1993). Children in immersion classes, who have studied school subjects through their second language, are found to develop language skills that match their native-speaking peers on listening skills and pronunciation, but lag behind in grammatical accuracy and precision. It seems that focusing on meaning is important, but is not enough for continued language development.

Language for young learners raises more problems with the notion of 'real' or 'authentic' language use. Many children do not use the foreign language much outside the classroom, except perhaps on holiday, with tourists to their country, and when using computers. Beyond these limited domains, their outside lives do not readily provide a needs-related syllabus for foreign language learning. Furthermore, their adult lives and possible needs for the language are still too far away to give content to lessons; 7 and 8 year olds have little need to book holiday accommodation or even give directions! What 'real language use' (Skehan 1995: 23) is for these children is not obvious; it might be seen as the language used by native speaker 7 and 8 year olds, but by the time they have learnt it, they will be 9 and 10 year olds, and will no longer need to talk about, say, teddy bears or dolls. The best we can do is aim for *dynamic congruence*: choosing activities and content that are *appropriate* for the children's age and socio-cultural experience, and language that will *grow with* the children, in that, although some vocabulary will no longer be needed, most of the language will provide a useful base for more grown-up purposes.

From this point of view, school activities *are* congruent with children's lives, and using English to take the register or sing songs is quite real enough. It seems appropriate that tasks can be defined as *classroom* activities. However, not all activities that take place in a classroom will qualify as 'tasks'; an activity can be any kind of event that children participate in, but a task has further features. As with our demand and support analysis of the grid task at the start of this chapter, learner participation is the pivot around which classroom tasks are to be examined. There must be something unified and coherent, for learners, about a task. Rather than taking outcomes as criterial as in Willis' and Skehan's form of TBL, the focus is on how the *goals* and *action* create a *unified whole* (Coughlan and Duff 1994). A classroom task will have a clear beginning and end; it may be quite short or it may last over several lessons. For the child, a classroom task should have a clear purpose and meaning; for the teacher, the task should have clear language learning goals. Key features of classroom tasks for children learning a foreign language are summarised as follows:

Classroom tasks for children learning a foreign language

- have coherence and unity for learners
  (from topic, activity and / or outcome)

- have meaning and purpose for learners

- have clear language learning goals

- have a beginning and end

- involve the learners actively

If we think about these features in singing songs, we can see that although any instance of singing is an activity, only the more carefully planned and structured events using songs will be classed as 'language learning tasks'. This perspective turns the song into a tool for language teaching and learning, that can be effectively planned, implemented and evaluated.

2.7 Stages in a classroom task

In this section, a further aspect is added to the framework of classroom tasks, and that is the notion of steps or stages. In teaching reading skills, it has been common practice for many years to plan reading activities in three stages: pre-reading, reading and post-reading. The three stage format has been applied to listening, to mainstream task-based learning (Skehan 1996) and to activity-based language learning in primary classrooms (Vale 1990). I adopt it here too, with the following labels:

PREPARATION $\longrightarrow$ CORE ACTIVITY $\longrightarrow$ FOLLOW UP.

The 'core activity' is central to the task, just as the earth has a hot, molten core or an apple has its pips inside the core. Without the core, the task would collapse. The core activity is set up through its language learning goals. Preparation activities prepare the learners to be able to complete the core activity successfully, and might include pre-teaching of language items or activation of topic vocabulary. The 'follow-up' stage builds on successful completion of the core, perhaps with a public performance of work done in the core or with written work based on oral language used in the core. Since one task can lead to another, the follow up of the first may be, or lead into, the 'preparation' stage of the next.

As an example of how the stages can combine to produce a task, we can return to Hani and his weekend, and place the production of oral sentences from the grid as the core activity in the centre of an imaginary task. We can then fill out the task with possible preparation and follow-up activities.

2.8 Hani's Weekend: Possible preparation and follow-up activities

Given the core goals of pupils saying sentences about each picture in the grid, it seems helpful for the preparation stage to activate the vocabulary that will be needed, i.e. the action verbs and the names of objects and places in the pictures. This can be done using the pictures from the grid in Figure 2.1, but with a small adjustment: the pictures are used one-by-one rather than in combination, and are blown up in size for whole class work (or changed into big, quickly done sketches by the teacher straight on to the board). Each picture can then be used with the class as support to recall words for objects, people, places, and actions. In the core activity, the same pictures will be used, and the link made at preparation stage between picture, form and meaning will be available as support for sentence production.

There is however a more weighty demand for pupils in this task than the lexis: having to understand why a past tense form is needed, constructing the past tense form, and producing it in a sentence with the

		24.2.01	
mending	→	*mend<u>ed</u>*	☐
riding	→	*<u>rode</u>*	☐
watching	→	*watch<u>ed</u>*	☐

Figure 2.2 The board divided into two, to highlight meaning and form of Past verb tenses. (Note: the boxes represent pictures.)

time phrases such as *on Thursday evening*. To support these demands, the teacher could make one small but crucial change to the information and then use simple graphics. The small change that I suggest might really help pupils understand the meaning of the grammar, i.e. why the Past Tense is needed, is to add *dates* (e.g. 24th, 25th February, when the class takes place in March) to the grid, so that it is not just any weekend that is being talked about, but a *particular weekend that has passed*. Alternatively, the weekend could be some holiday or festival that has just passed. Either way, making the weekend clearly specific to the pupils gives a support to their understanding that the weekend activities need to be talked about in the past tense.

It is likely that when shown the pictures, pupils will produce verb forms such as *mending*. The teacher can then use a graphical prompt to support the production of the correct form, dividing the board into two with a vertical line, and writing the selected (past) date on one side (Figure 2.2). Holding the picture on the undated side, the teacher can use the form *mending*; moving the picture to the dated side, the teacher can produce the past form *mended*, emphasising the ending with stress or, if the word is written down, with a different colour or underlining. Other verbs can be practised in the same way.

Practice with the past tense forms and pictures (still separately, rather than in the grid) could be done by pupils in pairs, as extra preparation.

At the end of the preparation stage, pupils should be ready to move on to the core activity, supported by the teacher first modelling for the students how to 'read' information from the chart. A large grid could be constructed on the board, placing the large pictures one by one on to the grid as the sentences are modelled. Follow-up activities could develop written production, by pupils writing down the sentences about Hani, and then writing about their own weekend, using the same phrases or ones that they choose.

The task is summarised on the grid in Figure 2.3. The three stages of the task appear in the columns. For each stage, working downwards

TASK	Say sentences about Hani's weekend		
	Preparation	*Core activity*	*Follow up*
Language learning goals	Activate previously learnt lexis. Practise past forms of verbs.	Oral production of sentences from grid.	Written production of Hani sentences. Composition of own sentences.
Activities	Teacher-led: (1) Use of single pictures to prompt recall of lexis. (2) Divide board into two and recall/ practise past forms. (3) Pairs practise with single pictures.	(1) Whole class introduction of grid and teacher model-ling of sentences. (2) Pair production of sentences: e.g. P1 points to a box and P2 says sentence.	(1) Teacher writes key words on board, next to pictures. (2) Teacher models writing sentence from grid. (3) Pupils write sentences. (4) Pair checking of accuracy.
Demands on learners	To recall lexis, or to re-learn. To understand idea of past events and use of tense to express this.	To recall lexis and verb forms from preparation stage. To 'read' the grid. etc. (see Table 2.1).	Writing in English (see Ch. 6). Remembering words and forms from core. Finding words for own activities.
Support for learning	Pictures of familiar events. Teacher modelling of lexis and forms. Pair work.	Familiar pictures. Addition of dates to grid. Preparation stage practice of forms. Teacher modelling. Pair work.	Teacher modelling. Key words on board. Teacher feedback while writing. Teacher provides new words for pupils' own sentences.

Figure 2.3 Hani's weekend: turning an activity into a task

through the column, we first see the language learning goals that are set for the stage. The activities that will take place are then listed in the next box. Below that, the activities are analysed in terms of demands and support. The grid as a whole displays the planning that would underpin the task.

Of course, none of the activities I have suggested are groundbreaking, or even very exciting! However, I have tried to show how thinking about demands, support and goals can help to plan carefully linked stages that scaffold the pupils' language use towards language learning. We should also notice the important point that making very small changes to the information (adding dates) or to the activity (using separated pictures singly) can lead to very large changes in the task as experienced by pupils. This is a very powerful tool: if teachers have repertoires of such small changes, they can use them to adapt and adjust tasks found in course books to suit particular learners.

2.9 Task-as-plan and task-in-action

At the beginning of this chapter, we used the metaphor of the task as *creating an environment in which learning can occur.* We have seen that this environment can be better understood by analysing the demands and support of activities. In the last section, the course book task has been adapted by adding more activities to produce an environment in which (imaginary) students might be able to meet the demands and achieve language learning goals. In many ways, this analysis was an unrealistic exercise, because we did not know much about the specific pupils or teachers who might use the grid, how the teacher might introduce it, or what language pupils would bring to making sense of it. If we had that information, we could have produced a much tighter analysis. However, it would still have been an analysis *of a plan*, and we still would not know what actually happened when the activity was used *in action with a particular class*, unless we observed and recorded the lessons. In order to help maintain a clear distinction between what is planned and what happens in practice, we can label the two 'task-as-plan' and 'task-as-action' (after Breen 1987).

Until the task is turned into action, it cannot be fully evaluated for its usefulness or effectiveness. However, the different aspects of tasks introduced in this chapter can all be used for evaluating tasks-in-action, once they have been identified in the task-as-plan. In the next chapter, data recorded in classrooms will allow us to analyse a task-in-action, as we use the grid and task analysis to discuss an oral task from a Norwegian primary school, and oral skills development more generally.

3 Learning the spoken language

3.1 Learning the spoken language: guiding principles

Following the division of language skills set out in section 1.7, this chapter deals with the development of children's skills in using the spoken language. The chapter is built around two 'guiding principles' for teaching.

> - **Meaning must come first**: if children do not understand the spoken language, they cannot learn it.
> - To learn discourse skills, children need **both** to participate in discourse **and** to build up knowledge and skills for participation.

Central to the chapter is an analysis of children using their foreign language in a real classroom task-in-action (section 2.9); we will see how the teacher and task construct an environment for the use and learning of the language.

The chapter begins by establishing how the term 'discourse' will be used. Section 3.3 turns to meaning in discourse; a child's search to find meaning in language can drive language learning but will need support from the teacher. The differing demands of speaking and listening as a discourse participant are set out. In section 3.4, the talk of pupils and teacher on a classroom task is analysed in some detail, using the concepts of demand and support. Section 3.5 draws on the literature about children's discourse development to explore the discourse skills that we might expect from child language learners. Section 3.6 presents ways in which classroom activity can support children's discourse skills development in the foreign language. Examples of short language practice activities that can be developed from a single set of pictures are given in section 3.7. After consideration of the relation between spoken and written language in the classroom, section 3.8 discusses the use of dialogues in the classroom and their relation to learning the spoken language.

3.2 Discourse and discourse events

The term 'discourse' is used in two ways in the literature. Firstly, *discourse* is contrasted with *text* to emphasise that it concerns *use of the language*. While 'text' means nothing more than a piece of language, if it is considered as 'discourse', we must include the context of use and the users of the text. A very simple example is a shopping list. If we consider the shopping list as a text, we have a list of items. If we consider the shopping list as discourse, then we have the text but we must also consider many other elements around the list: that it was written by a woman, who has a family and a house to look after, who was planning a trip to a supermarket, that the list was written on the back of an envelope, that it was intended to be used while walking around the supermarket (although in my case would be as likely to be left on the kitchen table and have to be remembered from the writing of it!). These use and user factors are part of any analysis of discourse, and help explain content and form.

The second use of *discourse* is in contrast to *sentence*, when it refers to a piece of language longer than the sentence. The sentence has traditionally been taken as a basic unit for grammatical analysis, broken down into clauses, phrases and then words. Once we move from sentences to paragraphs or to books, articles or other large units of text, we are in the world of discourse. When we think about spoken language, discourse in this sense refers to conversation or to larger units of talk, such as stories or songs.

The first sense of discourse is, for me, the most important, because all language is used in a context and develops as a result of contextualised use. The second sense can be seen as springing out of the first, in that, when people use language for real purposes, they tend to do so in time-bounded chunks of talk or writing. These real units of language use are very seldom restricted to the length of a sentence or smaller – although they can be, as when a sign on the edge of a building site says *Keep Off!* or *Danger*. The term 'discourse event' will be used here to describe a naturally bounded use of language of any length.

'Discourse' in foreign language learning needs both senses. Discourse as real language use is the target of teaching: we want children to be able to use the foreign language with real people for real purposes. Part of this requires that children know how the foreign language works in conversations and longer stretches of talk and text. Furthermore, discourse occurs in language classrooms: when teachers and learners interact on tasks and activities, they are involved in a discourse event.

3.3 Meaning first

3.3.1 Children's drive to find meaning

Piagetian and Vygotskyan theories of development, set out in Chapter 1, see children as actively constructing meaning from their experiences in the world. Vygotsky emphasised the shared construction of meaning with other people, and Bruner's notion of scaffolding develops this idea to show how adults can support children in the construction of understanding. From early childhood, the desire to connect emotionally and communicate with other people seems to drive speaking. As children move through infancy, they begin to communicate with others about things in their shared world, and develop their vocabulary of labels alongside their developing abilities to categorise (Locke 1993). Underlying any social interaction, including scaffolding, is the human desire to make contact with other people, to cross the gap between their thoughts and one's own. Even if, ultimately, we must acknowledge that we never have complete access to anyone else's mind, we seem to be driven to keep trying. In this quest to connect with another's thoughts, language is the primary tool we have. When we interact, we use words to try to capture our own and other people's 'sense', our own particular contextualised understandings and connotations for events and ideas (Vygotsky 1962). For infants, language often seems to play a secondary role to the social and affective, and less attention is paid to the actual language content of talk than to its probable social meanings. Locke (1993) describes three year old English speakers who were happy to respond to an adult who spoke to them in Spanish that they did not understand. The children seemed to use the social context and intonation as guides to how to respond. Locke points out that we need to be aware that young children must inevitably have to operate with only partial understanding of much of the language that they hear every day, but that this does not stop them interacting. As they get older, so they build up knowledge of word meanings from a wider range of contexts, and language gradually becomes a more precise and effective tool for communication. The move in language use from partial to more complete understandings must also be experienced by foreign language learners.

Donaldson's work with children taking part in experimental tasks showed how they use their experience of intention and purpose in human activity to make sense of what they are required to do (Donaldson 1978). As human beings, we are driven by a need to 'make sense' of, and to, other people. In what has been described as 'an innate drive for "coherence"' (Meadows 1993:72), children cope with the continual novelty of the world by seeking sense, bringing all they know and have already experienced to work out a meaning in what someone says to them or in what they see happening. Research with autistic children adds further evidence to support the idea that children are normally driven to construct understanding; these children are *not* able to make coherent sense of these events but seem to see them as bewilderingly unconnected. The use of first language is driven by a socially-motivated search for understanding and a need to share understanding.

Let's then imagine children, who we have described as actively trying to make sense of new situations and events, sitting in a foreign language classroom. The social and affective drive to share understanding will still operate (unless it is trained out of them, which can happen). When they encounter new language, we can expect that they will try to make sense of it by bringing their 'social knowledge', i.e. what they know already about how the world works, how adults, in this case teachers, talk to children and what kinds of things those adults have previously wanted them to do. This knowledge and experience will help children find social purpose that can be used as a key to understanding. It will also help children understand the foreign language *as a means of communication*, as words and phrases are learnt to fit familiar contexts, such as greeting and naming. When children are put in a situation where they want to share understanding with other people through the foreign language, they will search their previous language-using experience for ways to act in the foreign language. If their language resources are not sufficient, then the social motivation to construct shared understanding, what Skehan has called 'communicative pressure' (Skehan 1996), is likely to lead to use of first language or mixtures of L1 and the foreign language. This tendency towards communication at any cost affects learners of all ages. We discuss the implications of this further in Chapter 9. In the learning-centred approach to classroom activity adopted here, the human drive to find and share meaning is harnessed to support language use by being built into task demands.

3.3.2 Why teachers need to check that meaning is accessible

I have already (in section 2.1) briefly referred to the possible dangers if children *cannot* construct understanding in foreign language lessons. If adults find themselves in a situation where they cannot make sense of what they were told or asked to do, they will probably ask directly for clarification or find some other way to understand. Children are importantly different in this respect because it takes some years for them to become equal participants in interaction, and to see that each participant has responsibility for making themselves understood to the other (Ricard 1993; Meadows 1993; Anderson and Lynch 1988). Generally respecting and wanting to please their teachers, children may continue with activities even if they do not understand. They will continue to speak in the foreign language and continue to perform classroom activities, without understanding. And, if they are not understanding, they cannot be learning. It is not unusual to see pupils in lessons 'mouthing' the sentences in the text book back to their teacher, appearing to complete an activity, but understanding, and learning, nothing. We will look at ways of evaluating children's understanding in Chapter 10. Here though we should note the importance of teachers continually putting themselves in the child's position and asking:

Can the child find or construct meaning in this language / activity?

It is crucial for teachers to take the responsibility for checking whether their pupils understand the language being used and the purpose of activities being carried out.

3.3.3 Meaning in speaking and listening

Speaking and listening are both active *uses* of language, but differ in the mental activity involved and demands that they make on learners of language in terms of finding and sharing meaning. Listening can be seen as (primarily) the active use of language to access other people's meanings, whereas speaking is the active use of language to express meanings so that other people can make sense of them. The labels 'receptive' and 'productive' uses of language can be applied to listening and speaking respectively.

To construct understanding in a foreign language, learners will use their existing language resources, built up from previous experience of language use. In active listening, the goal of the mental work is to make sense, e.g. of a story or instructions, and is thus naturally meaning-focused rather than language-focused. For example, children listening to a story told in the foreign language from a book with pictures will understand and construct the gist, or outline meaning, of the story in their minds. Although the story may be told in the foreign language, the mental processing does not need to use the foreign language, and may be carried out in the first language or in some language-independent way, using what psychologists call 'mentalese'. If we were to check what the children understood, we might find they could tell us the story in their first language, i.e. they could recall the meaning, and they might recall some words or phrases in the foreign language. It is very unlikely that they would be able to re-tell the story in the foreign language, because their attention has not been focused on the words and syntax of the story but on its underlying meaning. Different types of listening activities are required to ensure a language-focus (Field 1998).

To speak in the foreign language in order to share understandings with other people requires attention to precise details of the language. A speaker needs to find the most appropriate words and the correct grammar to convey meaning accurately and precisely, and needs to organise the discourse so that a listener will understand. When listening, the nuances of meaning carried by grammar or discourse organisation can often be constructed from other clues, but speaking doesn't allow for this so easily. The demands of re-telling a story in the foreign language after listening and understanding should not be underestimated: the language needed at word, sentence and discourse levels must be found and produced. Speaking is much more demanding than listening on language learners' language resources and skills. Speaking activities, because they are so demanding, require careful and plentiful support of various types, not just support for understanding, but also support for production.

The terms 'Input' and 'Output' are often used to refer to listening and speaking (and reading and writing) respectively. This terminology reflects a computer model of the human brain that sees language used by other people as 'information', which is received as input, is mentally processed, and the results produced as output. The computer metaphor has been helpful, but is not adequate to describe listening and speaking in a foreign language because the key processes between input and output, that we have described as finding and sharing understanding, are down-graded in importance.

For some time in the 1980s, it was suggested that 'comprehensible input', i.e. listening to or reading English and making sense of it, was not just necessary for learning a language but would be enough on its own to drive language development (Krashen 1982). Research in immersion situations, however, showed the limits of this comprehensible input theory. Pupils in Canadian schools who learnt their school subjects through French as a second language received plenty of meaningful and comprehensible input. Evaluation of their language skills and resources showed that their listening comprehension skills were very good, but that their production often showed a lack of precision and grammatical accuracy. It was clear that, in addition to being exposed to large amounts of comprehensible input, learners need to use their *production* resources and skills, if they are to develop knowledge and skills to share their understandings fully and accurately (Swain 1985, 1995).

41

Cognitive differences between listening and speaking help us understand why the metaphor of input and output is inadequate for language learning. For a computer, input leads to output through invisible processes. The metaphor directs attention away from the crucial learning processes which happen between input and output, both in the classroom and in learners' minds, and from how these learning processes may be supported by teaching and tasks. Recent work on 'input processing' (Van Patten 1996) attempts to work with these in-between processes to help language development. We look in some detail at these ideas in Chapter 5.

3.3.4 Summary

In this section, we have further developed the idea of discourse as meaningful use of language, and children as participants in the discourse, searching out meaning and coherence in what they hear around them and in the contributions they make to the discourse. Discourse in the foreign language makes different demands on children from in their first language, and if they are to use their meaning-making capacities to help in language learning, the teacher must support them by making meaning accessible. The theoretical differences between understanding and participating in foreign language talk described in the last subsection will be seen more clearly when we move to look at real discourse in the next section.

3.4 Analysis of a task-in-action

We will now look at young language learners participating in discourse, and analyse how they use their foreign language to understand and to share meaning with their teacher. We will see how some succeed better than others in producing talk and participating in discourse. The classroom talk will later provide examples of several aspects of discourse skills.

3.4.1 The setting and the task

The classroom discourse event was recorded in a small school in northern Norway. The headteacher of the school taught English, and in this Grade 4 class he had just seven pupils, who were around 11 years old and had been learning English for a year. Although the school was in a tiny, isolated village, many pupils used English on their home computer games and all had television showing programmes in English, with Norwegian sub-titles; they were in these ways linked into a global English-speaking community. Their lessons usually followed the course book quite closely, and the class had just completed the reading of a dialogue about animals who live in the arctic areas of the far north and had discussed it a little. In the first extract from the talk, we see the teacher (T) setting out the task-as-plan that he intends the pupils to complete:

Note
All transcribed talk will use the following symbols:

(.)   micro pause   ?????   indecipherable talk on tape
(1.0)   pause of approx. 1 second, etc.   an::d   extended syllable or phoneme
?   rising intonation suggesting question   <?   'ski-jump' question

Extract 1
1   T: um (4.0) there were some (1.0) polar (3.0) some some animals (.) there
              mentioned (2.0)
              er (2.0) could you please (2.0) think of (3.0) *(blinds pulled down)*
              any animals (.) you know (2.0) um (3.0) A (.) and then B (.)
5   could you please (2.0) go to the blackboard (.) and write (.) down (2.0)
              the name of an animal you know
*A and B (boys) go to the blackboard and write 'reindeer' and 'foks'. Teacher helps
with spelling of reindeer.*
     T: what is wrong about fox? (6.0) A (.) could you (.) correct it?
Correction made to 'fox'
     T: yes (.) now it's right (2.0)
              er (.) while you are on the blackboard (.) could you please tell us a little
10   about (.) arctic fox (.) what kind of animal is it?

In line 3, the teacher addresses the whole class and asks them to *think of any animals you know.* He then chooses two pupils to go to the front of the class and write the name of an animal on the board. The boys do not know at this point what they are going to be asked to do with the names; this comes later in line 9: *could you please tell us a little about arctic fox.* Here then is the oral task as set by the teacher to pupil A, standing by the board with pupil B next to him:

Task-as-plan

   ## tell the class about the animal you have chosen.

This task sets the initial conditions for the use of English by pupils (and teacher). As it unfolds, it creates the environment of language use and learning.

The demands and support of this initial task-as-plan can be analysed as follows:

Cognitive demands: access previous knowledge about the animal
supported by previous knowledge and by allowing pupils to choose an animal they know about.
Language demands: to find words and phrases to describe the animal, speak them
supported by open choice as to what to describe; by the earlier reading of the text.
Discourse demands: extended talk is required
supported by previous work on the topic.
Interactional demands: to tell your classmates and the visiting researcher with tape recorder
supported by familiar people to talk to (except the researcher!).
Involvement demands: to be motivated to create an interesting description
supported by the arctic context which links to pupils' lives; being able to choose the animal to talk about.

3.4.2 The task-in-action

In the next extract, we see what happens as pupil A talks about the arctic fox. You will notice that the planned extended description is not produced, but instead the teacher helps out the pupil by asking questions. As you read the extract, notice how this change of plan occurs, the different types of questions that the teacher uses, and the pupil's responses to them. Notice too the different aspects of the animal that the teacher encourages the pupil to talk about.

Extract 2

```
10  T:  what kind of animal is it?
    A:  it's a ( . ) fox
    T:  it's a fox ? ( . ) yes it is ( . ) laughs
        um ( 3.0 ) could you tell us ( . ) describe it ( . ) ?
        is it big? or is it small? (1.0) how does it ( . ) look like?
15  A:  little ( . ) and white ( . ) er (5.0)
    T:  is it a big or a small ( . ) animal?
    A:  little one (1.0)
    T:  a small one ( . ) yes ( . ) rather small ( . ) compared with (1.0) for instance
        ( . ) polar bears ( . ) yes ( . ) um (1.0) have you seen an arctic fox?
20  A:  no ( . ) er ( . ) on TV yes
    T:  not ( . ) the real one? ( . ) no (2.0)
        do we have ( . ) the arctic ( . ) foxes ( . ) in ( . ) Norway?
```

44

A: I don't think so

T: no I don't think so too (.) I think (.) you have to go to (.) further (.)

25   further north to get them (2.0) yes thank you (.) um (3.0)

The task-as-plan is altered very quickly. The teacher's opening question (line 10) is very broad in terms of possible answers. Pupil A's response in the next line seems to surprise the teacher, probably because saying *it's a fox* does not answer the question at all. In line 13, the teacher asks again, *tell us . . . describe it.* This broad invitation to speak is narrowed down almost immediately in line 14, by asking more closed questions: *is it big? is it small?* Rather than leaving the pupil to decide which aspect of the fox to talk about, the teacher's questions decide for him that size/appearance will be topics. This 'yes/no' type of question offers a lot of support to the pupil because it contains within it the vocabulary that the pupil needs. The last question in line 14, *how does it look like?* opens out the talk again by offering the pupil more choice of answer topic. Pupil A responds in line 15 with his own vocabulary choice. Sticking with the teacher's topic of size, he chooses *little* to describe the fox, and then adds the colour word *white*. Notice that the teacher's planned task of describing the animal is being carried out, but only in single words.

The teacher response to pupil A in line 18 takes up the topic of size and contains a more complicated piece of language comparing the fox and a polar bear. Having taken over the lead role in the talk, the teacher then tries to hand it back to pupil A, by asking if he has seen a fox. Again, A seems to understand but replies very hesitatingly, in single words and with the short phrase: *on TV.*

In line 22, the teacher tries again to get the pupil to speak, this time with another closed question that only needs *yes* or *no* as a response. The pupil does a bit better than this, producing the phrase *I don't think so*. Finally, the teacher elaborates this answer by saying that they are further north.

What has happened to the task-as-plan? Clearly, the pupil has not managed to tell the class about the fox or describe the fox in a piece of extended talk. The teacher has had to take over control of the task and uses questions to construct some interactive talk about the animal. Pupil A, we might surmise, found the task in some way too demanding. In the next extract from the discourse, we will see what happens when pupil B is asked to talk about the reindeer. Again, notice what happens to the planned task, and how this comes about through language use, particularly through questioning.

Extract 3

	T:	B (.) you have written (.) reindeer (.) could you tell us a little about (.) reindeers? (3.0)
		have you seen reindeers?
	B:	yes (3.0)
	T:	yes (.) how (2.0) do they look like?
30	B:	it's (.) er (.) white (.) and (4.0) ?????
	T:	yes (.) the colour is white (.) and
	B:	an::d grey
	T:	yes
	B:	and (3.0) they are er (3.0) bigger (3.0)
35	T:	yes (1.0) rather big
	B:	*(quietly)* rather big
	T:	yes um (2.0) have you seen one?
	B:	yes
	T:	where?
40	B:	in (2.0) Salten
	T:	Salten?
	B:	yes
	T:	yes (.) but (.) I think we have reindeers in Hameroy (.)
	B:	yes
45	T:	yes in fact (1.0) I saw some last (.) week (.) when I was (.) in (.) ????? (2.0)
		so (1.0) we needn't go to (.) Salten to (1.0) see (2.0) I think we have some here in ????? too (1.0) I have seen some (.) in ????? (4.0)

After establishing that the pupil has in fact seen a reindeer, the teacher again uses an open question to prompt pupil talk: *how does it look like?* (line 29). With the help of the 'ski-jump' question in line 31, pupil B describes the colours, and in line 34 offers a sentence about their size. The teacher corrects the word *bigger* to *rather big*, and the pupil repeats the phrase. In this interaction, as with A, the pupil does not seem to be able to produce an extended description using several sentences together, but instead the teacher and pupil together construct a description, using phrases or words elicited through questions. In lines 37–41, the elicitation process becomes very marked, with very closed questions and single word replies. As B's turn comes to an end, the teacher offers a short piece of information about seeing reindeers in their locality. B's task changes from speaking to listening.

After A and B, two more pupils were asked to talk, and the discourse proceeded in a similar way, with an early move from open to closed teacher questions. Again, the teacher closed the talk with a little story or narrative:

Extract 4

T: yes (1.0) they are very dangerous (1.0) in fact (.) some (.) months ago (2.0) a person were killed (.) on Svalbard (.) by a polar bear (.) two ladies were out walking (.) tourists (.) were out walking (.) and (.) were (.) attacked by (.) a polar bear (.) and one of them was killed (1.0) so they're (.) very dangerous (1.0)

It seems that a pattern of talk, or a format, occurs in these extracts from the task-in-action, in which the original task of producing an oral description has changed under the pressures of production and become a task of answering the teacher's questions, with a concluding piece of information or an anecdote from the teacher.

The final extract from this classroom activity is very different. It shows pupil E not just responding to questions but taking the lead in the talk. This pupil selected a *budgie* as his animal; this is a small, brightly coloured bird that comes from the tropics and is only found elsewhere as a pet. In choosing a budgie as an arctic animal, E is 'subverting' the task (Cameron 1999) and makes the task work for him in ways that the other pupils did not. As you read this extract, look for differences between E's talk and that of the other pupils; also, notice how the teacher's talk is different. What is driving these differences?

Extract 5

T: yes (.) alright (.) we were talking about (.) er (.) arctic animals (1.0) I haven't (.) *laughs*
85   I haven't seen a budgie in the Arctic (.) alright
       pupils laugh
       let's see (2.0) budgie (1.0) could you describe a budgie?
E: er (.) she can (.) have many colours
T: yes (.) she can (1.0)
       what kind of animal (.) is it?
90 E: it's a bird
T: yes (.) it's a bird (2.0) yes?
E: and (2.0) and she (.) and she talks a lot
T: yes (2.0) do you have a budgie?
E: yes
95 T: and she can talk?
E: yes
T: what's her name?
E: Gia
T: what's her ? (.) yes?
100 E: Gia
T: sorry (.) Gia? (.) yes (2.0) we had a budgie (1.0) er (.) some months ago (1.0) it died (.) huh *laugh*
Ps: *pupils laugh*
T: suddenly it was (.) dead (2.0) made (1.0) terrible noise (2.0)

105   many strange (.) sounds (3.0) yes (.)
             um (1.0) where do (.) budgies (.) come from? (2.0)
             well (.) they come from eggs (.) that's OK (.) but (1.0) from which part
             of (1.0) the (1.0) world do you think?
    E: um (.) I read (2.0) in a book (.) and er (.) um (.) and it's (2.0)
110   it say it's (.) a little parrot
    T: it's a little parrot (1.0) yes (.) it's (1.0) perhaps it's like a parrot (1.0) I'm
           not very familiar
    E: but I don't know where they come from
    T: I think (.) they are (.) from (.) the tropic zone (2.0) yes (.)
           okay (.)

This extract feels different from the others. Let's first see how it is different, and then ask what has made the difference. The open teacher question in line 87 receives a full sentence reply from E: *she can have many colours.* In line 92, E offers a further piece of information, *she can talk,* with only *yes?* as elicitation from the teacher. Again, in line 109, pupil E takes the initiative and answers a teacher question with an extra piece of information; the sentence does not flow out fluently but is full of hesitations and pauses. What strikes me about this exchange is how pupil E appears to be working *at the edge* of his oral skills, pushing himself to produce sentences where other pupils used just single words.

In line 114, the teacher produces an answer to the question he had asked earlier (107). This is a further indication that the teacher's involvement in this task was greater too. He earlier (102) contributed a story about his own budgie that everyone found quite amusing.

It may be that pupil E has learnt more English than the other pupils, and that he thus finds the task easier, but, even so, his hesitant talk shows that he does not find the task easy. The other difference may be the choice of an animal that E is familiar with and attached to. By choosing his pet budgie, E increases his involvement in the task, and has more things to talk about that he possibly knows better, and cares about. The budgie information carries *personal meaning* for him that was missing with the reindeer or the fox. The meaning that the teacher wants to share is also personal. The involvement with the topic has perhaps created an incentive for talking in order to share understanding, which was much less strong in the previous extracts.

The task created opportunities for pupils and teacher to share meanings through the use of the foreign language. However, only pupil E seemed to respond to the opportunity in a way that might also help in language learning, introducing personal meaning into the task. In the first three extracts, pupils seemed to have problems in finding anything to say: perhaps they could not find the English, or perhaps they could not find information about the animals to share through talk. Either

Table 3.1 *Language produced by children on the oral description task*

Pupil A	Pupil B	Pupil C	Pupil E
it's a fox	yes	bear	she can have many colours
little and white	it's white and	no	it's a bird
little one	grey	yes	and she talks a lot
no	and they are bigger	big	yes
on TV yes	rather big	polar bears	yes
I don't think so	yes	white?	Gia
	in Salten	yes	Gia
	yes	dangerous	I read in a book
	yes		and it say it's a little parrot
			but I don't know where they
			come from

way, it is clear that these pupils needed more support to be able to do the oral description.

3.4.3 Language used in the task

We now look a little more closely at the language that the children produced in the description task to examine the type of utterances used. The question of how children might learn from participation in discourse begins to be addressed.

The pupils' talk clearly demonstrates that speaking is much more demanding than listening; although they had read (and understood) a text about arctic animals and although they could understand when they listened to the teacher talk about the animals, when they were asked to produce a description, they mostly used single words and phrases. Table 3.1 lists the language produced by the pupils.

3.4.4 Use of formulaic language

Looking at Table 3.1, we can see some phrases that seem to have been produced as whole chunks, rather than being put together word by word. Sometimes these pre-fabricated phrases have a structure that does not quite fit into the talk or they are longer than the rest of the child's utterances. I would hypothesise that the following phrases are produced formulaically, although further evidence from the children's talk in English would be needed to confirm this:

it's a fox / bird
little one
on TV

I don't think so
it's white

The heavy mental demands of speaking are believed to be one of the causes of the phenomenon of formulaic use of language (Wray 1999). In all types of language-using situations, first and second, child and adult, speakers seem to rely on such 'chunks' of language that come ready made and can be brought into use with less effort than constructing a fresh phrase or sentence. The 'formulaic sequences' or chunks can be learnt as wholes, or may be 'fused', i.e. they are not encountered as wholes but are made into chunks in the mind of the learner. Chunks are likely to be produced as whole units, and help to avoid long pauses while taking part in talk.

The potential benefits of using and learning chunks are not fully understood yet, but the first and the last phrases illustrate how they can be useful in talk by providing a basic pattern [*it's* . . .] with 'slots' that can be filled by different nouns or adjectives. In child first language acquisition, there is some evidence that phrases learnt formulaically are later broken down into individual words that can be combined with other words, giving new ways of speaking. For foreign language learning, it seems likely that even if formulaic phrases were not taught as such, some stretches of language would be learnt formulaically. The debate continues as to whether and how formulaic use of language can be exploited for learning, with some suggesting that direct teaching of formulaic phrases will help discourse skills development (Nattinger and de Carrico 1992; Myles, Mitchell and Hooper 1999).

Examination of young learner course books show that many choose conversational phrases as units of language to be taught, and that they seem to expect these to be learnt as formulae. Phrases are presented to children through stories, songs, rhymes, dialogues, and through classroom language. In Chapter 5 we will consider how these learnt-as-whole phrases might be used for later grammatical development.

3.4.5 Selecting and adapting language on-line

The hesitations in pupil E's long utterance about where the budgie comes from suggest that this language was constructed on-line, or there and then, rather than being produced formulaically as a chunk. E selected from both vocabulary and his grammatical knowledge to try to communicate his meaning.

Learning and use are tightly interconnected – when a child *uses* English, adapting his or her oral skills to the task in hand, a micro-level instance occurs of *learning* in action. Over a longer timescale, these accumulating experiences of using language will produce more obvious changes in language resources that constitute learning. What we might call language 'knowledge' or 'proficiency' is the overall effect of many separate uses of the language, in each of which ways of talking or understanding are *selected and adapted* to fit the specific situation or task. Over time and many, varied uses of language, the child will move from partial to more complete understanding of aspects of language and develop a greater range of language resources and skills; when the child is then put into a new language-using situation, there are more language resources and skills to select from and the language can be adapted more precisely to fit. Language-using experience in a variety of situations means that the child's language resources can be used across an increasing range of contexts; where at first a child can count in the language only in a recited sequence: *one, two, three, four*, etc., gradually the numbers become available for use in more and more linguistic and situational contexts: *I'd like four apples*. The repeated use of the same words in different physical and language contexts helps to construct in the child's mind the sound, shape, and use of the word. Language learning is the continual changing of these resources of words and phrases and of grammar, contextualised initially, and de-contextualising as it develops.

Explicit attention to language resources is not ruled out by this idea that use drives learning. As will be suggested in later chapters, skilful teaching about language can play an important role in helping language development.

3.5 Discourse skills development in childhood

This section sets the discourse skills demanded by the task in a broader picture of discourse skills development in childhood. Was it unrealistic to expect an 11 year old to give a description of an animal? Could they do that in their first language? What can we expect of young learners in terms of the types of discourse they can use English for? We will see how the foreign language discourse development of children is constrained by their cognitive and social development. Although it is important to take account of maturational constraints, plenty of scope remains, and the rest of the chapter will look at how teachers can most effectively help discourse skills development.

3.5.1 Conversation and extended talk

The teacher's plan was to generate extended talk in the form of a description. What actually happened was much more interactional, and took the form of a teacher and pupil conversation, directed largely by teacher questions. The teacher also produced stretches of more extended talk within the conversational interaction, in the form of little stories about polar bears attacking tourists and his budgie dying.

Conversational interaction and extended talk are the two major types of discourse that can be developed in both first and foreign languages (Brown and Yule 1983). Empirical research has shown that the two types involve different discourse skills and developmental patterns for young children in their first language (Snow 1996), as mentioned in section 1.6. This work has shown that, not only do these two types of discourse develop at different rates for different children, but that the rate and quality of development is connected with how much children are exposed to and participate in each type.

The key differences between conversation and extended talk are *length* of turns and degree of *interaction*. Both require attention to other people. In conversation, the social interaction is more obvious, as each short turn responds to previous turns and contributes to the development of the talk. But extended talk, if done well, also needs to take account of the listeners and how they will understand the longer talk turns. The teacher's little stories seem to be well adapted to his pupils' understanding.

3.5.2 Development of conversational skills in childhood

Taking responsibility for how other people will understand what you say and for making sure that you understand them, is an aspect of discourse that develops with age. Young children are not very good at taking other discourse participants into account and shaping what they say to fit the needs of others. The effects of age on communication skills have been shown in various empirical studies into children's (first language) listening comprehension and communication strategies (a useful summary is given in Anderson and Lynch 1988; also, Ricard 1993; Nelson 1996). Young speakers between five and ten years lack awareness of how to cater for other participants in discourse, and are not very skilful in planning their talk. As listeners, they understand other people's talk relative to their current level of social and cognitive resources; across the full young learner age range this can be different from an adult understanding. Children up to age seven seem to blame themselves if they do not understand something said to them, rather than judging that what was said to them might have been inadequate. Even 10 and 11 year olds who have problems in understanding something may not ask for more information. Researchers have tried to train children to be more effective communicators, but have found that training is only effective for older children, above about eight years of age.

Children's limited communication skills have been explained in terms of their growing understanding of how they and other people think, act and communicate. Children seem to begin to really develop their understanding of other people's actions and minds around four years of age, but it takes much of childhood to gather enough experience and use it to construct a full awareness of how people operate socially and mentally. Indeed, as adults we continue to develop this sensitivity to other people and everyone can probably think of someone who still seems to have problems seeing into the minds of their fellow adults! While some theorists invoke the idea of a developing 'theory of mind' in children (Frith 1989: 178), others posit that this understanding is a socially motivated process, in which (first) language use plays a key role in creating and learning from experiences with other people, initially in the family and then beyond (Nelson 1996).

The maturation of social and cognitive understandings over the 5–12 age range has implications for foreign language use and learning. When children are asked to take part in conversations that are beyond their development, they cannot fully participate and may be forced to repeat without understanding. Discourse in young learner classrooms should follow patterns children find familiar, from their home and family, or from their school experience, and should not demand more of children than they can do, in terms of imagining someone else's state of mind or expressing causes and beliefs. We can see that children may have difficulties in estimating what other people will understand from what they say; even if the pupils in our Norwegian class had managed to produce a description of an animal, they might not have been able to judge very accurately what their fellow pupils would understand from their talk. Summarising someone else's point of view is also likely to be a demanding task for a child.

Familiarity of content and context in foreign language use will help children as speakers and as listeners. Learner training in communication from eight years on may help children to be able to say when they do not understand what they hear and to formulate helpful questions to understand more. The final implication takes us back to the teacher's responsibility for ensuring that children understand and can make sense of the foreign language they hear. The developmental constraints on children's ability to do this for themselves give a further emphasis to the need for teachers to act *on behalf of the child* in this respect, carefully monitoring how they talk to their pupils in terms of what and how their pupils can find meaning in that talk.

3.5.3 Developing children's discourse repertoires

Learners of a foreign language will increase their range or *repertoire* of discourse skills and types. They will learn to interact conversationally with an increasing range of people, in different situations, with different goals and on different topics, moving from the familiar settings of home, family and classroom to situations in the wider world. Children develop skills to produce different types of talk and increasingly long stretches of talk, including:

– narratives
– descriptions
– instructions
– arguments
– opinions
(Brown and Yule 1983, McCarthy and Carter 1994).

In contrast to the social demands of conversational talk, extended talk makes heavier cognitive and linguistic demands because ideas have to be held in the mind and organised so that the links between them will make sense to listeners. Language forms are need that display the links between ideas, for example cause and effect, and sequencing in time. Listeners to extended talk will face interpretive demands to unpack meaning from the language they hear. In young learner classrooms, we cannot expect pupils to produce extended talk of these forms beyond what they can do in their first language. Again, the first language research provides some help in working out what might and might not be possible in a foreign language.

Here we will concentrate on narrative and description, since these are probably the most accessible to young learners. Other discourse types – instructions, arguments, opinions – can be analysed in similar ways for their content and organisation. They require sometimes more developed skills in communicating with other people, understanding their points of view, gathering and ordering information and shaping discourse to persuade or to illustrate ideas.

The primacy of narrative

In the child development literature, 'narrative' appears not just as a discourse form but as a mode of mental organisation that is found in memory construction and that features in the early social experiences of children. Key features of 'narrative' are the organisation of events in time, the intentional actions of participants, cause and effect, and the resolution of problems, often through some surprising event. Narratives have 'thematic' structure as well as temporal structure: sequences of actions have some underlying meaning or driving force. In the large-scale and culturally significant stories of societies, such as myths and fables, we find recurring themes, such as love triumphing over loss or bravery outwitting greed or cruelty. Story telling also acts to socialise children by showing accepted ways of living and behaving.

Bruner (1986) argues that narrative discourse and mental organisation is primary in children's development. We can note that young children encounter narrative in many types of talk and visually too: in story books, in songs, in cartoons, on TV and video, in computer games, and as part of everyday talk in the home and in school. Snatches of narrative occur frequently in conversation, just as the story about polar bears attacking tourists occurred in the classroom talk. A switch to narrative mode is marked by raised pitch and change in intonation patterns (Nelson 1996). Children are included in narrative production when their parents encourage collaboration. The adult may initiate a narrative for the child to participate in: *let's tell daddy where we went today*; and will provide questions and suggestions to help the child keep the sequence of actions going: *what did we see next? and what was the lion doing?* Children are thus exposed to narrative from very early ages, they participate in narrative and they develop their skills in producing narratives. Such skills and knowledge are brought to foreign language learning; what is lacking is the language to express them.

The language of narrative

In their first language, children develop the language for doing narrative quite early, with sentence grammar and discourse grammar appearing to develop interdependently (Nelson 1996). Constructing cohesive narrative requires the use of relative clauses, connectives, pronominal reference, and of adverbs, verb tense and aspect to convey temporal relationships. Even the youngest children can use the connectives *so, when, then, because, if . . . then, or, but*. Some types of relative clauses are learnt very late (see Chapter 1). Pre-school children master the use of past and present tenses, and use temporal adverbs and adverb phrases, such as *yesterday* or *some months ago*. An interesting phenomenon with time words and phrases is that use often precedes full understanding for children. A child may use a phrase like *in a minute* because she has heard adults use it, but without knowing exactly what it means. Contextual information has helped the child get a rough idea of a phrase's meaning, and a model of its use, but it will take many more exposures and uses in a range of contexts before the full and specific meaning is available to the child. Coming to understand the reality of *minutes* or *days* may take until a child reaches 8 or 9 years of age.

In English (L1) narratives produced by young children, verbs can refer to the past (*the giant chased Jack*) or to the future (*then we'll get the train and go home*), and sometimes use the simple present as a timeless form (*giants love the taste of boiled boys*) (examples from Nelson 1986). Very seldom do they use the present continuous that is so often found in young learner text book 'stories': *Annie is sitting in her garden*. This tense has historically been the first taught in English as a foreign language, perhaps because it is easy to support through actions and pictures. It is not, however, authentic in stories.

Non-narrative discourse: description

Narrative is contrasted with '*paradigmatic*' mental organisation, which is concerned with categorising the world, and naming objects and characteristics. Paradigmatic discourse is also found in early childhood social interaction, when parents teach children their colours or name animals they see together. Such talk can be seen as leading to formal, abstract concepts and logical argument that are the central focus of education, particularly at and beyond secondary level. Development will be seen in increasing precision in use of language resources, and in increasing complexity in language resources available to express more complex ideas.

There is some evidence that the balance between narrative and paradigmatic discourse in early childhood varies within and across cultures. Mullen (1994) describes Korean parents who emphasise paradigmatic organisation in their talk with their infants.

A description clearly derives from paradigmatic organisation: objects, animals or people and their parts, features and habits are labelled and described. Parts are linked to other parts, and to wholes.

The describing talk about the budgie from Extract 4 includes:

Appearance:	*can have many colours*
Habits:	*talks*
Categorisation:	*is a bird (as kind of animal)*
	is a little parrot
Origin:	*comes from eggs*
Natural habitat:	*comes from the tropics*

A description might also have included:

Appearance:	*feathers*
Structure:	*wings, beak, feet, head*

Habits:	*flies, nests*
Food:	*fruit*
Pet habitat:	*cage, bell, mirror, perch*

If pupils are to produce successful descriptions, they will need to access their prior knowledge of such descriptive features and the language to express them. By building up the language components of a description, the teacher can carry out more effective preparation for extended talk.

The discourse of description also requires that these components are put together to form a whole. As with narratives, there are prototypical forms of description, such as those found in biology texts, and simplified forms that are accessible to young children, such as those found in children's information books and TV programmes. Even the simple example of the budgie illustrates how our world knowledge requires categorising and expressing relations between categories. Being able to do this in the foreign language is crucial if that language is ever used as a medium of instruction, and cognitively beneficial even if it is not.

Summary

This section has developed the justification for the second guiding principle: that to learn discourse skills, children need both to participate in discourse and to build up knowledge and skills for participation. To be able to do the 'whole' that is a description, children need to learn the 'parts', or components of a description, and to practise integrating those parts into the whole.

To effectively develop the discourse skills of young learners, teachers may be helped by an awareness of the following:

- types of discourse
    their organisation and components;
    the language forms typically used in their construction;
- an understanding of children's developing communication skills and cognitive abilities;
- the importance of working outwards from the familiar;
- the primacy of narrative;
- the educational significance of paradigmatically organised discourse.

There is much that teachers can do to gradually build up children's discourse skills in their foreign language. Classroom tasks and teacher's use of language create the environment in which new forms are met and familiar ones expanded. In the next section, we focus on how this information about children's developing discourse skills can be most effectively brought to bear on classroom practice.

3.6 Effective support for children's foreign language discourse skills

The previous section has demonstrated that to use the foreign language to produce narrative or description requires the assembling of ideas into organised discourse patterns, in ways that will make sense to listeners. We can translate this idea to the teaching of foreign languages in order to see how teachers can support children's oral skills development. The task of producing a short spoken description of an animal will be used again; readers will be able to transfer the ideas and suggestions to other tasks.

3.6.1 Support through motivating topics

The first point to be made is that if children are to talk meaningfully in foreign language classrooms, *they must have something they want to say.* Pupil E's talk makes this point very strongly – he *wanted* to talk about this budgie, and his motivation seems to push him to manage to do so. A and B did not have the same motivation to talk about the fox or the reindeer. Pupil E re-created the teacher's task so that it gave him the opportunity to talk about something that interested him, but for every confident pupil like E, there are many more like A and B who won't take control and whose opportunities for language using and thus for language learning are thereby reduced. Once again the teacher must take on the responsibility for adjusting tasks and topics so that they relate to pupils' interests. A sure way to do this is by building in to a task an element of *choice* for pupils. Encourage them to choose which animal they will talk about, and if they lack information they may at least be motivated to discover it. Find things in which the children are experts, whether that is the life of budgies, how to program the computer, or football teams, and use these interests in tasks.

3.6.2 Support through task structure

Children usually benefit from knowing what is going to happen at the different stages of a task. I suspect that when A and B wrote fox and reindeer on the board, they did not know that they would be asked to describe them. By the time E's turn came, he might have worked out what the task was and have deliberately chosen the budgie because he knew he could talk about it. Sharing with the pupils the *expected outcomes* of the task will usually help pupils.

It helps too if a task has a clear goal or *purpose*. Here purpose means a communicative or interpersonal purpose – why was one pupil to tell the rest about an arctic animal? To construct a human purpose for a task, we try to imagine a realistic reason for why one person might want to say these things to another person. Why might the class need to know the descriptive information? Why would the pupil want to tell them? As the task was set up, no clear purpose was given. In the final extract, pupil E changes the task and seems to create a real, human purpose for his talk; the teacher wants to find out about this budgie. This simple purpose might be enough to motivate and support talking – telling people what they don't know, but are interested to find out about. Human beings are generally interested in the lives of other people. Such interest underlies our fascination with soap operas, and magazines that show the houses and parties of film and TV stars.

Other more intricate purposes might be constructed. One way to do this is to think of an imaginary situation or event in which such language would naturally be used. Perhaps a very unusual animal had been spotted in the neighbourhood – a polar bear wandered down from further north or a pet lizard escaped. Then a news reporter might describe the animal so that people could look out for it. Perhaps someone has lost a valued pet and prepares a description to be read out on local radio to encourage other people to help find it. Sometimes real situations can be created – perhaps the class is preparing a video, CD-ROM, or cassette and pictures about local animals to exchange with a school in another country. Each of these situations supports the production of language by linking it to real people and purposes; each situation or event produces constraints on who would say what, and how, that limit the language that is needed while, at the same time, provide a reason for using it.

The final way in which tasks can support oral skills development is through their *structure*, and in particular through the preparation stage. If producing a description is the core activity in our task, with goals and outcomes decided on, then the preparation stage allows for preliminary work to assemble ideas, vocabulary and sentences, and to put together and rehearse the extended description. Willis (1996) suggests various ways this can be done, and many of her ideas can be adapted for younger learners. In section 3.7, I give examples of short language practice activities that can build language resources and discourse skills either immediately before a description task or in the weeks and months building up to one.

3.6.3 Support through language practice

Interest in a topic and purpose for a task, though important, are not enough. Even when talking about his budgie, pupil E still needed more support with his English, at word, phrase and clause level. All the pupils needed support at discourse level to organise their talk into an extended description. The pupils are learning English *as a foreign language* and we need to accept that this differs in important ways from learning it as a first language. Unlike first language children, foreign language learners are not immersed in a continual stream of spoken discourse, from which they can pick out words and phrases while also being helped by adults to participate in the discourse. Foreign language teaching needs to compensate for this lack of exposure to the language by providing other learning opportunities. I suggest that, although participation in discourse is the *target* of foreign language learning, it is not the only *means of reaching the target*, and that direct language practice at word, phrase and sentence level has an important contribution to make in building discourse skills (see also Widdowson 1998). The part-skills of using the language at word, phrase and sentence level can then be combined and integrated through discourse-level practice.

General language learning principles and research show that language learners need the following, and young learners need much the same but in shorter bursts and more frequently:

– models of language use to listen to, notice and appropriate;
– plentiful opportunities for repeated listening;
– plentiful opportunities to say the words and phrases;
– feedback on production to improve fluency and accuracy.

Producing extended talk in addition requires:

– preparation time;
– support for remembering the information to be included, while talking;
– rehearsals of large chunks of talk, as well as words and phrases.

In addition, the central message of this chapter bears repeating yet again – all these types of language practice should *make sense to the child*, as an activity and as meaningful language.

3.7 Short activities for learning the spoken language

The set of pictures in Figure 3.1 is taken from the work book of a Norwegian course for young learners. A range of listening and speaking activities at word, phrase and sentence level can be generated from the set of pictures, and can be adapted for other topics. Most will work with all ages of children. They can be used with language that the children have only recently met for the first time, or to revise language

*Figure 3.1 Animal pictures from 'Young People', Activity Book 4, p. 124.
NKS-Forlaget, Norway*

learnt in earlier years. Because many of these activities will seem like games – they are fast moving and sometimes have a competitive edge – they are likely to keep pupils' interest.

It is assumed that each child will have his or her own set of pictures, although sometimes a pair or group will work with a single set. While the set can be used as it is, as a 4 x 4 matrix, cutting up the matrix and using 16 small pictures (which can be kept in envelopes between activities) gives a lot more flexibility in the possible range of activities. The pictures can be used over and over again for increasingly difficult activities. They can also be used for reading and writing activities, but all the activities below can be done orally. The activities are roughly organised in terms of the learning opportunities they offer the children.

3.7.1 Listening and doing

In these activities, the main learning focus for the children is to listen to the names and characteristics of the animals so that the English words and phrases become familiar, and the children begin to notice features of the English. After playing the games a few times, the children will begin to speak as well as listen, and can gradually take over the teacher's role and play in pairs or groups. Most of the games produce an outcome, e.g. one picture left or a scenario completed, that can be talked about as immediate revision of the language.

(1) Listen and identify

In its simplest form, the teacher says the name of an animal and the child points to the picture or puts a counter on it. The teacher can see at a glance whether the pupils understand the spoken word.

The game can be developed by the teacher describing a picture in more detail:

> *This animal has fur, four legs and barks.*

(2) Bingo

Each pupil chooses six animals, and puts the other pictures back in the envelope. The teacher says the names of the animals at random. When a pupil hears one of his or her animal names, she or he turns that picture over. The first one with all the pictures turned over shouts 'bingo!' and is the winner.

As with (1), this can be developed by the teacher saying the features rather than the names, or by pupils taking turns to say the names as the game is played in a small group.

(3) Listen and take away

Pupils start with the full set of pictures. The teacher instructs them to take away certain animals:

> *Take away all the animals with wings / beaks / who live in hot countries.*

This continues until only one animal is left. Anyone who has that animal is a winner.

Again, the moving of the pictures gives the teacher information about who is understanding and who is not.

(4) Find the odd one out

The teacher says the names of four or five animals. The pupils pick them out and have to decide which one is the odd one out:

> e.g. *budgie, cat, dog, lion – the budgie is the odd one out because it can fly.*

Pupils may not be able to say in English the reason for being the odd one out but they can try, and the teacher can then give the full phrase or sentence. As the game progresses, they may begin to learn the *because* phrases.

Pupils will enjoy doing this for each other, although they may come up with weird and wonderful differences that stretch the patience of their partners!

(5) Listen and put

Pupils draw a cage, a house and a field on a sheet of paper. They follow the teacher's instructions of where to place the animal pictures:

> *The lion lives in a cage. The cat and the dog live in the house.*

This is a form of picture dictation that can be adjusted in many ways:

(i)   The activity can be varied by changing the original picture. The pupils might draw a zoo and be told where the animals go, or use a map of the world to place the animals by their original habitat.
(ii) Pupils could draw the animals rather than using ready-made pictures.
(iii) At the end of the activity, pupils tell a partner about their picture.

3.7.2 Listening and saying

Each of these activities requires pupils to say something, either as individuals or all together in chorus.

For some, it is useful for the teacher to have a set of much larger pictures that can be held up for the whole class to see. Again, pupils can take over the teacher's role and the games can be played in pairs or groups.

(6) Look and say

At its simplest, the teacher holds up a picture and the pupils say the name of the animal.

The large pictures can be placed on the board and pointed to. By moving around the pictures very quickly, the pupils get lots of enjoyable practice in saying the names.

(7) Listen and choose

The teacher gives the pupils a description that fits several animals. Each pupil chooses one animal and tells the class or his / her partner what s/he has chosen.

> e.g. *Choose your favourite pet / an animal with four legs and a tail. I chose a dog.*

This can be developed into a class survey by collecting the results together and displaying them on a graph.

(8) Listen and sort

The teacher names some animals and pupils pick out their pictures. They then have to describe the group that they have, e.g. *dangerous animals.*

(9) Tennis game

Pupils are divided into two teams across the classroom. A pupil from the first team says the name of an animal and a pupil from the other team responds with another animal. The teams keep going for as long as they can. The winner is the team who knows most animals.

This is an excellent vocabulary revision activity that can be played in a few minutes, with a range of topics: animals, parts of animals, things animals eat, places animals live in etc.

(10) Guess my animal – questions

The teacher (or pupil) chooses an animal but does not tell. The pupils have to guess by asking *yes / no* questions. The simplest version uses the name of an animal: *is it a lion?*

Pupils can also use descriptive language to ask more powerful questions: *does it have wings?*

More open *wh-* questions are more challenging to answer: *what does it eat?*

Note that the questions will need to be modelled by the teacher first.

The guessing can be done about a category of animals that have been chosen, as in 8.

(11) Guess my animal – actions

In this guessing game, a pupil chooses an animal and other pupils tell him or her to act like the animal using different verbs: *sleep / eat / walk like your animal.*

They have to guess by watching what the chooser does.

3.7.3 Focus on sounds in discourse

These activities work at two levels: discourse and phonological. The sounds of the language interact with the meaning of the words and the form of the whole. They allow attention to the pronunciation of words and of the rhythms of the spoken language. In a kind of 'language play' (Cook 1997), intonation and stress can be exaggerated dramatically, allowing children to notice (probably not consciously) and practise aspects of the foreign language that may be different from their first language.

(12) Poems or chants

Simple poems can be very easily put together from the earliest stages. Many can be composed and learnt orally. Poems also provide meaningful writing practice, as they can be carefully copied out and illustrated. Once the poems are composed, they become part of the class repertoire to say or chant together in any odd moments.

(i) The class chooses an adjective to go with each of 3 or 4 pictures. A miniature story can be produced by sequencing the lines carefully!

> *Hungry tiger,*
> *Hot lion,*
> *Sleeping rabbit.*

The pictures can be placed on the board or drawn in a children's book in the same sequence, so that they serve as a memory prompt.

(ii) Use numbers to structure the poem

> *One lion walking tall*
> *Two rabbits crouching small*
> *Three birds in the tree*
> *Sing out loud – don't eat me!*

The animals could be chosen at random first and put in sequence, and then the rest of the line added to make a drama or story.

(iii) Acrostic

These poems need to be written for the full impact. They work with just one animal, with the letters of the name arranged vertically downwards, and a sentence or phrase made up that begins with each letter. Just the name can be written on the board, with the phrases held in memory.

T   *terrible teeth*
I   *in the jungle*
G   *goes gently*
E   *early in the morning*
R   *roaring!*

(13) Tongue twisters

Pupils and teacher make up phrases or sentences about the animals, with each word beginning with the same sound, and try to say them as quickly as possible

> *ten terrible tigers*
> *big beautiful blue budgies bite biscuits with their beaks*

3.8 Supporting the spoken language with written language

In classes of older students who have mastered reading and writing, written texts often support the learning of spoken language. In young learner classrooms, however, the helpfulness of the written language is limited, and using reading passages, writing up words of songs or using written labels for new vocabulary may cause serious difficulties for pupils. Later in the book when we explore literacy in depth, we will consider the many linguistic and educational factors that influence literacy development. For the time being, a generalised picture of literacy development will suffice to highlight the primacy of spoken language for children. Formal literacy skills in the first language are generally introduced to children from around five or six years of age. At the beginning, children struggle to make letter shapes with their pencils and to recognise printed words and letters. After a year or so, they can read simple texts but still need to work hard to make sense of new words; for several years, writing remains a laborious process that requires careful attention to shapes and spelling. All through this time, children communicate much more easily through talk than they do through written language. As reading and writing skills develop and become more automatic, so literacy becomes less of a struggle and more of a tool that can be used to assist communication. At some point in the development of literacy skills, the written language becomes for the child a *more efficient* source than spoken language for some purposes, such as finding out information or exploring ideas in writing. It is as if there is a switch between literacy and oral skills in terms of efficiency and helpfulness to learning. For children learning to be literate in their first language, this switch begins to happens at around 8 or 9 years of age. Before the switch point, oral language is more helpful than written language; after the switch point, written language can be functionally more useful.

Holding this idea of the switch point in mind, we can bring into the picture the learning of literacy in the foreign language. Generalising and simplifying again, we need only to agree that foreign language literacy is likely to lag behind a child's first language literacy development. We can then see that the foreign language is likely to have a later switch point; the written form will continue to be a burden rather than a help for a longer time. In young learner classrooms where children are still learning to read and write in the foreign language, they will generally find it easier to learn new language through listening and speaking than from written text.

There are many situations in secondary and adult language classrooms where written text is used to support learning, and these have to be re-thought for young learners who are still struggling with writing and reading. We can't, for example, ask young learners to '*make a quick note*' of new vocabulary items learnt in a lesson, because writing a list of words for a six- or seven-year-old child may still be a slow and demanding process that would take most of a lesson. We can, though, give them a set of simple pictures of the new vocabulary that they can point to and say, colour in and talk about with a partner, and take home to show and say to parents. Similarly, it is of little use writing key words from a story on the board if pupils cannot read them easily. We can, though, have large cut-outs of key characters and places in a story that we pin or stick on the board, to build up the story as it is told, and that can be used later to support all sorts of talk and drama.

I am not here insisting that listening and speaking must always precede reading and writing. As usual, children's learning is more complex and interesting than that over-simplification allows, and there is interesting evidence that literacy skills work can produce gains in speaking, which we will examine in Chapter 6. What is being emphasised is the need to assess the demands that the use of written English in classroom activities makes on learners, so that these demands can be lightened or increased in line with the language learning goals of the activities. For children of 5–7 years beginning foreign language learning, very little use of the written form is appropriate, because the demands would be altogether too high. At all stages, if the learning goals of an activity are about oral skills development, then written language used to support oral skills would have to be well within the current level of literacy development of the learners.

So preparing for a spoken description by writing a draft is probably not appropriate for young learners, although it might well be at secondary level. Pupils like those in the Norwegian classroom we met earlier might benefit from purposeful *listening* to written descriptions read aloud that were sufficiently simple for them to understand. Listening might provide them with models of the discourse pattern and style that they can try to reproduce. On the other hand, a follow-up activity may have literacy skills goals, using the spoken work as preparation for reading or writing.

3.9 Using dialogues

3.9.1 Dialogues and discourse

It is very common to find dialogues in children's foreign language course books. At first sight, it may seem that dialogues are exactly what we need to give children practice in discourse-level talk. However, a closer look suggests that the course book dialogue is a rather strange invention. Here is an example from Cambridge English for Schools, Book One (Littlejohn and Hicks 1996: 52):

ANNE: Gosh! How beautiful!
PAT: Yes, it is.
ANNE: Where do they live?
PAT: In trees of course.
ANNE: I know that. I mean where in the world do they live?
PAT: Oh, sorry. Well, they live in North America and South America. Countries like Mexico and Brazil.
ANNE: How do they fly like that?
PAT: Well, they move their wings very fast. They drink nectar from flowers.
ANNE: Oh. You're clever. How do you know all this?
PAT: I've got this magazine at home.
ANNE: Oh!

Dialogues are an historical legacy to children's foreign language teaching that have been bequeathed to us from the adult language learning. Course book writers have adapted the idea for young learners, by using child-friendly characters, by changing the content, or by turning dialogues into cartoons with speech bubbles, but the basic idea remains: that the dialogue provides communicative phrases that children can learn.

Course book dialogues are unlikely to be very close to natural spoken discourse, for several reasons. Firstly, to get into a *book*, they have to be written down, which inevitably produces a tidied-up version of talk. Furthermore, they are usually specially composed for language teaching and, compared to natural talk, seem very artificial. The dialogue above has some interesting parallels with the classroom extracts used earlier in the chapter. It sounds, however, very different from how two girls would be likely to talk to each other in its tidiness, precision and linearity.

3.9.2 The language learning opportunities of dialogues

Text book writers who produce dialogues may have quite other goals than showing how speakers engage in discourse to find out information, to get something done, or just to make contact with another person. The dialogues *may* be included to show learners how spoken English sounds, but may also be there to provide samples of new vocabulary to be learnt, or to give grammar practice. The example given above is followed by practice in asking questions beginning with *Where does . . . How does . . .*, so that the dialogue provides a model of these question types. By examining the repeated patterns of language in a dialogue, teachers can see how a dialogue might best be used.

Dialogues may offer:

– genuine samples of spoken language;
– contextualised sentence patterns that are not very like the spoken language;
– written sentences that resemble what people might say;
– practice of sentence patterns – a grammatical drill in disguise;
– scripts, rather like short theatrical plays.

Deciding how to use dialogues must take into account what they have to offer and what their limitations are. It is no good thinking that pupils are being helped to practise talking in the foreign language if they are actually being drilled in sentence patterns.

We may decide that the dialogues are so different from the types of talk we want our pupils to practise that they are best used just for listening practice, to contextualise new vocabulary (see Chapter 4), or for reading comprehension and writing practice. Some parts of a dialogue may offer useful phrases that could be learnt by heart.

Working with written dialogues, or with pictures supported by cassettes, is different from participating in real discourse because of the absence of the support to understanding that is given by the presence of another person, their gestures and facial expressions. Taking part in discourse produces time pressures to answer or respond on the spot, whereas reading a dialogue produces quite a different set of pressures to decode written words and map on to sounds. Nevertheless, even the most artificial dialogues can usually provide a starting point for more improvised talk, because they offer situations, characters and events, and thus the possibility for narrative and for conversational talk.

The example dialogue in section 3.9.1 would be interesting for the Norwegian children to *listen to* after their oral description activity, because they could be encouraged to *notice* the form of correct questions and answers of the sort that they themselves had been trying to use. Their involvement with these bits of language might lead to greater learning and a desire to try again more accurately. Willis uses the idea of listening to native speakers do a task, after having tried it, in her approach to task-based learning (Willis 1996).

3.9.3 Other sources of spoken discourse

Stories offer ready-made dialogues that can be extracted and practised (see Chapter 8). Some songs and chants are in the form of dialogues, e.g.:

> *Tommy Thumb, Tommy Thumb, where are you?*
> *Here I am, here I am. How do you do?*

New situations can be set up through the text book pictures and text, or by the use of props such as large pictures or blackboard drawings that create a place and a problem. Then characters are needed who would talk to each other in that situation. These can be puppets, figurines or pictures of people, or pupils wearing hats or masks that put them in role. Class and teacher can then work together to construct the dialogue (no writing needed!) as a piece of drama with actions and props to support understanding and memory. The teacher will need to provide the phrases and sentences that the children want to include, and will model how to say them, gradually handing over the speaking to the children.

3.10 Summary

This chapter has explored the development of discourse skills in children's foreign language learning, building from the assumption that the major part of teaching and learning for young learners will be oral. A child participating in discourse will seek to understand and to share meanings, and this can drive language learning if conditions are suitable. The following key points have emerged:

- the meaning and purpose of discourse needs to be made accessible to the learners;
- personal involvement in the talk will increase participation;
- speaking (contributing to discourse) makes different demands from listening and understanding;
- when demands are too high, children will tend to produce single words or formulaic sequences;
- children are capable of participating in narrative and simple descriptive discourse;
- short practice activities can help build productive language to use in discourse;
- children need experience of a range of discourse types to increase their skills with types beyond narrative;
- a dialogue should be seen as a text that offers learning opportunities; these will not necessarily be for discourse skills development.

We will return in later chapters to ways of using these types of discourse for foreign language learning. Meanwhile, the next chapter explores children's learning of vocabulary in the foreign language.

4 Learning words

4.1 Introduction

The previous chapter was concerned with children using the foreign language as discourse in the classroom and how such use might work to promote learning. This chapter deals with the development of vocabulary as a language resource.

Building up a useful vocabulary is central to the learning of a foreign language at primary level. While opinions differ as to how much grammar of the foreign language can be taught, children are clearly capable of learning foreign language words through participating in the discourse of classroom activities. Vocabulary has moved to centre stage in foreign language teaching in recent years, backed by substantial and increasing research (e.g. Carter and McCarthy 1988; Coady and Huckin 1997; Schmitt and Meara 1997; Singleton 1999; Read 2000). Alongside the growing importance of vocabulary, there are fascinating and, I suspect, very significant, changes taking place in how we think about the relative nature and roles of vocabulary and grammar. The more we find out about how words work in language and how vocabulary is learnt, stored and used, the more difficult it becomes to uphold the traditional split between vocabulary and grammar. Much important grammatical information is tied into words, and learning words can take students a long way into grammar. This suggests that if we give a high priority to vocabulary development, we are not thereby abandoning grammar. Rather, vocabulary learning can serve as a stepping stone to learning and using grammar. The interrelation of vocabulary and grammar in language learning will be taken further in the next chapter.

The chapter begins with an overview of vocabulary development. Children are still building up their first language vocabulary, and this development is intimately tied up with conceptual development. In planning and teaching a foreign language, we need to take account of this first language background to know what will work and what may be too difficult for children. It also becomes quickly apparent that learning a new word is not a simple task that is done once and then completed.

The second part of the chapter covers the many different aspects of vocabulary knowledge involved in learning words, and sets out principles for teaching that can help learners build up these different aspects and make links between them. The third section applies these principles to activities for vocabulary learning. The final section of the chapter draws on strategy research to consider how children can be helped to develop their autonomy as self-directed vocabulary learners.

4.2 Vocabulary development in children's language learning

4.2.1 The word as unit

Vocabulary development is about learning words, but it is about much more than that. Vocabulary development is also about learning more about those words, and about learning formulaic phrases or chunks, finding words inside them, and learning even more about those words. Even the idea of what counts as a 'word' starts to become confused when linguists try to produce watertight definitions (Singleton 1999). However, we will start from words in the recognition that infants, children and adults talk about 'words' and think in terms of a word as a discrete unit. Children will ask what a particular word means, or how to say a word in the foreign language, and, in learning to read, the word is a key unit in building up skills and knowledge.

The role of words as language units begins with the early use of nouns for naming objects in first language acquisition, and of use of other words to express the child's wants and needs, e.g. *'more!'* or *'no'*. Infants go through a period of rapid vocabulary growth as they start to name, as well as interact with, the world around them. There is an interesting coincidence in timing between infants learning to point, and a well-documented sudden increase in the rate of acquisition of nouns for naming objects, as if the two reinforce each other by enabling the children to get helpful adults to label the world for them. Many of these words are 'names for things', acquired through ostensive definition, i.e. by the child seeing or touching the object that a word refers to. Very often early words are used to do things, so that when a young child says *'daddy book'*, she may be trying to get her father to give her a book or to read a book to her, with the context of use making the intended meaning quite clear.

We need to be aware, as Vygotsky warned, that although children may use the same words as adults, they may not hold the same meanings for those words (Vygotsky 1962; Wertsch 1985). The acquisition of word meanings takes much longer than the acquisition of the spoken form of the words, and children use words in their speech long before they have a full understanding of them (Locke 1993). We can think of words as rather like flowers growing in the soil. All we see above ground is the flower, but that flower is kept alive and growing by roots that spread underneath it. Underneath the flowers of spoken words lie the roots, a connected web of meanings, understandings and links. All through childhood, words are used with only a partial understanding of the full meaning system that underlies them. This is true for adults too; you only have to think about technical words that we use quite happily, but whose full meanings are not known, such as *carburettor* or *hard disk*. We can use words with 'good enough' meanings for them; if we had to have complete knowledge of words before using them, we would be restricted to very limited vocabularies. In this sense, our production races ahead of our comprehension, and vocabulary development is a continuous process, not just of adding new words but of building up knowledge about words we already know partially.

For children learning the vocabulary of a foreign language, this partial knowledge issue is compounded. Some of the foreign language words will map on to word meanings that are already fully formed in the first language. Many of the words, however, may link to first language words and concepts that they are in the process of learning about and have only partial meanings for. In addition, the first and foreign language words may not map straightforwardly one on to another, but may have different underlying meanings because of cultural or other differences. What these complications emphasise is that vocabulary development *is* about learning words, but that learning words is not something that is done and finished with. Learning words is a cyclical process of meeting new words and initial learning, followed by meeting those words again and again, each time extending knowledge of what the words mean and how they are used in the foreign language. Each time children meet familiar words again, they too have changed and will bring new first language and conceptual knowledge to the vocabulary. The root system of word knowledge continues to grow and become thicker and more tightly inter-linked, so that the flowers of word use are more and more strongly supported.

4.2.2 Vocabulary size

Having acknowledged the complexity of knowing words, and before pursuing it in more detail, we will briefly focus on vocabulary development in terms of building up a greater number of words. Some useful work has been done on measuring the size of learners' vocabularies that will put a helpful perspective on classroom foreign language learning.

When researchers set out to measure vocabulary size, or how many words someone knows, they have to make many simplifying assumptions and decisions. For example, in many measures, only receptive knowledge is measured: a person is said to 'know' a word if they can recognise its meaning when they see it. Vocabulary size is usually measured to the nearest thousand, and counts 'word families', in which a base word and all its inflected forms and derived forms counts as one e.g. the word family is the base form *walk* plus *walking, walked, walks, a walk*. The English language is said to contain around 54,000 (54K) word families, when these are counted in a large dictionary (Nation and Waring 1997). No one person knows all the words in the language, of course, and figures for native speaker adults range from 20K for a student of about eighteen years of age starting university (Nation and Waring 1997) to the 37K that Shakespeare is alleged to have used, although he did invent many of those! Child native speakers of English have about 4 or 5K word families by the age of five, to which they add about 1K each year. Second language learners of English who attend English speaking school have also been found to add about 1K per year, but the 4–5K gap between them and their native speaker peers remains (Nation and Waring 1997). Nation (1990) reports studies of foreign language learners in India and Indonesia that showed children reaching 1 or 2K word families in English after five years of regular lessons.

These figures show that the gap between vocabulary size in first and foreign language is very large, and seldom closed, even by adult FL learners after many years of study. They also suggest that a realistic target for children learning a foreign language might be around 500 words a year, given good learning conditions.

To put the numbers into some perspective, it is important to note that not all words are equally useful in using a foreign language. When words are considered in terms of their frequency of use in written texts, it seems that the most frequent 2K English words account for a large proportion (80% or more) of all texts (Nation 2001). Vocabulary teaching can be focused to help learners build up a knowledge of words in ways that will enable them to use the language efficiently and successfully. We return to this later.

4.2.3 What it means to know a word

To illustrate the many types of knowledge involved in 'knowing a word', consider the following classroom extract, in which a native-speaker teacher is talking with a second language learner of English about the equipment needed to draw a pie chart (a circular graph that shows proportions like a pie or cake cut into slices).

    1 T: a compass (2.0) you need a compass (.)
           what else do you need for a pie chart? (2.0)
           because you're measuring angles aren't you? slices of the cake
           (.) so to speak (.)
           so what do you need for angles?
    5 P: measure (.) angle measure
       T: what's it called? is there a special name for (.) the piece of
           equipment that we use for measuring angles? (.)
           go on (.) you've started
       P: ????? *(unclear utterance)*
   10 T: protractor

The extract of classroom talk helps consider what the pupil knows about the word *protractor* and what he still has to learn about it. If we ask the naive question – Does the pupil know the word *protractor*? – we would have to answer that he does seem to know something about it, since he tries to say it in line 9, and in order to do that, he must understand the meaning of what is being talked about. Word knowledge is always then a matter of degree, rather than all or nothing. The pupil seems to have some receptive knowledge of the word, but not yet to have sufficient productive knowledge to be able to produce it automatically on demand (line 5). Because the pupil did not himself say the word in this piece of discourse, we cannot tell whether he can pronounce the word acceptably, i.e. has phonological knowledge of the word.

This exchange was spoken, so that, even if the pupil's productive spoken knowledge of the word has increased and he remembers the word next time he needs it, he still may not recognise it when he sees it written down (decoding knowledge) or be able to spell it (orthographic knowledge).

Notice that, in the last line, the teacher tells the pupil the word *protractor*, but only gives him the single word. As a result, the pupil does not receive any grammatical information about how the word works in clauses or phrases. For example, he needs to know that we say *a* or *the protractor* (it is a countable noun and needs an article), that the plural form is *protractors*. There is further information about the **use** of the word, its pragmatics, that is part of knowing it: to know that a protractor is a technical term for the piece of equipment used when talking mathematics (knowledge of style and register); to know that in English certain other words are likely to occur in surrounding discourse, we *use a protractor to draw / divide a circle/ measure angles* (collocational knowledge). A further type of knowledge about a word is metalinguistic, concerning the formal properties of the word, e.g. to know that *protractor* is a noun.

These different aspects of word knowledge are summarised in Table 4.1, which combines similar lists from Ellis and Sinclair (1990: 99) and Schmitt and Meara (1997: 18). These in turn drew on work by Richards (1976) and Nation (1990).

Table 4.1 *Knowing about a word*		
Type of knowledge	*what is involved*	*example*
Receptive knowledge: aural / decoding	to understand it when it is spoken / written	
memory	to recall it when needed	
conceptual knowledge	to use it with the correct meaning	not confusing *protractor* with *compasses*
knowledge of the spoken form: phonological knowledge	to hear the word and to pronounce it acceptably, on its own, and in phrases and sentences	to hear and produce the endings of verb forms, such as the /n/ sound at the end of *undertaken*
grammatical knowledge	to use it in a grammatically accurate way; to know grammatical connections with other words	*she sang very well* not * *she sang very good;* to know that *is* and *be* are parts of the same verb
collocational knowledge	to know which other words can be used with it	*a beautiful view* not * *a good-looking view*
orthographic knowledge	to spell it correctly	*protractor* not * *protracter*
pragmatic knowledge, knowledge of style and register	to use it in the right situation	*would you like a drink?* is more appropriate in a formal or semi-formal situation than *what can I get you?*
connotational knowledge	to know its positive and negative associations, to know its associations with related words	to know that *slim* has positive connotations, when used about a person, whereas *skinny* is negative
metalinguistic knowledge	to know explicitly about the word, e.g. its grammatical properties	to know that *protractor* is a *noun;* to know that *pro* is a *prefix*

In summary, knowing about a word involves knowing about its **form** (how it sounds, how it is spelt, the grammatical changes that can be made to it), its **meaning** (its conceptual content and how it relates to other concepts and words), and its **use** (its patterns of occurrence with other words, and in particular types of language use). The next section looks more deeply into different types of meaning and their development in childhood.

4.2.4 Developing meanings in childhood

Empirical research shows that increasing the depth of word knowledge does not happen automatically in a foreign or second language, even in what seems like the most favourable circumstances where children are immersed in the language through their schooling. Verhallen and Schoonen (1993; 1998) have shown that Turkish children at school in Holland know fewer meaning aspects of Dutch words that their native speaker peers, and also know fewer meaning aspects in their first language than in their second. Schmitt's research with adults learning English as a foreign language showed that they too are often working with a limited set of meanings for words (Schmitt 1998). Learning a word takes a long time and many exposures to the word used in different situations.

Conceptual knowledge grows as children experience more and more of the world in their daily lives. There are also maturational factors that seem to affect the nature of conceptual knowledge about first language vocabulary at different ages, and that can be expected to have a knock-on effect for foreign language learning. One of these factors is the 'syntagmatic-paradigmatic shift' that occurs between five and ten years of age (Miller and Johnson-Laird 1976; Singleton 1999). This shift refers to the types of associations that children make between words and ideas. Children in word-association experiments are given a word and asked what the word brings to mind; as they get older, so the types of words that come to mind seem to change. When given a cue word like *dog* or *table*, younger children tend to make syntagmatic associations, choosing a linking idea in a word from a different part of speech, or word class, so the noun cue words might produce verb responses *bark* or *eat*. We can also think of these links as 'thematic', in that the ideas link together in a kind of theme. Older children are more likely to respond to cue words with words from the same word class: *animal* or *chair*. These are called paradigmatic responses (Verhallen and Schoonen 1998: 454; Singleton 1999: 76). Recall that the word 'paradigmatic' was used in section 3.5.3 to describe discourse that is organised through categories, rather than temporally as in narrative. Children's shift to paradigmatic responses probably reflects other developments: they become more able to deal with abstract connections, such as 'a dog is a kind of animal', and they build up more knowledge of the world, words to go with it and ways of organising it. Schooling has a major impact on how children's knowledge and vocabulary develops because it introduces them to formal logical thinking. As they move through school, so they learn how to sort things into sets, how to classify and label sets and categories according to characteristics, how to compare and contrast categories. The categorising, labelling and talking about categories is, moreover, increasingly carried out in the language of the adult world, as children learn the ways of thinking and using language that is characteristic of subject disciplines such as science and history. Schooling also moves children from the concrete to the abstract as they no longer only work with what they can see and touch, as happens at home and in nurseries, but develop skills for working with ideas and talking about what is not immediately present.

As children deepen their word knowledge, they increase both syntagmatic and paradigmatic knowledge, but also shift over the years of childhood towards more emphasis on the paradigmatic and the abstract. Because these developments occur deep in a child's mind, they will be applicable to foreign language learning too, in that children will increasingly be able to handle paradigmatic aspects of word meaning, and words with less concrete meanings.

4.2.5 Categorisation and word learning

Research into the types of categories used in early childhood has shown that the middle of a general to specific hierarchy is particularly significant for children, and hence for their foreign language learning (Lakoff 1987; Cameron 1994). Here are two examples of hierarchies with the most general concept, or superordinate, at the top, and the most specific, labelled subordinate, at the bottom:

Superordinate	FURNITURE	ANIMAL
Basic level	CHAIR	DOG
Subordinate	ROCKING CHAIR	SPANIEL

In each case, the hierarchies could be extended upwards and downwards. However, it is the middle, or 'basic', level that is of interest. The words for basic level concepts are the most commonly used words, they are learnt by children before words higher or lower in the hierarchy, they are the shortest words, and they are the words used in neutral contexts e.g. *We have always kept dogs* is more likely to be used than *We have always kept spaniels*. Conceptually, the basic level is the highest level at which objects have similar shapes, are used in similar ways and at which a single mental image can be used for the whole category (Lakoff 1987). So, we can create a single image of a chair, but not of furniture, and we interact physically with all chairs in the same way (sitting on them), but interact differently with different examples of furniture. At the basic level, a child's experience with the physical world links directly into the development of concepts and vocabulary, serving as an 'entry point' for learning.

In the foreign language classroom, basic level concepts are more likely to have been mastered than superordinate and subordinate levels that develop through formal education (see section 4.2.4 above). When teaching vocabulary around a topic or lexical set, e.g. *food* or *space travel*, we can begin from basic level items, such as *pizza* or *rocket*, moving over time to superordinate or more general vocabulary (such as *vegetables* or *vehicles*), and downwards to more specific words (*sprouting broccoli* or *moon landing module*).

4.2.6 Cultural content in word meanings

Words and their meanings are connected in syntagmatic and paradigmatic patterns as described above. These patterns create networks of connections in the mind that have been variously called 'schemas' (or 'schemata'), 'scripts' and 'frames'. When a word is encountered, the schema that they are part of will be activated, and the network of activated meanings becomes available to help make sense of the discourse and the words at a holistic level.

While the detailed theory of schemas is not necessary here, the general idea of networked and connected ideas in the mind is a useful one in thinking about vocabulary. In particular, it is helpful to remember that, for foreign language learners, these schemas are usually being constructed throughout childhood (and onwards) **within the first language culture**. When foreign language words are learnt, they are likely to be mapped on to first language words and to thereby enter schemas that have already been built up. However, this mapping of foreign language words on to first language schemas may lead to problems, because different cultures organise aspects of the world differently. The schemas that foreign language words are placed in may be appropriate for the first language but less so for the second. For example, if someone living in Britain says, '*I'll go and fetch the milk*', they are (still) quite likely to mean that they will go to the front door and pick up the bottles of milk delivered by a 'milkman'. The schema of *milk* includes doorstep deliveries; for someone living outside Britain, this is unlikely, and fetching milk may involve a trip to the supermarket.

Hsia *et al.* (1995) found that Chinese learners of English in Hong Kong used their first language schemas in organising their foreign language words. One learner put together the words *early* and *light*, explaining this as 'when light first appears at dawn'. The same Chinese character is used for *early* and *morning*, so that the learner may have associated the word *early* with the schema for *morning*.

4.2.7 The development of children's vocabulary: Summary

What implications does vocabulary and conceptual development across the early years at school have for vocabulary development in children's foreign language learning? Conclusions from this section and principles for teaching are listed below:

– The types of words that children find possible to learn will shift. Five year olds learning a foreign language need very concrete vocabulary that connects with objects they can handle or see, whereas older learners can cope with words and topics that are more abstract and remote from their immediate experience.
– Vocabulary development is not just learning more words but is also importantly about expanding and deepening word knowledge. Children need to meet words again and again, in new contexts that help increase what they know about words. Teaching needs to include the recycling of words.
– Words and word knowledge can be seen as being linked in networks of meaning. Meeting a word will activate the network and thus provide support for understanding and for learning.
– Basic level words are likely to be more appropriate for younger children, or when learning vocabulary for new concepts. Older learners can benefit from building up superordinate and subordinate vocabulary linked to basic level words they already know.
– Children change in how they can learn words. Whereas the very young learners will learn words as collections, older children are much more able to make connections between the words they learn and to use the paradigmatic organisation of words and concepts as a help in vocabulary learning.

4.3 Organisation of words in a language

The idea of vocabulary items and meanings linked in an increasingly complex web of connections in the mind is important for learning, and for teaching. Further ways of thinking about links between words in the foreign language are considered in this section. These connections are primarily linguistic i.e. to do with the language as formally analysed, but they can also be useful for learning by organising the words taught in lessons and activities.

4.3.1 Function and content words

The words of a language split roughly into two groups according to how they are used to construct sentences. Content words are those that carry a lexical meaning, even out of context, whereas function words seem to be mainly used to carry grammatical meaning. In the following sentence, the content words are underlined, and all the others are function words:

The *little house* in the *street* was *built* when my *mother* was a *child*.

The distinction is based on meaning but maps fairly neatly on to word class, and on to potential for coining new words. So content words are nouns (e.g. *house*), lexical verbs (e.g. *built*), adjectives (e.g. *little*); function words are modal and auxiliary verbs (e.g. *could, was*), articles (e.g. *a, the*), and prepositions. Content words form an 'open set' in that new content words can be invented, whereas the set of function words is 'closed'. New nouns like *calendarisation* (adding the date to a document automatically) are constantly being added to the language, but new prepositions are very rare. The distinction between content and function words is not unproblematic (Singleton 1999), but it does capture an important idea for language teaching. There is also some neurological evidence that this is an important distinction: research into reading is showing that function and content words may be stored in different parts of the brain. As we have seen, content words are mentally linked in schemas or networks of meaning. Networks are less important for understanding and remembering function words. Function words are a much smaller set, and are used very frequently: for example, the first 71 words in order of frequency of occurrence in the Cobuild corpus of English are function words, and only six content words come in the first 150 most frequently used words (Carter and McCarthy 1988: 149).

Content and function words need different teaching approaches. While the meaning of content words can be explained and talked about, it is very difficult to do this with function words. Children will learn function words incidentally, through continued use in a range of different discourse contexts, rather than through direct teaching or explanation. Content words can be taught in more planned and explicit ways.

4.3.2 Sense relations

Content word meanings in a language can relate to each other in a range of ways, called 'sense relations' (Lyons 1995), also labelled 'semantic relations' or 'lexical relations'. The types of sense relations that hold between words include:

- *antonymy* being opposite in meaning e.g. *alive – dead*;
- *synonymy* having (nearly) the same meaning e.g. *rich – wealthy*;
- *hyponymy* one is an example or type of another e.g. *furniture – chair*;
- *meronymy* one is part of another: e.g. *army – soldier*.

Hyponymy overlaps with the idea of basic level words introduced in section 2.2.5.

4.3.3 Organisation of words in the language: summary and teaching principles

Content and function words work differently in the language, and will be taught and learnt differently. Function words will be acquired through repeated use in different contexts. Content words can be taught more directly.

Content words can be linked as sets of related ideas in various ways. This organisation can help in analysing text book demands, in choosing teaching activities and in extending learners' vocabulary beyond the text book. Text book writers and syllabus designers often use the various types of word organisation to write and structure courses. As a result, we can also use them to analyse the content and demand on learners. It is important in considering the suitability of texts for learners to set the vocabulary demand (4.3) against conceptual development factors (4.2). Vocabulary input may be well organised but may still not be compatible with the age and developmental point of the pupils.

4.4 Learning and teaching vocabulary

The information about mental development, categorisation, and lexis in language is now taken forwards into the practicalities of the young learner classroom. After considering what is known about the path of vocabulary learning, we examine what text books, lessons and activities can usefully offer the young learner.

4.4.1 The dynamic nature of vocabulary learning

In the previous paragraph, I deliberately chose to use the word **path**, rather than **steps** or **stages**, to emphasise the **dynamic and continuous** nature of vocabulary learning. Hatch and Brown (1995: 372) describe five 'essential steps' in vocabulary learning based on research into learners' strategies:

(1) having sources for encountering new words;
(2) getting a clear image, whether visual or auditory or both, for the forms of the new words;
(3) learning the meaning of the words;
(4) making a strong memory connection between the forms and meanings of the words;
(5) using the words.

We have seen that there is a lot to be learnt about a word and that children's capacities for learning change as they get older. So the learning of words is a process that continues, but that changes in nature as it continues. To use a metaphor, learning words is not like ticking off items on a shopping list when they have been bought. It is more like the continual process of trying to keep a house clean; the cleaning (or learning) can be done one day, but needs doing again the next. Floors and furniture need to be cleaned in different ways, but both need to be clean for a room to look clean, just as function and content words, or superordinate and basic level words, may be learnt in different ways.

Vocabulary needs to be met and recycled at intervals, in different activities, with new knowledge and new connections developed each time the same words are met again. Looking at the five steps, we can see that each 'step' is in fact something that needs to happen over and over again, so that each time something new is learnt or remembered. Nation (1990) suggests that a new word needs to be met at least five or six times in a text book unit before it has any chance of being learnt. I am emphasising the need for words to recur, not just in a unit, but across units or chapters, and across levels and years. For children who start language learning young this is particularly important. Although some of the words learnt early on may become redundant because they refer to childish things e.g. *doll*, many others will be useful later, but only if they can be recalled. Recycling makes recall more probable.

In the following sections we examine what may help learners at various points in the learning process.

4.4.2 Learning the meaning of new words

Nation (1990: 51) listed basic techniques by which teachers can explain the meanings of new words, all of which can be used in the young learner classroom:

> *By demonstration or pictures*
> (1) using an object
> (2) using a cut-out figure
> (3) using gesture
> (4) performing an action
> (5) photographs
> (6) drawings or diagrams on the board
> (7) pictures from books
> (to these we might add moving images, from TV, video or computer)
>
> *By verbal explanation*
> (8) analytical definition (as in the teacher's description of a *protractor*, on page 76, lines 6 and 7)
> (9) putting the new word in a defining context (e.g. an *ambulance* takes sick people to hospital)
> (10) translating into another language

Verbal explanations (8) and (9) clearly require greater pre-existing knowledge of the language, but even at a fairly simple level, definitions and explanations can help activate schemas or networks that will in turn help understanding. If children know *hospital*, then mentioning it will help them construct a meaning for *ambulance*, by activating scenarios connected with hospitals.

Notice that all except (10) require the learner to do some mental work in constructing a meaning for the new foreign language word. The amount of mental work done by learners affects how well a new word is engraved in memory; the more learners have to think about a word and its meaning, the more likely they are to remember it. This hypothesis about the importance of 'deep processing' (Craik and Lockhart 1972) can be complemented by noting that methods that involve relatively 'shallow' processing, such as repetition and learning lists by heart, can also help memorising (Schmitt 1997). However, it is important to realise that the immediate translation of a new word takes away from the child any need or motivation to think about the meaning of the foreign language word or to hold the new word in mind. As a result, although understanding may be rapid and painless, longer term remembering is less likely.

Sometimes a new word is first explained in the foreign language or with pictures, but is then immediately translated in the first language. Pupils will soon realise the pattern of their teacher's explanations and learn that they don't have to concentrate on working out the meaning, because the translation is predictably given afterwards. As a general principle, it would seem useful to avoid translation as a regular way of explaining new words, and to try other techniques, both for variety and for promoting learning. Often when new words are introduced, pupils will produce the first language translation. Then the teacher can accept the translation, as useful evidence of understanding, but can still proceed with explanations in the foreign language that will provide useful input.

Nation suggests that an explanation is quickly followed by a check of understanding, using a different technique. So, having explained *ambulance* through a defining context, learners' understanding can be checked by asking them to identify an ambulance in a picture. If the new word has not been understood, a further explanation can be given.

4.4.3 Attending to form

Form – how a word is pronounced and how it is written – is a key part of word knowledge. For young learners, the spoken form should have priority, but written forms can be introduced either soon after, for learners who are literate in the foreign language, or some time later as reading and writing skills are developed. With a focus on discourse and embedding new words in a discourse context, we may be at risk of forgetting that form is difficult to notice when a word is encountered in a sentence. Pupils need to hear a new word in isolation as well as in a discourse context, so that they can notice the sounds at the beginning and end, the stress pattern of the word, and the syllables that make up the word. They will need to hear the word spoken in isolation several times to catch all this information. If we again use the example of *ambulance*, then the teacher's explanation could be followed by saying the word by itself several times, before returning it to a discourse context. The teacher talk might look like this:

> *An ambulance takes sick people to hospital.*
> *Ambulance*
> *Am-bu-lance*
> *Ambulance*
> *Can you see the ambulance in this picture?* (child points to picture)
> *Yes, there's the ambulance arriving at the hospital.*

When children encounter the written form of a new word, their attention should be drawn to its shape, to initial and final letters, to letter clusters, and to its spelling.

4.4.4 Making strong memory connections

Having met and understood a new word, and paid attention to its form, the pupils' vocabulary learning process has begun. The word has entered the learner's short term memory, and the next teaching issue is how to build up the memory of the word so that it is available for use in the longer term. Memorising activities are needed at the point of learning new words for the first time, and at regular intervals to recycle vocabulary, so that it stays active and ready to use.

Vocabulary memorising activities can make central use of the idea of networks of meaning that have been discussed in some detail earlier in the chapter. As we revisit these links below, each type is followed by examples of vocabulary memorising activities. Many of the organisational networks lend themselves to diagrams or pictures, and the use of different media can help memorising.

(1) Thematic organisation of vocabulary

Things that go together or happen together. A theme can be seen as including:

> people + objects + actions + processes (combinations of actions) + typical events + places.

Children can build up a collage on the theme of shopping that will practise newly learnt words such as *shopping bag, change, assistant,* and at the same time recycle earlier learnt words for *food.* To make sure the words are actually used, the teacher might give the pupils a list of things to be included in their collage; the learners then decide how to share out the list between them and set out to find and cut out pictures in old magazines. Before making the collage, each learner has to report back to their group and show the pictures they have found of their allotted items. The large collage pictures can be used as a background context to introduce and practise further vocabulary for actions and processes e.g. *stack the shelves, pay the bill, push the trolley.*

More formally diagrammed grids and sets can be used to organise vocabulary, providing practice in the process, e.g. sorting pictures of sports equipment, famous players, clothing (or the words) into sets of basketball / football / tennis, etc. Nation (1990: 99) has a version for older learners who can cope with grids and tables.

(2) Organisation of vocabulary through relations of wholes to parts

For example, *body – arms / legs – fingers / toes*.

When parts of the body are to be learnt, initial explanations are easily done by pointing and touching. Memorising activities could include singing the song '*Heads, shoulders, knees and toes*', in which moving and touching link with saying the words. Alternatively, children might work in pairs on a 'listen and do' activity, each giving the other instructions to draw an imaginary animal or monster: '*draw two blue heads, six legs, a long tail*'. The completed monster pictures can be used for further practice through listening: they are all placed on the wall or board, the teacher describes one and pupils identify which it is, and through speaking: a pupil selects one picture secretly and the others have to guess by asking yes / no questions such as '*does it have two heads?*'

(3) Organisation of vocabulary in general to specific hierarchies

For example, types of *food – vegetables – cabbages*.

Activities to sort and categorise will practise vocabulary through this type of organisation. If food words are being learnt, children can sort real items into vegetables and fruit, naming the individual items as they go.

Some language games also exploit this type of organisation. The game 'Shipwreck' puts pupils into teams with pencil and paper. They are given three minutes to list all the *drinks* they can think of, then all the *food*, then all the *clothes*. Then one team reads out their list item by item, and if another team has also written an item, it has to be crossed off everyone's list. Teams can only keep items that no-one else has listed. At the end of the game, teams have to imagine themselves landing on a desert island after a shipwreck, with only those items left on their list (usually an amusing selection of odd things).

'Word Tennis' splits the class into two teams. The teacher names a category e.g. *sports*, and teams take it in turns to give examples in a kind of tennis rally. The winner is the last team to find a word. The game then repeats with another category.

These kinds of games bring together previously learnt vocabulary in organised groups, recycling them and embedding them back more deeply in memory. Played at odd moments in lessons, they can help keep words active.

(4) Organisation of vocabulary through words and antonyms

Some words that have meanings related through antonymy can be placed on lines or clines (sloping lines) that give a picture of the degrees of difference, e.g.:

hot – warm – cold

With young children this can be done with real objects or pictures to support the foreign language words e.g. food that is hot, warm and cold, rather than with written words. New words can be inserted between known words e.g. *cool* would be placed between *warm* and *cold*.

Organising words by their related meanings can help with memorising and recycling more abstract words, e.g.:

always – usually – sometimes – never

For older learners, these words could be written on cards that have to be placed in order by meaning. A further set of pictures of activities could then be sorted and placed under the appropriate adverb e.g. *eating breakfast, taking the bus to school, going to the cinema.*

A game that exploits these graded adverbs has a pupil construct a description of someone famous or in the class from a set of sentences, each using one of the adverbs. The rest of the class has to guess who they are describing. For example: '*he always succeeds in his tasks; he usually helps people in need; he sometimes flies through the air; he never tells anyone his identity*' (answer: Superman).

(5) Organising vocabulary in 'ad-hoc' categories

This is the name given to collections of things put together on the spur of the moment e.g. *things to take on a picnic* (Barsalou 1987). A nice example of how this can be exploited for vocabulary practice comes from a Malaysian text book unit on the topic of equipping an office (Moving On, Year 6). The unit has a set of vocabulary items introduced through pictures: *files, a typewriter, stapler, paper clips, envelopes, a filing cabinet*, etc. Later in the unit, pupils are asked to look at the items and say which can be brought back from the shop and which will need to come later in a lorry. This is a simple activity, but one which requires pupils to think and use the new words, and thus helps those words become part of the learners' longer term vocabulary resources.

4.4.5 Extending children's vocabulary beyond the text book

The vocabulary of course books for young learners is fairly predictable. Most start with words connected to the family, the house, the school, and work outwards from the child's world, bringing in other countries, topics from history and so on. As is conventional in foreign language teaching, vocabulary input is limited. It is clear from talking to teachers that many pupils either fail to learn, or forget, a lot of the vocabulary they meet in their early years and that is vital for future language learning. Often, text books do not help because pupils only meet new words briefly and there are insufficient recycling and consolidation activities. Extra recycling and consolidation activities need to be added.

However, there is another concern about vocabulary learning that at first sight seems quite the contrary to this: are children encouraged to learn a wide enough vocabulary in their foreign language?

Children are getting more and more global in their interests through the Internet, television and video, and computer games. Their worlds are much bigger, from much younger ages, than used to be the case. It may be that young learners could take on much more vocabulary than their course books and syllabuses give them access to, given the opportunity.

The two issues may be connected: difficulties in learning vocabulary may result from that vocabulary not being sufficiently connected to pupils' real lives, rather than the lives that text book and syllabus writers think they should lead!

Here are three ways in which the vocabulary that children are given access to could reach beyond the text book.

(1) Working outwards from the text book

Start from the topic of the text book unit, but do not stop with the words that are given. The idea of thematic organisation will help extend the words. Take the Malaysian example of 'Setting Up an Office' that I have already referred to. Vocabulary extension could begin by asking what other types of equipment would be needed for a really up-to-date office (*computer, laser printer, mobile phone*). It can then move to the people who work in an office (*manager, clerk*) and the jobs they do (*filing, faxing*), and to the events that happen in offices (*meetings, appointments*). We could then pick up the general-specific organisation of words, and note that the set vocabulary in the book is mostly basic level. Perhaps some superordinates would be helpful (*furniture, stationery*). Subordinates would recycle *large / small* envelopes or *plastic / metal* paper clips.

The idea of moving outwards from a given topic is very powerful in adjusting a text book unit to suit learners; it will be recycled when we look at working with stories.

Such vocabulary extension techniques can also help if a text book unit contains too many different topics with insufficient repetition of vocabulary. Instead of following the book to the letter, teachers can enrich and recycle vocabulary from just one of the topics, including the spoken language activities or grammar learning set out but just changing the background or situational context.

(2) Learners' choice

Vocabulary learning around a topic could begin from the learners rather than from the book, by asking them directly what words they already know and what words they would like to learn in the foreign language. Here is a positive use of first language that leads to the foreign language, rather than away from it as translation does. Suppose the book has a unit on wild animals. The teacher could write 'wild animals' on the board and ask learners what they already know and which words they would like to know in the foreign language. The words are then written on the board, the unknown ones in the first language and then translated into the foreign language (from Phillips 1993).

In doing this activity, learners will meet the word in isolation but also within the larger meaning context of the topic. The first language words can be rubbed off the board, leaving just the foreign language words to be copied down, perhaps illustrated with a quick picture to serve as a reminder to meaning.

(3) Incidental learning of vocabulary through stories

Young children learn many of their first language words through social interaction with adults, and the use of stories in young learner classrooms would seem to offer similar rich opportunities for learning vocabulary indirectly, or incidentally, while attending to something else. Additionally, words encountered in stories are heard in linguistic and discourse contexts, so that important grammatical and collocational information is available about words. Moreover, the plot and characters of a story are likely to form a thematic organisation for many of the words, thus assisting understanding and learning.

The potential of stories for learning must not be assumed, but should be based on empirical evidence, and it must be said that very little research evidence is available. One study carried out by Elley (1989) investigated how 7 and 8 year old children learnt words from stories in their first language. He found encouraging results: that useful amounts of vocabulary were learnt, and retained over several months, and that the lowest ability children improved most. Several factors influenced learning: the number of occurrences of a new word in the story; the number of times the word was pictured; the helpfulness of cues to meaning in the text. When teacher explanations of new words were added to the process, gains in vocabulary doubled. However, he found that different stories had different effects on vocabulary learning, and suggested that children's involvement in a story affects what they can learn from it. We should also recall that learning words takes a long time and that some of the effects he found might have been due to previously partially known words becoming better known.

It is important to note the need to match stories to children's interests and language levels; if there are too many new words, a story might make no sense to the learners. Views on how many new words should be in a text vary from 1 new word per 15 words to 1 per 50 words (Nation 1990).

4.5 Children's vocabulary learning strategies

By vocabulary learning strategies we mean the actions that learners take to help themselves understand and remember vocabulary. Schmitt makes a useful distinction between 'discovery' strategies, such as looking up a new word in a dictionary or guessing it from its context, and 'consolidation' strategies, such as learning a list of words by heart or asking someone to test you (Schmitt 1997).

4.5.1 Empirical evidence on the usefulness of strategies

Much empirical work has been done on vocabulary learning strategies, although again unfortunately very little with young language learners. Schmitt (1997) contains an overview and a taxonomy of strategies. Some studies though have investigated strategy use by secondary level pupils just slightly older than our age group (Ahmed 1988, Schmitt 1997, Schouten-van Parreren 1992). These show that strategy use changes with age and that successful and less successful learners vary in what strategies they use and in how they use them.

Schouten-van Parreren investigated Dutch 12–15 year olds working out the meanings of new words in reading French as a foreign language. She found that weak learners, who generally had smaller vocabularies in their first language too, did not make systematic use of the information about a word available in the text. Unlike the strong learners who picked up information from the linguistic context, from the topic, from illustrations, etc., the weak learners tended to focus on just one or other source of information that seemed salient to them. This meant that they often guessed the meaning of words without enough information to get them right. They also did not embed new words in tightly connected networks of information and meaning, and so were less successful at remembering them. They were also less 'flexible' as learners, not looking beyond what was salient and staying with a meaning when they had guessed it, even if it was clearly not right. The differences between learners suggest useful strategies that teachers can encourage learners to adopt:

- guessing meanings by using all the information available in a picture or text;
- noticing grammatical information about words from the way they are used;
- noticing links to similar words in the first language;
- remembering where a word has been encountered before and how that helps with its form and meaning.

Both Schmitt's and Ahmed's studies compared secondary level learners with older learners, in Japan and the Sudan respectively. They both show changes with age, although this seems to be affected by culturally determined educational practices, such as whether the use of monolingual dictionaries is encouraged in place of bilingual dictionaries. In Japan, older learners did more guessing words from context and creating images of words to help remember them, and they made less use of written repetition of words and study of word spellings or words in lists. In Sudan, younger learners who were successful used other people to help find meanings, but with increasing use of dictionaries as they moved up the school.

4.5.2 Strategies and young learners

The evidence is somewhat inconclusive as to whether it is useful to train young learners in strategy use and, if so, which strategies are most helpful. Schmitt (1997) suggests introducing children to a range of strategies so that these are available for learners to choose from as suits their individual learning styles. Certainly, many of the strategies used by older learners can be seen as having their roots in what happens earlier. It is clear too that learners may not adopt strategies automatically, and thus some explicit training may be helpful. The general principles of helping children to learn (Chapter 1) apply:

- Teachers can model how to use strategies and draw children's attention explicitly to aspects of strategy use. For example, teachers can show how to find clues to the meaning of a new word in a picture or in other words in the same sentence.
- Teachers can teach the sub-skills needed to make use of strategies. For example, to use a dictionary efficiently requires knowledge of alphabetical order and lots of practice with it.
- Classroom tasks can include structured opportunities for using strategies. For example, when reading a story, teachers can explicitly encourage prediction of the meanings of new words.
- Independent strategy use can be rehearsed in classrooms. For example, children can be helped to prepare lists of words that they want to learn from a lesson, can be shown ways of learning from lists and later can be put in pairs to test each other.
- Young learners can be helped to reflect on the learning process through evaluating their achievements. For example, at the end of a lesson they can be asked how many new words they have learnt, and which words they need to learn more about. Through regular self-evaluation, children can come to understand more about what they are learning and how.

4.6 Summary

Vocabulary has been seen as a major resource for language use. Early foreign language learning offers the chance for learners to build up a solid core of words useful for further learning, together with words that are learnt because they interest or excite young learners at that age. However, early vocabulary learning may be ineffective if words are not consolidated and used regularly. Children entering secondary education will have varying amounts of words, some they have mastered really well, some only partially learnt and some that they have met once or twice but not remembered. It should not be assumed that children know what they have been taught, i.e. the content of their course books or syllabus. They know what they have learnt.

Progression in vocabulary learning has been examined from several different perspectives:

1. Over the timescale of primary education, progression in conceptual development impacts on vocabulary learning. As children get older, they are more able to handle abstract ideas and words as well as concrete and the here-and-now; and to work outwards from basic level concepts to more general and more specific concepts and vocabulary.

2. Over lessons and years, knowledge about particular words can be seen as a progression from partial knowledge of their meaning, use and form to fuller knowledge.
3. Over tasks and lessons, progression in vocabulary learning moves from receptive and initial understanding of what a word means to being able to use it appropriately.

Two key ideas for teaching that have emerged are that the linking of words and meaning in connected networks can be exploited for meaning and memorising, and that recycling previously met words in varied contexts and activities is essential to keep learnt words active.

In the previous chapter, we considered the development of discourse skills. Vocabulary is fundamental to using the foreign language as discourse, since vocabulary is both learnt from participating in discourse, and is essential to participating in it. Teachers' planning may separate vocabulary as a resource from discourse skills, in order to think about which words are to be learnt and how, but from a pupil's viewpoint the separation should be much fuzzier. They will encounter new words in a discourse context, which will provide many clues to their meaning and use; they will begin to use new words in a discourse context that makes sense to them and which contains many better known words; they will eventually have those words ready for use in discourse to communicate their own ideas. When words are assembled into discourse, what holds them together is grammar, and it is to grammar that we turn our attention next.

5   Learning grammar

5.1 A place for grammar?

It could be argued that grammar has no place in a young learner classroom, that it is too difficult for children or is not relevant to their learning. In this chapter, I want to open up the idea of 'grammar' and to explore grammar from the learners' perspective. By doing this, I hope to convince readers that grammar does indeed have a place in children's foreign language learning, and that skilful grammar teaching can be useful. Opening up what we mean by 'grammar' will remind us that it is something much more than the lists of labels and rules found in grammar books, and that grammar is closely tied into meaning and use of language, and is inter-connected with vocabulary. We will then see how some current methods of helping learners develop their grammar can be adapted for younger learners.

To start the chapter, a short conversation with a young learner will help focus on grammar and meaning. The following conversation took place between a seven year old boy and myself in Malta, where children start learning English from five, mostly nowadays as a foreign language. I was visiting his English class, where the children had been working on a dinosaur project, and he was showing me his drawing of a Tyrannosaurus Rex. Our conversation, in which he was a mostly silent partner and I did nearly all the talking, went like this (A = adult; P = pupil):

> A: what's that?
> P: it's T Rex.
> A: is it big or small?
> P: big
> A: how big?
> ((silence))
> A: this big? ((demonstrating small size with hand a few inches off the floor))
> ((Child shakes his head to indicate 'no'))
> A: this big? ((demonstrating a waist-high size with hand))
> ((Child shakes his head to indicate 'no'))
> A: this big? ((demonstrating a human size with hand))
> ((Child shakes his head to indicate 'no'))

A: THIS big? ((demonstrating as high as the ceiling with hand
   stretched up))
((Child nods his head to indicate 'yes'))
A: yes, it was VERY big!

By the end of our short conversation, not only had we reached
agreement on the size of T Rex, but I had modelled for the child a new
piece of grammar, which he seemed to need to express what he already
knew about the dinosaur, that *it was very big.* Moreover, the little boy
had understood the meaning of the new piece of English grammar; the
topic of our talk was clear from the picture, and the idea of size was
clear from the gesture and his knowledge of *big.*

Without the grammatical structure *it was very big* in his language
resources, the child could not tell me all he knew about his dinosaur.
With the adjective *big,* he could begin to express his knowledge, but he
needed more to express meaning precisely. By beginning the process of
introducing the new grammatical form, I was helping him expand his
language resources and his communicative possibilities.

Of course, it is possible he did know how to say this, but was too shy.
In that case, the argument still holds: the form had not yet become part
of his language resources available for communication, and this incident
may have helped it move a little towards automaticity by hearing it used
again in a meaningful context. Any one instance of grammar modelling
or use is not itself a guarantee of learning, but should be seen as one
contribution to the learning process; as with vocabulary learning in the
previous chapter, much recycling and meeting again of partly known
forms will be needed. The child would need to hear *very* used with
other words and to have opportunities to say the word himself.

The simple phrase that I introduced to the boy – *it was very big* – may
seem more like vocabulary than grammar, just adding a new vocabulary
item – *very.* To me this was an episode of 'grammar' teaching, because
very by itself has little or no 'meaning', rather, it creates meaning
through its use, intensifying the meaning of any adjective it is placed in
front of. Learning how to use *very* adds not just a single word to the
pupil's language, but a whole new resource for intensifying that could
be applied to previously learnt language to produce new forms, such as
very hot or *very hungry.* If the child had been more advanced, a similar
conversation could have been used to introduce other new pieces of
grammar, e.g. *it was too big to get in the classroom; it was as big as a
house.*

It is also possible that, from our conversation, the child did not notice
the grammar of the sentence, but instead may have caught the whole
phrase, as a chunk. This kind of learning of pre-fabricated phrases, or

chunks of language, is also on the fringes of grammar, but it is probably very important in the early stages. The chunk may be used as a whole for some time, but it is available to be broken down and parts re-used with other words, e.g. *it was very dangerous*. The breaking down and recombining of previously learnt chunks of language is a process of grammar construction, and appears to be a useful part of language learning.

The short conversation about T Rex has illustrated several starting points for thinking about grammar and young learners:

- grammar is necessary to express precise meanings in discourse;
- grammar ties closely into vocabulary in learning and using the foreign language;
- grammar learning can evolve from the learning of chunks of language;
- talking about something meaningful with the child can be a useful way to introduce new grammar;
- grammar can be taught without technical labels (e.g. 'intensifying adverb').

In the next section, discussion of three different meanings of the word 'grammar' helps to clarify what is happening when children learn the grammar of the foreign language. Section 5.3 reviews current views on grammar learning. Section 5.4 gives a historical overview of how grammar teaching has developed towards the current approach of 'focusing on form'. These theoretical sections yield a set of principles for learning-centred grammar teaching that are set out in section 5.5. Techniques and sample activities that put these principles into action are then developed in section 5.6.

5.2 Different meanings of 'grammar'

The word **grammar** has been used so far to refer to an aspect of how a language, in this case English, is conventionally used, i.e. to the **structure** or **system** of a particular language. But it is a slippery word, and is also used to refer to the way that system is described by linguists, as in 'Chomskyan grammar'; 'systemic functional grammar', and to the internal mental representation of the language that an individual has built up, as in the 'learner's grammar'. Before proceeding, I should like to briefly clarify these different meanings of *grammar*.

5.2.1 The grammar of a language

Think for a moment about the foreign language in use as a first language: for example, French being spoken in French-speaking homes, schools, shops, factories, television; in Canada, in France, in Togo. Every time native speakers of French use the language, they re-create it to express their ideas or needs to other people, and each time French is used, it changes a little for the people using it. A 'language' does not really exist as an object or entity, separate from people; we tend to think of it that way, but we might also think of it as a collection of all its uses. As such, a language is constantly changing, i.e. it is dynamic (Larsen-Freeman 1997). If you are in contact with teenagers and listen to how they talk to each other, the dynamic nature of language is very obvious; new words and ways of talking come and go in days.

To teach a language to non-native speakers, we need to stop it, to fix it so that we can understand it as a more static set of ways of talking, and break it into bits to offer to learners. Breaking a language into word-sized bits produces 'vocabulary', finding patterns in how words are put together produces 'grammar'. So English has the pattern, i.e. a regularity across many or most native speakers, that expresses the idea of intensification by placing *very* in front of adjectives. These patterns are often called 'rules', but we should notice that patterns are rules in so far as they **describe what people usually do**, rather than being like 'school rules' or 'rules of football' that teachers or referees ensure are obeyed.

5.2.2 Theoretical and pedagogic grammars

Theoretical linguists concern themselves with finding and describing the patterns in the use of a language. The way they fix and then describe the language depends on their theoretical views about language use and their objectives. Chomskyan linguists aim to describe language as it is internalised in the mind / brain, rather than as it is produced by speakers. Their main goal is to explore, and unify, on a theoretical level, similarities in syntax across all languages, and this work has little, if any, application to the language classroom. At one stage in this research programme, the idea of a 'generative grammar' was developed. Hallidayan linguists, on the other hand, view language as a tool for expressing meaning, and so they categorise language in terms of how meaning is expressed, and produce 'functional grammars'. Now that computers can hold very large samples of a language (the Cobuild Bank of English at the University of Birmingham has over 320 million words at the time of writing), a new generation of 'corpus linguists' are producing grammars based on real data about frequency and patterns of use, rather than on the intuitions of native speakers that were used earlier. New ways of analysing these large datasets are producing new theoretical concepts of language; for example, examining the way certain meanings are expressed can produce 'local grammars' of topics such as definitions and evaluation, which are part of a more 'global' grammar of the language (Hunston and Francis 1998).

These various descriptive grammars aim to be theoretically sound, elegant and complete. They are not primarily designed for the foreign language classroom and, if they are to be used to inform foreign language teaching, need to be adapted with learning and teaching in mind. Such adapted and adjusted grammars are known as 'pedagogical grammars', and familiar examples might be Quirk and Greenbaum (1975) or the Cobuild Grammar (Sinclair 1990).

Pedagogical grammars are explicit descriptions of patterns, or rules, in a language, presented in ways that are helpful to teachers and to learners. Teachers need an overview and description of the whole of the language that is to be taught, but learners will encounter the pedagogical grammar bit by bit, as parts of it are introduced in text book units. While older learners may use a learners' pedagogical grammar, such as *English Grammar in Use* (Murphy 1994), which sets out and explains a description of the language on paper, it is doubtful that learners younger than about ten years of age could benefit from formal pedagogic grammars because of their cognitive demands.

5.2.3 Internal grammars

Learners will meet pedagogical grammar, if not directly from a learners' grammar book, then indirectly through lessons, teacher explanations and text books. A further key distinction needs to be made between this 'grammar', and what any individual learner actually learns about the patterns of the language: his or her 'internal grammar' of the language. Every learner's internal grammar is different from every other's because each has a unique learning experience. Internal grammar is sometimes referred to as 'interlanguage' or as 'linguistic competence'.

I want to emphasise the distinction between external theoretical or pedagogic grammars and internal grammars because it helps us understand why a learner may have been taught a piece of grammar on the syllabus, but may not be able to use that grammatical form in talking or writing. It is essentially yet another way of pointing out the difference between teaching and learning, so that learning can be made central to teaching.

5.3 Development of the internal grammar

In section 3.5.4, I set out a view of language learning as emerging from language use, in which repeated, meaningful encounters with forms of the language produce dynamic and evolving language resources. As the book proceeds, so we are making that general picture more specific, and in this section, we trace a more explicit view of the development of the language resource that is an 'internal grammar', before considering it in the wider context of classroom language teaching and learning.

5.3.1 From words to grammar

There is evidence from adult second language learning and from school-based foreign language learning that, in the beginning stages, learners seem to use words or chunks strung together to get their meanings across, with little attention paid to grammar that would fit the words or chunks together in conventional patterns (Klein and Perdue 1992; Mitchell and Martin 1997; Weinert 1994). We saw examples of this in many of the phrases produced by pupils in the polar animals task in Chapter 3. The question then arises of how these collections of items turn into something more like a language with patterns of grammar.

Cognitive psychology suggests that our brains / minds work always with a limited amount of attentional capacity (or mental attention) that is available to concentrate on getting a task achieved. When that task is communicating an idea or message through the foreign language, then it seems that finding the right words takes up attention early on, but that, once those words or chunks are well known, using them takes up less capacity, and attention is freed for grammar. This will be a repeating process of moving from lexis to grammar, as language resources get gradually more extensive. As a counter-balance to that, social factors will influence the actual need for grammar to communicate. If you can get your message through without grammar, as when a very small knowledge of a language makes it possible to buy food in a foreign shop by naming the item and amount, then there may be little impulse to drive grammar learning. It seems increasingly likely that paying attention to grammatical features of a language is not something that happens automatically in communicating, and that therefore some artificial methods of pushing attention are needed, i.e. teaching!

Weinert's research into Scottish children aged 11–13 years learning German showed that they used formulaic phrases or chunks both for communication and for developing grammar (Weinert 1994). Chunks that had been learnt by rote were sometimes split up into their parts and those parts re-used with other words to make new sentences. Mitchell and Martin, investigating English learners of French (also 11–13 year olds), also found evidence of breaking down of chunks and substituting new words as children struggled to express meanings, in an 'evolution from chunks to creativity' (Mitchell and Martin 1997: 23). Applying these empirical findings to even younger learners suggests that rote-learned chunks of language will make up a substantial part of early learning, and that learnt chunks also provide a valuable resource for developing grammar, as they are broken down and re-constituted. Ways of teaching that help learners notice words inside chunks and how other words can be used in the same places may help with the development of grammar.

5.3.2 Learning through hypothesis testing

Hypothesis testing is the rather grand name given to mental processes that are evidenced from a very early age: for example, as a baby drops her spoon, watches someone pick it up for her, and then drops it again so that it will be picked up again. The baby appears to have constructed a hypothesis 'If I drop my spoon, it will be picked up for me', and to be testing it through repeated trials. Of course, eventually the child learns that the hypothesis was right, but only for a limited number of drops, after which 'adult fatigue' sets in, and the spoon probably disappears!

It is suggested that something similar happens when children learn the grammar of their first language, once they move past holistic use of language chunks. Children do not just produce random word orderings and forms, but they somehow work out how to use the language and then try out their hypotheses in saying things, amending them when they hear alternative versions. It is as if the child has worked out a 'grammar rule' and is testing it out. Evidence that children work naturally with rules and patterns comes from their creative productions of utterances that they can never have heard anyone say but that seem to follow an internal rule the child has constructed: e.g. *he tookened my ball* (= took), in which a new past form is created according to the child's current hypothesis. Later on, the form will change to the conventional *took*.

Such refining of language and of ideas is characteristic of mental development, and is thus likely to occur in foreign language learning too, as children build hypotheses about how the foreign language works from the data they have received from their limited experience with the language. As they get more input, so the hypotheses will change. The set of hypothesised patterns at any point would form the internal grammar.

Changes can be steady and continuous, or can involve more dramatic shifts as whole sections are re-organised in the light of new information. These dramatic changes have been called 'restructuring' (McLaughlin 1990). In the following extract, two 12-year-old Norwegian children are retelling a story called 'The Playroom' that they had read previously. The narrative part of the story was written in the past tense and if we look at the past tense verbs they use (italicized), we can see how they get some right and others wrong, but also how their errors show their use of rules:

Pupil 1

1 grandfather *show* Joe around in the house and they *come* to the playroom
2 Joe *gasped* when she saw the playroom
3 it *looked* more like a toy shop . . .
4 in the far corner of the room there *was* a toy castle
5 this castle my father *maked* with me when *was* in your age
6 I *made up* stories about knights and dragons

Pupil 2

1 my father *make up maked* this tower when I *was* in your age
2 and my father and my great and they *used* to make up stories when I *was* a knight
3 after supper Joe *climbed* up to the bed

Notice how Pupil 1 in line 1 uses an unmarked form of the verbs *show* and *come*, with no endings, but how *gasped* and *looked* do have the endings. This kind of mixed accuracy often characterises learning 'on the edge', or in progress. *Gasped* and *looked* may be being used as memorised chunks, whereas *show* and *come* have been stored not just as past tense forms but as 'raw' verb forms that can be assembled to express meanings, and will eventually be given the endings they need. *maked* in line 5 adds more evidence that the pupil is moving from chunk learning to grammar: here, the base form of the verb has been given a regular past tense ending. It is incorrect, but it is strong evidence that the child's internal grammar is at work, and we can confidently expect that in time, and with more data, the internal grammar will separate regular past tense forms from irregular, and will produce *made*. In line 6, the verb *made up* is either produced as a memorised chunk, which seems to me more likely, or is an instance of forming the irregular tense correctly. Pupil 2 has two attempts at getting the past form of *make* and also produces a regularised form *maked*.

Errors in language use can often act as a window on to the developing internal grammar of the learner, and are signals of growth. They can also suggest what types of teacher intervention may assist learning.

5.3.3 Influence of the first language

It will be apparent that constructing hypotheses about the foreign language is much more difficult than for the first language, simply because the learner has relatively little amounts of data to work on. When you have only encountered 500 words and maybe 50 phrases, it is quite hard to work out grammatical rules, and hypotheses are likely to be over-generalised and incomplete. So children learning French may assume that *je suis* (= I am) can be translated as the pronoun *I* and use it together with other verbs:

  * *je suis appelle.*

In Chapter 3, the pupil who replied to the teacher's polar animal question *Is it big or small?* with *little one*, perhaps assumed that the phrase meant 'small'.

When data is limited, learners are more likely to use the first language to fill the gaps. So that learners may assume, as a kind of default, that the foreign language grammar works like the first language grammar. I surmise that the phrase *I was in your age* is a transfer of the Norwegian grammar to English in the extracts above.

In Chapter 1, we encountered the Competition Model of language use. In this theory, the sensitivity to how the first language works that children develop in early infancy explains the transfer of first language comprehension and production strategies to foreign or second language use. Learners instinctively listen out for cues to meaning in word order or word form that work for them in their first language, and they may miss cues that the foreign language offers. For example, Malaysian learners of English often miss the information carried by the endings of verbs, e.g. the difference between *work* and *worked*, because in their first language, the ends of words do not carry useful information. English learners of Spanish can be confused by the position of pronouns; in English, word order is a very reliable cue and the first word in a sentence is generally the subject, but, in Spanish, the first word may be an object pronoun (Van Patten 1996). If the foreign language cues are not particularly obvious, the probability of them being noticed and used is even smaller. Harley (1994) suggests that it is precisely these cross-linguistically different and low-profile features of grammar that need form-focused instruction.

5.4 A learning-centred approach to teaching grammar: background

5.4.1 Trends in teaching grammar

Young learner classrooms are inevitably affected by the trends that sweep through foreign language teaching, as can be seen from the development of 'task-based' syllabuses in Malaysia, of the 'target-oriented' curriculum in Hong Kong, and of 'communicative' syllabuses in many other countries. Some of these trends turn out to be good for learners and learning; others are less clearly beneficial. Young learner contexts also start trends, but less frequently; Prabhu's work on task-based learning in India in the 1970s was influential in early developments in task-based language teaching, for example.

Grammar teaching in recent years has been as susceptible as other aspects of FLT to trends, the most significant of which for our purposes has probably been the swing away from grammar-translation methods through communicative methods and on to current ideas about 'focusing on form'. Each of these perspectives on language teaching takes a different view of learning processes, and we can clarify what is important about each by examining practice through the lens of research on learning.

5.4.2 Teaching grammar as explicit rules: learning as building blocks

Underlying traditional grammar-translation methodology, and other forms of grammar-centred language teaching, is the notion that the most important part of the language is its grammar, and that language learning is the accumulation of mastered rules of the grammar. Grammar rules are introduced one-by-one, explicitly, to the learners. Metalinguistic labels are used to talk explicitly about the grammar, e.g. 'the past perfect tense', and the terms and organisation needed to talk *about* language become another part of what has to be learnt. Learners are expected to learn the rules and to practise using the rules to construct sentences. After more practice, the assumption is that the rules get to be used automatically. To teach the language this way, the structures or rules are sorted into a sequence, assumed to progress from 'easy' to 'difficult', and the sequence forms a syllabus.

Some learners, particularly those who are academically successful, can do well using these methods and reach high levels of language proficiency. It is known from language testing, that students who do well on grammar tests often also do well on reading and writing tests, reinforcing the possibility of a link between more formal educational success and success via formal explicit grammar teaching. This in turn has implications for younger learners, who, as we have seen, are only beginning to get familiar with formal institutionalised 'scientific' concepts. The ways of thinking needed to cope with learning through explicit grammar rules are likely to be difficult for younger children. The building block sequencing also does not fit very comfortably with younger children's tendency for the thematic or narrative. We need a more organic metaphor for the growth of internal grammar, that does not see it as the piling up of discrete blocks of knowledge, but that captures the idea of non-linear and interconnected growth: grammar grows like a plant, perhaps, watered by meaningful language use, and pushing out new shoots while older stems are strengthened.

As we will see, explicit teaching of grammar patterns can have a role even in this metaphor, but it is more like the occasional application of fertiliser at certain key points in the growing season. Even the youngest children are intrigued by the way their first language works and this curiosity is likely to be felt about the foreign language. Children notice patterns as they make sense of the world around them and it may be fruitful to make use of curiosity and pattern-noticing in foreign language learning. As we saw with the T Rex extract at the start of the chapter, talking about patterns in language does not need complicated technical metalanguage. However, metalanguage is a useful tool in more advanced language learning, and can have a place in the language classroom. Young children are quite capable of learning terms like *word*, *sentence*, *letter*, moving on to learn about word classes and their labels (*nouns*, *verbs*, *adjectives*, *adverbs*, *prepositions*), about sentence construction (from seeing punctuation in written English) and early ideas about clauses as parts of sentences (e.g. a sentence with two clauses joined with *and*). Graded introduction of metalanguage across the primary years, if done meaningfully and through discourse contexts, can give children a solid foundation for later study of languages. We will return to this idea in section 5.6.5, and again in the next chapter, since working with the written language makes form visible and more easily talked about.

5.4.3 Communicative approaches: no grammar needed

Being able to talk about the language is very different from being able to talk in the language, and it was a reaction to the lack of fluency and ease with the foreign language, experienced by many of those taught by grammar-translation, that led to the development of communicative language teaching (CLT) in the late 1970s and 1980s. A central tenet of

CLT was that learners would learn the language by using it to communicate with others. In its strongest form, the process of foreign language learning was supposed to resemble child first language acquisition, where it all just happens without any direct or explicit teaching. It is questionable whether such a strong form of CLT was ever adopted in practice. More likely is that various weaker forms were taken up, with attempts to make language practice activities more realistic. What certainly happened to grammar teaching was a downgrading of its importance in foreign language classrooms.

A form of CLT that is based entirely on listening to comprehensible input is Total Physical Response (TPR), and variations on TPR are found in many young learner coursebooks. In this method as developed by Asher (1972), students listen to commands in the foreign language and respond only through movement and action e.g. getting up and sitting down, turning round, putting things on shelves. The difficulty of the input is gradually increased and eventually students take over the teacher's role and give commands in the foreign language. In its manifestations in children's foreign language learning, TPR can involve listening and doing actions with a song or responding to commands. It is claimed that learners develop skills in listening and in speaking through TPR, and it has been shown to be particularly appropriate for beginners (Lightbown and Spada 1999). Along with other 'no grammar' approaches, however, there seem to be limits to what can be achieved without some attention to output and to grammar.

5.4.4 Focus on form: the revival of grammar teaching

One of the most important sites of language learning theory and research from the 1970s on has been the immersion programs in North America, in which, for example, French-speaking Canadian children might attend an English-medium school, or a Spanish-medium school in a US city might take in children using many different first languages, including Spanish. It was in this context that Krashen and colleagues set out the theory that second language learning could follow the same route as first language acquisition (Dulay, Burt and Krashen 1982), and immersion classes formed a huge experiment in learning through communicating in the foreign language. Recent evaluations of immersion programs show mixed results as to their success (Harley and Swain 1984; Harley *et al.* 1995). Children do pick up the foreign language quickly and develop very good accents and listening skills. They can achieve good results through the second language. But in terms of grammar, children taught through the second language do not develop the same levels of accuracy as native speakers and, without this attention to the form of the language, problems with basic structures continue (Lightbown and Spada 1994). In subject classrooms, where communicating meaning is the central aim, learners seem to bypass aspects of grammar, both in listening, where more attention is paid to the subject content than to the language that carries it, and in speaking, where teachers are able to understand what pupils want to say. Furthermore, if all pupils in a class are second language learners, the language that they use with each other can contain and reinforce inaccuracies in grammar.

What we are seeing now is that communicating through a language and learning a language can actually conflict with each other, and that focusing on meaning in classrooms does not automatically, as was assumed with CLT, guarantee continuing language development on all fronts. A similar point is emerging from work in task-based language teaching: if a task creates pressure to communicate, learners may respond with inaccurate use of language or with first language (Skehan 1996). Grammar may emerge naturally in first language, it may even be genetically determined (Pinker 1994), but the grammar of a foreign language is 'foreign', and grammar development requires skilled planning of tasks and lessons, and explicit teaching. From the learners' point of view, it is increasingly recognised that attention to form is vital (Doughty and Williams 1998), and that learners need to be helped to notice the grammatical patterns of the foreign language, before they can make those patterns part of their internal grammar (Schmidt 1990; Van Patten 1996). Van Patten suggests (for older learners) that instruction should include explicit suggestions for what to look for in an FL pattern and 'structure input' activities in which learners do not try to produce new forms but are required to manipulate language information in some way.

Not only are noticing and attention needed in input, but, in output too, learners need to be helped to focus on the accuracy and precision of their language use (Swain 1985, 1995). The potential of collaborative work in pairs and groups for grammar work is also being increasingly recognised (Kowal and Swain 1994; Fotos and Ellis 1991).

Batstone (1995) helpfully brings some of these ideas together in a suggested sequencing of grammar learning activities around particular patterns or structures:

(re) noticing
↓
(re) structuring
↓
proceduralizing

Noticing is, as we have seen, an active process in which learners become aware of the structure, notice connections between form and meaning, but do not themselves manipulate language.

Successful noticing activities will usually:

- support meaning as well as form;
- present the form in isolation, as well as in a discourse and linguistic context;
- contrast the form with other, already known, forms;
- require active participation by the learner;
- be at a level of detail appropriate to the learners – a series of noticing activities may 'zoom in' on details;
- lead into, but not include, activities that manipulate language.

Structuring involves bringing the new grammar pattern into the learner's internal grammar and, if necessary, reorganising the internal grammar (in processes like accommodation and assimilation; see Chapter 1). Batstone suggests that structuring usually requires controlled practice around form and meanings, and the learner must be actively involved in constructing language to convey precise meaning, thus perhaps prompting further noticing at a more detailed level.

In structuring activities:

- learners should manipulate the language, changing form in order to express meaning;
- learners can be given choices in content that require adjustments in grammar to express meaning;
- there will be limited impact on spontaneous use – most of the results of structuring work are still internal.

Proceduralisation is the stage of making the new grammar ready for instant and fluent use in communication, and requires practice in choosing and using the form to express meaning. In line with our awareness of the possible conflict between communicative pressure and accuracy, tasks used for proceduralisation **must** require attention to grammar as well as effective communication. By gradually adjusting task pressures, by decreasing the time allowed, for example, as the grammar forms are becoming automatised, teachers can help push proceduralisation forwards.

The most recent trends in language teaching remind us that grammar is needed, but we have also learnt from CLT and immersion programs that meaning-focused, communicative classroom activities do increase fluency in language use, and that there are interesting and meaningful ways to help learners with grammar. The final part of the chapter will consider how new, and not so new, ideas about grammar learning can be adapted for young learners, including noticing – structuring – proceduralising. Before that, the next section summarises the chapter so far.

5.5 Principles for learning-centred grammar teaching

Young learners need to be surrounded by and participate in meaningful discourse in the foreign language, and it would not be conceptually appropriate for grammar to be explicitly taught as formal, explicit rules in young learner classrooms to children under the age of 8 or 9 years. However, I suggest it is important for teachers to have an awareness of grammar issues, and to have a range of form-focusing techniques, so that they can take advantage of learning opportunities that arise when learners need grammar to take their language learning forwards and can bring grammatical features of stories, dialogues, songs, etc. to the attention of even the youngest children in non-formal ways. As children get older, so they are increasingly able to learn from more formal instruction, but we should remember that grammar teaching can often destroy motivation and puzzle children rather than enlighten them. Good learning-centred grammar teaching will be meaningful and interesting, require active participation from learners, and will work with how children learn and what they are capable of learning. As with all other aspects of learning and teaching, the socio-cultural context of foreign language lessons will strongly influence what actually happens in classrooms, but some general principles for learning-centred grammar teaching can be summarised:

The need for grammar

- grammatical accuracy and precision matter for meaning;
- without attention to form, form will not be learnt accurately;
- form-focused instruction is particularly relevant for those features of the foreign language grammar that are different from the first language or are not very noticeable.

Potential conflict between meaning and grammar

- if learners' attention is directed to expressing meaning, they may neglect attention to accuracy and precision.

Importance of attention in the learning process

- teaching can help learners notice and attend to features of grammar in the language they hear and read, or speak and write;

– noticing an aspect of form is the first stage of learning it; it then needs to become part of the learner's internal grammar, and to become part of the learner's language resources ready for use in a range of situations.

Learning grammar as the development of internal grammar

– the learner has to do the learning; just teaching grammar does not make it happen;
– grammar learning can work outwards from participation in discourse, from vocabulary and from learnt chunks;
– learners' errors can give teachers useful information about their learning processes and their internal grammars.

The role of explicit teaching of grammar rules

– teaching grammar explicitly requires the learner to think about language in very abstract, formal ways that some enjoy and some find difficult. The younger the learner, the less appropriate it is likely to be;
– children can master metalanguage if it is well taught; metalanguage can be a useful tool.

5.6 Teaching techniques for supporting grammar learning

In this section, we move to practicalities and consider how teachers may actually go about helping young learners develop their grammatical knowledge in the foreign language. We begin with seeing how common activities in the young learner classroom can offer opportunities for grammar learning. The middle three sub-sections take noticing, structuring and proceduralising, and present some examples of what young learner versions of such activities might look like. Finally, we turn to the issue of how to develop children's grasp of 'metalanguage'.

5.6.1 Working from discourse to grammar

Many types of discourse that occur in young learner classrooms have grammatical patterns that occur naturally, but that can be exploited for grammar learning. It requires teachers to think about their language use from a grammatical perspective, so that they become aware of opportunities for grammar that arise every day. Classroom discourse contexts and routines (see Chapter 1) can serve to introduce new grammar, with access to meaning supported by action and objects, or to give further practice in language that has already been introduced in other ways. Routines are an ideal context in which chunks can be expanded.

The language of classroom management

When children begin learning English, some very simple phrases for classroom management can be introduced, and as time goes by, these can be expanded. Some of the phrases originally used by the teacher can be used by pupils when they work in pairs or groups. The language of classroom management can thus act as a meaningful discourse context within which certain patterns arise regularly and help with building the internal grammar.

When organising practical activities, for example, the teacher may ask children to:

give out	the scissors
	the books
	the paper
	the pencils

The range of verbs to use with the nouns can be gradually increased:

give out	the scissors
collect	the books
tidy	the paper
find	the pencils
put away	

The noun phrases can be expanded to match or to extend grammar development:

give out	the small scissors
collect	the green writing books
tidy	the paper from the cupboard
find	the red pencils that are on my desk
put away	

Talking with children

As with the T Rex example where we started, conversations with individual children can be very powerful for language development, because they can pick up on exactly what an individual child needs to know next to talk about what interests him or her, the 'space for growth' as it was called in Chapter 1. If a child volunteers something, in the first language or in what they can manage of the foreign language, the teacher can respond in the foreign language, offering a fuller or more correct way of saying it:

Child: my mummy hospital
Teacher: oh! your mummy's in hospital. Why?

This type of 'corrective feedback' can also be used for expanding the talk. If a child offers a comment about a picture, for example, the teacher can respond with fuller sentences that pick up the child's interest:

Child: bird tree
Teacher: Yes. The bird's in the tree. He's sitting on the branch. He's singing.

Talk with children as a class can also offer incidental focusing on form. Although grammar may not be the central language learning goal of a task, it can be part of what is talked about, as in this example where a Norwegian teacher is working with the children we saw earlier in the chapter. This time, they are correcting a true / false reading exercise, but the teacher takes the chance to do some work on *make – made – made up*. Notice how she helps ensure children understand the meaning, as well as the form, by contrasting *made up* with *read*.

P: pretend
T: yes (.) or make (2.0) do you remember?
P: they made
T: yes (.) they made UP stories (.) didn't they?
    they didn't read the stories
    do you agree?

In another part of the same exercise, the teacher helps out a child who needs to find the opposite of *much bigger than*. Notice how the child tries to express the idea in line 5, and then how the teacher, in lines 7 and 8 offers alternative grammatical ways of expressing the same idea:

1 T: sentence ten (1.0) Christina
2 P: *(reads)* the strangest thing of all (.) was that Joe was
3   much bigger than the toy soldier (.) that's false
4 T: why?
5 P: because she (.) er (.) she was not bigger (.) not (.)
6   much bigger than the toy soldier
7 T: yes (.) that's right (.) she was not bigger than the toy
8   soldier

<pre>
 9   she was just as big as (.) this soldier
10   so she was quite small (.) wasn't she?
11   P: yes
</pre>

By becoming 'grammar-aware', it is possible to incorporate a lot of grammar teaching through this kind of incidental focusing on form that seizes on opportunities and operates in a child's space for growth.

5.6.2 Guided noticing activities

Activities in the previous section are those likely to lead to noticing of grammatical patterns in the language. It is possible to construct activities that make noticing even more probable, and which fit all or most of the criteria for good noticing activities listed in section 5.4.4.

Listen and notice

Pupils listen to sentences or to a connected piece of talk, e.g. a story or phone call, and complete a table or grid using what they hear. In order to complete the grid, they need to pay attention to the grammar aspect being taught. Halliwell (1992) suggests using a grid to practise prepositions (Figure 5.1). It is important that the top line includes at least two instances of each object with a different location, so that pupils have to listen to the preposition in the sentences to know which box to tick: e.g. *the cup is on the chair / the cup is under the chair.*

Presentation of new language with puppets

In language syllabuses that require teachers to present new language regularly to children, the idea of learner-noticing can be helpfully introduced into more traditional ways of teaching grammar. When introducing a new pattern, the teacher can construct a dialogue with a story-line, that uses a 'repetition plus contrast' pattern, to be played out by puppets. In one such story I have used (for children of 8–10 years), a crocodile (Croc) and a squirrel discuss going swimming; dramatic irony is added because the children know that Croc really wants a chance to eat Squirrel. The dialogue uses repetition and contrast to highlight how English expresses the idea of a regular routine event using the simple present tense. The meaning is supported by a picture on the board of Squirrel's house in a tree by the river, in which Croc swims, and a large calendar showing the days of the month with pictures of house cleaning in each Monday slot, grand-

Activity 2
Listening grid
****

Here is another activity suitable for your 'core'. It too is intended to provide active response to new language. For this activity, the children have to mark on a matrix or grid the information read out by the teacher. The example below is practising prepositions. The teacher has so far read out:

'The cup is on the table.'
'The cat is under the chair.'
'The girl is in front of the tree.'

Figure 5.1 Listening grid (from Halliwell 1992, p. 44, © Pearson Longman)

mother in each Tuesday, and so on. The children listen several times to the story-dialogue:

> s: I wish I could swim like you, Croc.
> c: I'll teach you to swim.
> s: Oh, will you?
> c: Let's start next week. Shall we go swimming on Monday?
> s: No, sorry. On Mondays, I clean my house.
> c: Shall we go swimming on Tuesday?
> s: No, sorry. On Tuesdays, I visit my grandmother.
> *Similar pattern for Wednesdays, Thursdays, Fridays, Saturdays.*
> c: ((wearily)) What about Sunday?
> s: Yes! On Sundays, I'm free.
> c: ((more excited; licking his lips)) OK. On Sunday we'll have our first swimming lesson!

The teacher can then recap the routine events by pointing to the calendar and saying the key pattern phrases on their own: '*On Tuesdays, I visit my grandmother*' etc. To help input processing, pupils may be given a blank calendar and be asked to complete Croc's regular routine from listening, making a distinction between routine events, '*On Mondays, I catch fish*' and, non-routine events '*On Sunday, I'm going to teach Squirrel to swim*'.

5.6.3 Language practice activities that offer structuring opportunities

In structuring activities the goal is to help learners internalise the grammatical pattern so that it becomes part of their internal grammar. The focus is on internal work that happens as a result of activities that demand accuracy, rather than on fluency in production. Various types of classroom tasks can be used with grammar structuring goals. Some manipulation and pre-planning by the teacher may be needed to ensure that the activities include plentiful practice of the particular form.

Questionnaires, surveys and quizzes

These are commonly found in young learner course books; after input on favourite foods, for example, children are asked to interview their friends to find out their favourite foods. The teacher needs to plan which language forms the pupils will be encouraged to use. Preparation and rehearsal of the questions is necessary to ensure accuracy, and the activity must be managed so that the questions are asked in full each time. The language use in a questionnaire activity can easily become reduced to something like *cakes? sweets? pizza?* Pretending to carry out the survey by phone, rather than face-to-face, would provide a realistic reason to require the full question, *Do you like pizza?* or *Which do you prefer, pizza or cake?* to be asked each time.

Once the information from several people has been collected, group work on compiling results can offer further opportunities for internalising or structuring the grammar patterns, but only if tightly organised. Remember that structuring requires learners to manipulate the language so that they produce the form with attention and accurately. The original question *Do you like . . .?* might have been produced as a chunk, whereas at this stage, the task can require the chunk to be broken down and re-used, as each child reports his or her individual results: *six people like pizza, and two people like cakes*. The numbers can be placed in previously prepared charts and added up. They can then be put on a graph that shows favourite foods, and a spoken report prepared, and then presented with the graph to the rest of the class. Again, the spoken report should be full and accurate, so that attention has to be paid to word form and word order. It should be practised by the group, and corrected by the teacher during the rehearsal stage so that accurate forms are said aloud in the final presentation.

Information gap activities

Activities with information gaps are often found in course books to practise oral skills. Again, with just small adjustments, they can be used with grammar goals rather than oral fluency goals.

A task that moves on from the Croc and Squirrel story but practises the same grammatical form through an information gap might use calendars. Children work in pairs; each has a calendar covering the same month, but with different entries (this is the 'gap'). Without looking, again perhaps pretending to talk by phone, the children are to find a time when they are both free, and can then decide what they want to do, e.g. go swimming, go to the cinema, go shopping. In finding out when they are both free, they should be encouraged to use the language form being practised, e.g. *Shall we meet on Friday? No, sorry. On Fridays, I go to the library.*

Helping hands

This is a nice practice activity that I came across in a Maltese classroom, and which offers opportunities for structuring the simple present for routines. The topic was helping in the house, and the children, aged 5 or 6 years as I recall, had drawn round their hands and cut out the hand shape (if this is too demanding on motor skills, the teacher can prepare cut out hand shapes in advance). On each finger they wrote one sentence describing something they do to help at home: *I wash the dishes. I play with my baby sister.* Each child's sentences could be different. The paper cut-outs were then displayed on the wall, making a kind of palm tree out of the hand shapes. It looked very effective, but was also interesting for the children to read, to see what their friends did at home.

Drills and chants

Drills have been used in language classrooms for decades, and are a useful way of giving all children some speaking practice when the class is too large for individual speaking. They also offer language and involvement support to children when used to practise new language, because the child can listen to others to pick up bits that she or he is unsure about, and drills can be lively and fun if the pace is kept up. The dangers of over-using drills occur mostly if the children do not understand the content, and drills are then a mechanical exercise in making a noise, rather than language learning opportunities. I shall take it for granted here that the meaning of the language being drilled is supported and made clear to children in appropriate ways. We can then ask whether drills can help in grammar learning.

Repetition drills, in which the children repeat what the teacher says, can help in familiarising a new form, but substitution drills are the ones that offer more for grammar structuring. In a substitution drill, the learners may transform the teacher's line, as here from *you want to* to *let's*:

> T: You want to play football.
> PS: Let's play football.
> T: You want to go swimming.
> PS: Let's go swimming.
> (Doff 1988)

Alternatively, the teacher may use single words or pictures as prompts for pupils to produce a sentence:

> T: Cinema.
> PS: Let's go to the cinema.
> T: Football.
> PS: Let's play football.
> (Doff 1988)

In each case, the pupils are doing grammatical work in their minds to produce their line in the drill, and this may help structuring.

5.6.4 Proceduralising activities

At this point, we want learners to automatise their use of the grammatical form so that it is available quickly and effectively for use in communication. Task design must ensure that grammar is *essential* for achieving task goals and that some attention to accuracy is required, but the idea is that attention to accuracy can gradually be relaxed as it becomes automatic.

Polar animal description re-visited

It will be helpful to recall what happened to the polar animal description task in Chapter 3. We looked at speaking activities on this theme in section 3.8, but here we can think about the task possibilities from a grammatical point of view.

We can see now that doing a description does need some grammatical knowledge that has already entered the internal grammar through 'noticing' and 'structuring'. The production of a description to the whole class might then be a useful proceduralising activity for those items of grammar. Because it is a public performance, it will justify attention to getting forms exactly right through rehearsing and perhaps writing down a text. The pupils could choose their animal, so that they will have to select and adapt the grammatical forms for their own particular choices. The presentation might be repeated several times: to another class, to parents, on tape for another school, and each repetition moves the child towards greater fluency with the new forms. A similar effect might be had by repeating the task, but describing a bird rather than an animal, or a tropical animal rather than a polar animal; there is practice in using the grammatical patterns, with attention to accuracy but with increasing automaticity leading to increasing fluency as well.

Dictogloss

This is a generic activity that offers many possibilities for young learner classrooms (as well as for older and adult learners) once reading and writing are established. Wajnryb (1990) describes various activities that pick up some of the learning opportunities of traditional dictation in more meaningful ways. Dictogloss is one of these. It was used by Kowal and Swain (1994) to investigate how well 13- and 14-year-old learners could reflect on their accuracy in language use, notice gaps in what they knew, and get help from their peers to develop their grammar. Although the study was carried out with slightly older learners, I would suggest that the idea can be adapted for young learners, perhaps as young as 7 or 8 years old.

The basic idea of Dictogloss is that the teacher reads out a text several times, the pupils listen and make notes between readings, and then reconstruct the text in pairs or small groups, aiming to be as close as possible to the original and as accurate as possible. During the collaborative reconstruction, learners will talk to each other about the language, as well as the content, drawing on and making their internal grammatical knowledge. Through this talk, a pupil may learn from another about some aspect of grammar. In Vygotskyan terms, if the text is carefully chosen, learners will be working in their zones of potential development and their peers may scaffold learning in the ZPD.

The length of the text and the difficulty of its content and language can all be adjusted to learners' needs, as can the amount and type of support given through key words written on the board, a skeleton frame for the text given, grouping pupils in mixed ability, and so on. We can imagine that a dictogloss around a description of an animal would be a helpful activity at some stage in the Polar Animal task, either as a follow up to listening to descriptions, or as a preparation to producing a group description.

Younger children might be given the words of a rhyme or chant on little cards. Their reconstruction task would be to put the cards in the correct order. This would probably lead to them repeating the rhyme many times over as they try to work out the order. They would need to pay attention to the form of words and the word order to complete the task, so that accuracy would be required at a level above spelling.

5.6.5 Introducing metalanguage

Explicit teacher talk

Here is a teacher doing some metalinguistic work with 11-year-old pupils on plural forms in English. Notice how he uses the repetition + contrast pattern, and how he formulates the 'rule' at the end, after the specific example:

> T: if we have many of them..two of them?
> P: cows
> T: horse?
> P: horses
> (*some more examples of regular forms*)
> T: sheep?
> P: sheep
> T: yes (.) we don't put the s at the end of sheep
> T: wolf?
> P: wolves
> T: how do we write it? yes?
> P: W..O..L..F..S
> T: you should (1.0) one should think so (.) but (.) it isn't
> so (2.0) yes?
> P: W..O..L..V..E..S
> T: yes (1.0) yes (1.0) it's a special word (2.0)
>   one wolf (.) with F
>   two wolves (.) with V

We can see that it is both useful and quite possible to talk about language without using technical terms. However, since these children seem to have the concept of plural and singular, the technical terms might be usefully introduced to them. This will also depend on whether they have learnt metalanguage terms in their first language lessons.

Cloze activities for word class

A new rhyme, song or poem could give a discourse context to focus on word classes through a simple cloze activity. The song, say, is written out with gaps; in one version, all the nouns are omitted, in another, all the verbs, and in a third, all the pronouns. The pupils would hear and sing the song a few times and then would be divided into three groups, each given one of the three cloze versions: the song 'This is the way we wash our hands' would look like this:

(1)	(2)	(3)
This is the ____	This __ the way	This is the way
We wash our ____	We ____ our hands	__ wash __ hands
Wash our ____	____our hands	Wash ____ hands
Wash our ____	____our hands	Wash ____ hands
This is the ____	This ____ the way	This is the way
We wash our ____	We ____ our hands	wash hands
Early in the ____	Early in the morning	Early in the morning

In groups, the learners would work together to fill the gaps. They can be told what is missing from their versions. After they have had a good try at completing the gaps, the groups are re-divided into threes, with one person from each of the previous noun, verb and pronoun groups working together. They then compare versions to complete one full version.

This kind of activity focuses attention on word classes and how they contribute to discourse, without going into any heavy grammar. It is more challenging with a less predictable content!

5.7 Summary

Developing the grammar of a foreign language is a long and complicated process; luckily, young learners have a long time ahead of them with the language. There is no need to rush into technical rules and labels that will confuse. For their ultimate success, it seems likely to be far better to give children a sound basis in using the language, while encouraging curiosity and talk about patterns and contrasts in and between languages, and introducing grammatical metalanguage slowly and meaningfully.

In this chapter, I have suggested that grammar does have a place in young learner classrooms. But the teacher of young learners can probably best help to develop children's grammar in the foreign language, not by teaching grammar directly, but by being sensitive to opportunities for grammar learning that arise in the classroom. A grammar-sensitive teacher will see the language patterns that occur in tasks, stories, songs, rhymes and classroom talk, and will have a range of techniques to bring these patterns to the children's notice, and to organise meaningful practice. To do this well requires considerable knowledge and teaching skills!

6 Learning literacy skills

6.1 Introduction

As with previous areas in the young learner classroom, literacy learning needs informed and skilled teaching, and this chapter aims to provide background information to issues in early literacy, and to suggest principles and strategies for classroom teaching based on our current understandings of how children learn to read and write. The reader should be warned in advance that second language literacy is a complicated area and, as far as young learners are concerned, there is much that remains unknown. In the absence of relevant research findings, we will often need to rely on clear thinking and carefully monitored practice as guides in the classroom.

It is important to begin with, and to keep returning to, the idea of reading and writing as language use for expressing and sharing meanings between people. Literacy in this sense is both social and cognitive. Socially, literacy provides people with opportunities to share meanings across space and time. Cognitively, literacy requires that individuals use specific skills and knowledge about how the written language operates in processing text.

The chapter is written in the midst of heated discussion and changes over the teaching of reading and writing in British schools, and also in a time of changing conceptions of reading processes in foreign language teaching. The two sets of changes are not unconnected, and both reflect a realisation that the cognitive and language processes of literacy operate with knowledge and skills at many different levels, and that every level matters. Amongst other things, readers and writers need to recognise individual letters, know how syllables make up words, use information from the whole text and the context. What makes for successful literacy is the integration of information from each of these processes in the larger process of making sense of written text. Foreign language reading debates since the mid-1980s have been dominated by 'top–down' approaches, that emphasise making meaning over the lower level skills of word recognition or knowing letter-sound links (Koda 1994). At primary or elementary school level, a similar opposition between top–down and bottom–up approaches has been created, between 'whole language' approaches and 'phonics' teaching (Beard

1993; Hudelson 1994). We can now see that such oppositions are artificial, and do a disservice to learners, who need it all.

The discussions of literacy skills in this chapter will focus on English as a foreign language, partly because more research is available for English than for other languages, but mainly because the discussions need to be about a particular language in order not to disappear into abstractions. We begin by identifying the skills needed to be literate in English, and then proceed to review research findings on learning to read in a foreign language, identifying factors that may impact on young learners of English as a foreign language. The second part of the chapter takes the background theory and research into the classroom, suggesting principles and techniques for teaching literacy skills at different ages and stages.

6.2 Literacy skills in English

In this section, the first / foreign language distinction is backgrounded, in order to describe first what is involved in becoming a skilled reader and writer in English. Section 6.3 will then address how literacy skills are developed in English as a foreign language.

6.2.1 Literacies and literacy skills

Literacy skills include being able to read and write different sorts of texts for different purposes. In most societies today, literacy is part and parcel of everyday life for children and adults, and life is full of different sorts of written texts: in the home, on the street, on television, and on computers. In societies where widespread literacy is more recent, schools may still make more use of written texts than homes, but information technology will probably bring rapid changes in the next few years. Literacy skills are then, not just an additional set of skills learnt in schools, but an integral part of people's lives. From their early infancy, children are involved in using writing and reading: for example, when they are helped to write their name on a birthday card to a friend or when they look at story books with adults.

An activity, such as story-book reading or sending birthday cards, in which reading and writing is involved can be described as a 'literacy event' (Barton 1994). People in their daily lives are regularly involved in a range of literacy events, in which they use skills that extend beyond writing and reading text. Participation in literacy events at home provides children with their first experiences of written language. If we take the wider view, that we each learn multiple literacies (Street 1996), we can see that becoming literate begins long before a child goes to school, and that the school has a foundation of literacy events and experiences upon which to build the narrower and more detailed skills of reading and writing.

Within the broader idea of literacies lies the narrower, and perhaps more traditional, view of literacy as reading and writing words and texts. While applauding the broadening of our thinking about literacy, especially for the way these new ideas expand our views of what children already know and are capable of, I remain convinced that learning the detail of how texts are written and can be understood is crucial to children's educational and personal development, and can be helped by good teaching.

6.2.2 Reading as dependent on visual, phonological and semantic information

Embedded in both the broader and narrower concepts of literacy is the idea that reading and writing are essentially about understanding: that readers will understand texts that they read by constructing a meaning for themselves, and that writers will try to ensure that their readers are able to understand what they write. Although reading for understanding is more than saying what is written down, on the way to understanding, reading does link to speaking, as written words are 'decoded' into spoken words. When skilled readers make sense of written text, they may appear to bypass turning text into talk and go straight to understanding. However, we know from recent empirical work that skilled readers do actually process every letter of words on the page; they just do it very quickly (Stanovich 1980, 1988; Oakhill and Garnham 1988). Fluent readers still have available the skill to speak the words of the text to themselves, the 'voice in the head' (Reid 1990: 91), and use it for difficult texts or texts that need special attention, such as poetry. Similarly, writing may involve turning spoken language into written words, but it also involves more than that.

Reading brings together visual information from written symbols, phonological information from the sounds those symbols make when spoken, and semantic information from the conventional meanings associated with the words as sounds and symbols (see Figure 6.1). All three types of information are used by fluent readers in reaching an understanding of the text, together with information about the social uses of the text as discourse. In addition, skilled writing requires mastery of the fine motor skills to form the written shapes and orthographic knowledge of how written symbols are combined to represent words through spelling conventions.

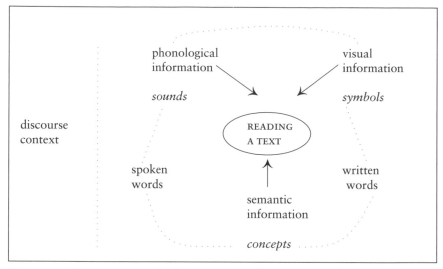

Figure 6.1 The integration of information in reading a text

6.2.3 The unnatural demands of literacy

Some of the most exciting developments in early literacy in the last few years have been around 'emergent' literacy and 'whole language'. These focus on how children work out for themselves the secrets of reading and writing from participating in literacy events. We will examine the implications for the foreign language classroom later, but in this section I want to explore why it is that many children do not develop literacy skills in natural and painless ways, but struggle to learn to read in their first language. It is important to remember that most children will need skilled teaching to help them become literate (Reid 1990; Oakhill and Beard 1999).

Some of the reasons for reading problems originate in the historical construction of literacy and the demands that are then placed on individual learners. Vygotsky (1978) describes the written language as 'second-order' meaning representation, to capture the idea of two stages between talk and written text in the development of literacy in societies. Spoken language was used first to represent mental ideas and meanings; in a socio-historical second step, written language was developed to represent talk. Different societies have produced different ways of writing down talk: English uses an alphabetic system, as does Arabic, but with a different direction; Japanese uses a syllabic system, with the syllable as unit, and a logographic system, in which symbols represent meanings directly. As the written form of a language develops, often over centuries, as a tool for representing the spoken language, conventions and rules emerge in the use of written forms that then have to be learnt anew by each successive generation of children. In the case of English, some spelling conventions date back to the 16th and 17th centuries, others were imposed in the nineteenth century and, because spelling has been fixed while pronunciation has changed, many of the conventions or rules of the written language do not match how English is spoken today (Stubbs 1980). To a modern child, the spelling of English does not offer a 'natural' match between written and spoken forms.

Similarly, certain specific text forms, or 'genres', have evolved over time within literate societies, with particular discourse patterns and organisations of texts becoming conventionalised. Genre theorists have argued that being able to use and understand a range of genres is an important educational goal that will empower children for adult life (Richardson 1998).

A second way in which written language is often much less natural than spoken language for children is in its social context of use. Spoken language is used in contexts that offer much support for meaning, often from familiar and helpful adults who know the child and interact with him or her regularly (see Chapter 1). A child faced with a written text has support only from previous knowledge, from what the writer can build in, or through pictures or diagrams that illustrate the text. The writer is much more distant from a reader than is the case with speaking, and this distance can place a high demand on a reader to construct an understanding of the text (Reid 1990).

Although recent developments in literacy have encouraged a focus on the natural and meaningful involvement of children in literacy events at home and in their communities, we should not forget these non-natural facets of literacy. The discussion in this section suggests two ways in which teaching can support children in mastering the demands of literacy. Firstly, English spelling conventions and the text organisation in some genres are far from obvious and so can benefit from direct teaching. Secondly, in the early stages of school literacy, children will need support as they move from the very contextualised use of spoken language to using the more isolated, or 'disembedded', information in written texts.

6.2.4 How skilled readers operate

In making meaning from a text, skilled readers use a combination of visual, phonological and semantic information, taken from the letters, words and sentences of the text. Readers build up an understanding of the text as they go along, sometimes called a 'text base' (van Dijk and

	context	------	space
	discourse	------	continents and oceans
a text read by	paragraph	------	mountains
a skilled reader	sentence / clause	------	motorways and cities
	words	------	houses, trees, fields
	letters / sounds	------	people, leaves

the earth seen by satellite

Figure 6.2 The analogy of reading a text as seeing the earth by satellite at different scales

Kintsch 1983; Kintsch 1988). The text base is a kind of dynamic and temporary meaning for the text, that draws on information processed at different scales. We can think of a reader working with a written text as like a satellite searching information about a landscape, and zooming in to different levels of scale to get information of different types at different scales. Pictures of the earth from space show it as a mainly blue sphere with continental masses set in oceans, while, at a much larger scale, British railways use satellite pictures to identify dangerous piles of autumn leaves that have fallen on railway tracks. To really understand the Earth, information is needed from all scales, from the leaf to continental masses; to really understand a text, information has to be integrated from the various scales at which a text can be 'read', from individual letters to discourse organisation. The various scales of reading a text are set out in Figure 6.2, in analogy with the satellite view of the Earth, and are then described in turn. The knowledge and skills used to extract information at the various text levels will be summarised in Figure 6.3.

Context

Context is used here to refer to any sources of information that are not inside the text but come from the reader's world. Adult readers usually choose their own texts and have good reasons for wanting to read them. For example, you may pick up a newspaper to get an idea of what is going on in the world, or you may buy a book on gardening in order to decide what to grow and where to plant it. Adults come to such texts with previous knowledge of using books and of the topic that will help make sense of what they read. Children on the other hand are often told what to read by adults, rather than choosing their own texts. Often children's previous knowledge is incomplete or inaccurate, and they rely on texts to supply knowledge. Children's reading is thus often much more demanding than it is for adults: if we did not know that the earth has oceans and continents, it would be much more difficult to understand the broad scale picture that is sent back from space.

Text

Skilled readers approach texts, not only with purposes for reading, but with expectations about how the texts will be organised. From previous experience with gardening books, for example, they may go straight to the index to find relevant sections, and will use the pictures and diagrams to supplement information from the written text. Skilled readers' knowledge of discourse organisation helps know where important information will be found, and they can thus direct their attention efficiently, focusing in on key passages and skipping more lightly over passages with less important information.

From their early experience, children are likely to be familiar with story or narrative structure (section 3.6.3) but to be less familiar with other types of text. Knowledge of discourse organisation in written texts develops through experience with them, and may also be developed explicitly through study skills activities. Until such knowledge is developed, children have a more difficult task than skilled readers and must work equally hard on all parts of a text to find out the useful information.

Paragraph

The paragraph is a discourse unit that is mainly used to deal with the development of topics in a text. Very often a paragraph contains within it, often right at the beginning, a 'topic sentence', which gives an overview of the whole paragraph (this paragraph began with one). From the topic sentence, the paragraph can move into more specific detail, through exemplification, expansion or explanation of the topic. Skilled readers will automatically recognise topic sentences and make mental links between its more general content and the more specific information in other sentences.

Children do not learn about paragraphs from their experience with spoken language. Many of the early texts they encounter will not be long enough to use paragraphing organisation. As their writing develops, so the need to use paragraphs will arise and links can be made with reading texts, to learn the conventions of paragraph patterns in English.

Sentence / clause

At this level in our metaphor, we are at a scale comparable to seeing man-made features on the physical landscape. We recognise the Great Wall of China, or a motorway network, on a satellite picture because we can mentally map their aerial shape on to our more close-up experience of them through pictures or real life encounters.

In understanding sentences and clauses, skilled readers draw on their 'close-up' grammatical knowledge of how words are connected to produce meanings. Groups of words with a sentence that belong together are automatically recognised as units and processed together, e.g. *once upon a time*.

Children, even in their first language, will not have encountered in talk some of the grammatical patterns found in written texts. Sentences with relative clauses, for example, are much more frequent in written texts than in spoken language. As with paragraphing, so experience with texts will broaden children's range of grammatical patterns. In the early stages, unfamiliar grammar may confuse young readers. Without the support that comes from recognising the syntactic pattern, early readers have to work on each word as a separate unit, working out what it is and storing it in memory while the next word is tackled. But memory spans are limited, and words can drop out of short term memory before the child reader gets to the end of the sentence and has a chance to work out the meaning of the whole.

Words

The word is a key unit of both form and meaning in reading and writing, perhaps equivalent to a 'basic level' in the hierarchy (see Chapter 4), comparable to familiar houses or fields in our satellite picture analogy. In terms of form, words in written text in English have spaces on either side so they are easy to spot, easier than in spoken language where words are often run together. Words are learnt often as wholes, and seem to be recognised on sight, without too much attention to the individual letters that make up the word. However, with the development of better measuring instruments, we now know that skilled readers do look at each component part of a word, and that any changes to a word such as a missing letter can disrupt the reading process.

Children's early reading often begins, naturally, with recognising whole words such as names or shop signs. This word recognition is meaning-driven, and links words to concepts. We must not assume, though, that children process words in the same way as skilled readers. They may pay more attention to what are, in the long run, rather irrelevant features, such as the length and shape of the word, and not notice other important intra-word features. Word recognition knowledge is a good start to reading, and from here, skills need to be developed upwards to sentences and downwards to smaller, intra-word, units.

Morphemes

To move inside words, we can take a visual or a phonological route. The morpheme is a visual unit, a part of a word that carries a meaning through its form, i.e. a grammatical unit of meaning. For example, in the word *walked*, two morphemes can be identified: *walk + ed*. The second does not 'mean' anything by itself, but, added to the first, it indicates that the action took place in the past. Morphemes are visual units because their shape and spelling mostly remains the same, although they may sound different in different words. Say aloud and notice the three different sounds of the *ed* morpheme:

<kissed>   <waited>   <carried>
/t/   /ɪd/   /d/

Note
Angular brackets <. . .> are used to show written form; slashes /. . ./ indicate spoken sounds, which are represented using the phonemic symbols for received pronunciation in spoken English.

Once the visual forms of morphemes are learnt, they are a (relatively) reliable source of information about meaning for readers, and for writers (Stubbs 1980).

Morphemes are the units that are represented by the symbols of a logographic language.

Syllables

Syllables are phonological intra-word units. In English, syllables contain one vowel sound, with the possibility of a consonant sound before and after the vowel as well. A syllable can be broken down further, into an 'onset' (the first consonant, if there is one) and a 'rime' (the vowel + final consonant, if there is one). So, within the word <caterpillar>, we find 4 syllables:

/kæt/ + / ə/ + /pɪl/ + /ə/ .

The first syllable has onset /k/ and rime /æt/; the second and fourth syllables are the weak vowel sound used as rimes; the third syllable has the onset /p/ and the rime /ɪl/.

Rimes are fairly often spelt consistently, not as reliably as morphemes, but reliably enough to provide very useful information for readers. The written form of a rime is sometimes called a 'phonogram'. Being able to notice the rimes within syllables is one aspect of phonological awareness, and research has shown that phonological awareness correlates highly with reading success in English. You need to be able to hear the sounds inside spoken words in order to understand how the alphabet can be used to write words. In the first language research, children with good levels of phonological awareness tended to become successful readers; children with poor levels of phonological awareness tended to have problems in learning to read, and, *vice versa*, poor readers often had poor phonological awareness. Furthermore, when poor readers have been helped to develop higher levels of phonological awareness, their reading skills have benefited (Bryant and Bradley 1985). Phonological awareness develops before children go to school, and seems to be linked to experience with rhyming words in songs and rhymes.

One of the key learning strategies available at this level is the use of **analogy** (Goswami 1991). A child who knows how to read the word *bell*, can use analogy to help read the new word *fell*, by noticing that the final rime *-ell* is the same in both cases.

Like many aspects of reading, phonological awareness continues to develop through experience with reading, so that reading and phonological awareness are interdependent and develop interdependently. However, the evidence is strong enough to support the inclusion in early literacy work of activities that will develop phonological awareness, and we will see how these can be adapted for the young learner classroom later on in the chapter.

Letters

With letters, we reach the bottom-most level of written text, equivalent to leaves or individual people in our satellite analogy. Written letters have names (e.g. L is called 'ell'), shapes, and sounds. These three aspects of letters must not be confused in learning and teaching. If children have learnt one aspect, this does not imply that they know the others. For example, learning the alphabet as a set of letter names ('ai, bee, see, dee' . . .) is often a key part of teaching reading. But this is not the same as learning how letters are used to represent sounds. Learning the names of the letters in alphabetical order does not help much in reading, whereas learning the sounds of the letters helps a lot. I did once have a pupil, who was learning to read in English as a second language, who did use the names of the letters to help him decode the words. He would look at a word like <did>, would say 'dee – aye – dee', and then read /dɪd/. I still do not understand how the process actually helped him to read! This is not to suggest children stop learning the alphabet; knowing the alphabet names and order will help with understanding the written language system and in using dictionaries later on. However, much more important for learning to read is children's growing knowledge of the links between the written letters and the sounds they represent.

The technical term for these links is grapho-phonemic relationships (grapho = written; phonemic = sound). Different languages have different types of grapho-phonemic relationships. In Italian and Spanish, for example, each written letter represents just one sound; there is said to be a 'one-to-one' grapho-phonemic relationship. English has a much less straightforward set of grapho-phonemic relationships between the 26 letters of the alphabet and the 44 sounds or phonemes:

- Some letters have only one sound: <b> is always pronounced /b/.
- Some letters have two possible sounds: <c> can be /s/ as in <ice>, or /k/ as in <come>.
- Two letters can produce just one sound: <ck> is pronounced /k/.
- Two letters can work to produce a single sound, but with two different possibilities: <th> can sound /θ/, as in <thin>, or /ð/ as in <the>.
- The sound of a letter can be affected by the other letters in the word: the sound of <a> in different in <hat> and <hate>, because of the <e> at the end, which itself is silent.

Fluent readers of English use knowledge of grapho-phonemic relationships automatically in reading words. A perennial question in teaching children to read in English is how much they can be helped by direct teaching about grapho-phonemic relationships (phonics teaching), or whether they should be left to pick up the rules indirectly through experience. It is rather like the grammar issue in language teaching, discussed in the previous chapter; we feel that if we could just explain the rules, learning could be made much more efficient but, on the other hand, explaining the rules gets so technical that most children cannot understand the explanations. The solutions in the two cases may be similar too: drawing children's attention to regular patterns, making sure they notice what is useful information; introducing technical metalanguage slowly and carefully; using explanations where they help and do not confuse; developing ways of explaining that make sense to young learners.

In British education in the 80s, many teachers dropped phonics teaching in favour of whole language approaches that stressed overall meaning. In the 90s, it was found that many children were not succeeding in reading, and the blame was put on lack of phonics teaching. Now phonics is back, but combined with top–down, and meaning-focused approaches to texts. The parallels with the move to form-focus in communicative language teaching are striking.

Summary

A skilled reader, faced with a text to read and understand, can access information from all the levels mentioned above, together with relevant previous knowledge of the world (Adams 1990). The skills and knowledge involved in constructing meaning from reading a text are summarised in Figure 6.3. As we have seen, the information from different levels is different in nature and in how it links into meaning; information can be predominately visual, phonological or semantic. In reaching an understanding of the text, all these different pieces of information are integrated with previous knowledge to construct a coherent meaning.

Children learning to read English need to develop knowledge and skills at the different scales. No 'right' way of learning to read has been found, and when we consider the complexity of what has to be learnt, this should not be surprising. What is clear, is that children need to progress within each scale or level, and need to practise integrating across the levels or scales. Just exposing children to one scale, e.g. learning lots of words by sight, or learning to sound out letters, may get them started, but to become skilled readers and writers they need to master techniques for using all the information available in a text.

6.3 Factors affecting learning to read in English as a foreign language

The previous sections have set out the learning task that children face in becoming skilled readers and writers of English. In this section, we consider the following factors in foreign language learning contexts that can influence that learning task:

- the nature of the written forms of the first language;
- the learner's previous experience in L1 literacy;
- the learner's knowledge of the FL;
- the learner's age.

6.3.1 First language

The Competition model of language use was set out in section 1.5.3. It embodies a theory that helps us think about how our minds are affected by the learning of our first language (or L1). Each language is structured differently, and the different structures offer users different cues to meaning. So when we learn our first language, our brain / mind 'tunes

> *skilled reading is a process of constructing meaning from written language*

knowledge		*skills*
• background knowledge of topic • functions of literacy in • uses of different genres / text types	**THE WORLD** ⇑ ⇓	• activate relevant knowledge of topic • activate vocabulary
• organisation and structure of texts • paragraphing • use and meaning of discourse markers	**TEXT** ⇑ ⇓	• recognise text type • locate key information • identify main points / detail • follow the line of argument • work out explicit / implicit meaning
• co-ordination and subordination • word order • meaning of punctuation • clause grammar	**SENTENCES** ⇑ ⇓	• work out how clauses relate to each other • identify verb and relation of other words to the verb • recognise formulaic chunks
• sight vocabulary • affixes • spelling • morphemes	**WORDS** ⇑ ⇓	• recognise by sight • guess meaning of new words from context • break words into morphemes • break words into syllables
• spelling patterns • meanings of common morphemes	**SYLLABLES** (spoken) **MORPHEMES** (written) ⇑ ⇓	• break syllables into onset and rime • spot same rime / morpheme in different words • use analogy to work out word
• grapheme-phoneme correspondences • the alphabetic principle • script • names / shapes of letters of the alphabet • letter clusters / digraphs	**SOUNDS –** **LETTERS**	• relate letter shape to sound • notice initial and final consonants in words • blend sounds to syllables

Figure 6.3 Skilled reading in English

135

into' the way the particular L1 works, and we learn to attend to the particular cues to meaning that are most helpful. When we meet a new language, our brain / mind automatically tries to apply the first language experience by looking for familiar cues. Part of learning a foreign language is developing new understandings about the particular cues to meaning that the new language offers, and that differ from those of our first language.

The ideas of the Competition model apply also to written languages. For example, written English offers cues to meaning at all the different levels set out in Figure 6.3; written Italian and Spanish have much more regular grapho-phonemic relationships, and so the phonological information offered at letter level is much more reliable. It makes sense to use this reliable information in reading, and reduces the need to attend to other levels of information. The features of the written language influence the skills and strategies that are most appropriately developed for using it. If L1 readers of Italian or Spanish begin to learn to read English, they are likely to transfer their skills and strategies to the new language. In this example, Spanish learners might need to learn some extra reading skills at the level of grapho-phonemic relationships to equip them for reading English. If we reverse the situation, and imagine English L1 readers learning to read Italian, then things are different, and simpler. A fluent reader of English will need to learn some new sound-letter relationships, but will then find reading Italian quite straightforward because s/he can use the skills and strategies used with English, and will have many fewer irregularities to deal with.

A fluent reader of English faced with Russian will need to learn a whole new alphabet, but otherwise similar strategies can be used because the way letters are used to make words is reasonably similar. Faced with Arabic, there is not just a new alphabet but also the right-left direction of writing. Faced with written Putonghua (Mandarin Chinese), the English reader must almost start from scratch!

The transferability of knowledge, skills and strategies across languages depends closely on how the two written languages work; it will be different for each pair of languages and for each direction of learning (i.e. which has been learnt first) (Koda 1994). What we can say is that English is a complicated alphabetic written language, and almost always requires learners of it as a foreign language to develop new skills and knowledge, in addition to what can be transferred. We can work out *what* needs to be learnt when learning to read English as a foreign language by comparing the content of section 6.2 with similar analyses of the learners' first language.

6.3.2 *The learner's first language literacy experience*

To complicate the picture still further, we have, as yet, only talked about fluent readers coming to read a foreign language. If, as happens with young learners, literacy knowledge and skills are only partly developed for the L1, then only some aspects are available for transfer, and those may be only partially mastered. It is also possible that learners will mix knowledge, skills and strategies between their languages, or even that 'backward transfer' (Liu *et al.* 1992) may occur, with foreign language reading strategies being applied to first language texts.

The methodology of teaching literacy skills in the first language must also be considered. The way the child is being, or has been, taught to read the first language will create expectations about how foreign language reading will be taught. While taking a quite different approach in the foreign language classroom may be a good idea, because it helps children to differentiate the languages and the literacy skills required in each, it may also confuse children by requiring them to cope with different definitions of 'good behaviour' or 'success' in reading.

Social aspects of first language literacy may also impact on learning to read in a foreign language, the extreme case being when a child's L1 does not have a written form, or when the medium of education is a second language, so that the child does not learn L1 literacy.

6.3.3 *The learner's knowledge of the foreign language*

Oral skills in the new language are an important factor in learning to be literate (Verhoeven 1990). Phonological awareness in the foreign language, the ability to hear the individual sounds and syllables that make up words, will develop from oral language activities, such as saying rhymes or chants and singing songs. Vocabulary knowledge is extremely important: (a) when a written word is being 'sounded out' or built up from its component letter or morpheme sounds, knowing the word already will speed up recognition, and (b) when a sentence is being read, known words will be easier to hold in short-term memory as meaning is built up. In the early stages, children should only encounter written words that they already know orally. If a text contains unknown words, then either the meanings of these need to be explained in advance, or the meanings must be completely obvious from the rest of the text.

Pronunciation skills in the foreign language will both affect literacy and be assisted by literacy development. Because written words are turned into spoken words in the reading process (and *vice versa* in the writing process), inaccuracies in pronunciation may hamper finding the right spoken word to match what is read. Seeing words written down can help towards accurate pronunciation because of the visibility of all the letters of a word; sounds that might be unstressed, and thus not noticed in listening, will be evident in written form. The reverse of this positive effect is that children may try to pronounce written foreign words using the pronunciation patterns of their first language.

In the broader understanding of literacies that was discussed in section 6.2.1 we recognised that children gain much literacy experience before they come to school. In the foreign language, this is less likely to happen, and the teacher can expand children's experience of literacy in the new language by creating environmental print for the classroom.

6.3.4 Age

Age of starting to learn to read clearly overlaps with first language reading experience. However, there are other factors that may make learning to read and write in English a very different experience for children of six or ten years of age. The youngest children are still learning how written text functions, so that they may not be able to transfer even the most general concepts about text and print. They are still mastering the fine motor skills needed to shape and join letters, and so producing a written sentence takes a long time, and, because their attentional capacities are also limited, they may only be able to write a small amount. Also because of constraints on memory, when reading a sentence, they may not be able to recall the beginning by the time they have reached the end. Given the importance of oral skills being established before beginning to read, if very young (under 6 years) foreign language learners do begin reading and writing, this should be at a very simple level, such as environmental uses of English text (see below), tracing their names, or reading single words or simple sentences around objects in the classroom.

Teaching children between the ages of 6 and 9 years to read and write in English as a foreign language can make use of some of the methods used with children for whom English is a first language, perhaps with extra stress put on those aspects of English literacy that contrast most strongly with the learners' first language reading and writing.

By the time children reach 10 years of age or thereabouts, their first language oracy and literacy are probably quite firmly established; they understand about how written text works; they are in control of the fine motor skills needed for writing; and they are able to talk and think about the differences between languages. So reading and writing can be part of foreign language learning at this age, even for beginners, although remembering the caveats about oral skills already mentioned – that only familiar vocabulary (and grammar) should be used initially in written form. Teaching reading and writing can utilise any transferable knowledge and skills from first language literacy, such as sounding out words and breaking words into syllables or morphemes, and can provide more focused instruction in skills and strategies that have not been used before and are needed for literacy in English.

The next sections move to practical methods and techniques of teaching literacy skills.

6.4 Starting to read and write in English as a foreign language

6.4.1 Objectives for readers up to age 7

Young children will benefit from a broad approach to literacy skills that includes activities from the different scales of Figure 6.3. Here is a suggested list of objectives for early literacy teaching that would provide a sound basis for further learning. Most can be learnt informally rather than through direct teaching. They are not listed in an order of teaching, but using the headings of section 6.2.4:

Text

- Attitudes to literacy: enjoy being read to from a range of books; enjoy looking at books.
- Print conventions: learn how text is written down in lines and pages, with spaces between words, capital and small letter.
- Participate in range of literacy events in school, and link to out of school literacy events.

Sentence

- Learn to copy short sentences that have a personal meaning, and read them aloud.

Words

- Learn a basic set of words by sight.
- Begin spotting words and letters in books.

Morphemes / syllables

- Listen to rhymes, chants and songs, and, by joining in with them, learn by heart, and be able to say or sing them.

Letters / sounds

- Learn the names, shapes and sounds of some initial consonants.
- Begin to learn the alphabet in order, by name.

6.4.2 Creating a literate environment in the classroom

The language classroom may be the only place where children will be exposed to environmental print in the foreign language, so it is helpful to make the most of the opportunities offered by the classroom environment.

Labels

Start by labelling the children's coat hooks, trays, and desks with their names. Bilingual or foreign language labels can be put on furniture and objects around the class and school, and will familiarise children with written forms. There should not be too many labels, and they should be changed after a week or so. Children should be encouraged to look at the labels and talk about what's on them. A student teacher of mine had the good idea of having a cut-out butterfly that would be found in a different place in the room each day. The children were excited by the challenge of finding the butterfly when they came into the class. If the butterfly (or star or . . .) moves from label to label, children's attention will be drawn to where the butterfly is and they will notice the word on the label.

Posters

Colourful posters that include quite a lot of text can be an on-going interest for children, as they gradually recognise more and more of the words. A rhyme that they are learning could be used for this – but notice that this is presenting children with the written words after they have encountered them orally, not before.

Advertising posters can be fun, but if teachers have ethical problems with using commercial adverts in class, then posters can be made to advertise healthy eating or teeth cleaning or borrowing library books.

Making posters for younger pupils would be a good writing activity for older children in the school.

Messages

Using written language for communication boosts children's motivation, and shows them some of the uses of writing. An English message board in the classroom may have simple messages from the teacher, like *Don't forget your crayons on Friday*, or more personal messages that children can write too: *My rabbit had seven babies*.

A 'post box' in the classroom can encourage children to write and send 'letters' to each other and the teacher.

Reading aloud

Reading aloud to young children by the teacher (or other adult) has an enormous range of benefits. It can be done in several ways:

- Teacher reads aloud, children just listen, and perhaps look at pictures;
- Teacher uses a 'big book', i.e. a large book with large enough print so that all children can see;
- Each child uses a text.

Each situation will create different demands on the child, and, if possible, all three modes of reading aloud should be used.

From listening and watching an adult read aloud, children can see how books are handled, how texts encode words and ideas, how words and sentences are set out on a page. Beyond these conventions of print, reading aloud familiarises children with the language of written English: the formulaic openings (*Once upon a time* . . .) and closings (*and so they all lived happily ever after.*); the patterns of text types – stories and information texts, and sentence types. Affectively, reading aloud can motivate children to want to read themselves.

Reading aloud is not only for the youngest children. Older children continue to benefit, if the texts that are read to them increase in complexity and range. Getting to know different text types through hearing them will have knock-on effects on their own reading and writing.

Teachers should ensure that children understand the overall meaning of what they hear and most of the individual vocabulary items in the text. Understanding can be supported by the use of pictures that show characters and action, and by talking about the text in advance and giving enough of the meaning, so that children have a 'skeleton' they can build on as they listen.

Having children read aloud to each other can help learning, but it has problems. If a child is asked to read to the whole class, she may well not speak loud enough for all to hear and, if she stumbles over words, the other children will lose the meaning and probably also the motivation to listen. Paired reading, where children take turns to read to each other in pairs, may be more helpful.

It is very important that children regularly read aloud individually to their teacher, since it is only by listening carefully to how children are making sense of written words that we can understand their progress in learning.

6.4.3 Active literacy learning

Making literacy teaching a multi-sensory experience

In learning to read and write, children have to make links from meaning to what they see (printed text), what they hear (the spoken language) and what they produce (written words). To assist the building and strengthening of all these various sorts of mental connections, we can use a range of modes and senses. Early literacy activities can provide opportunities for children to see, hear, manipulate, touch and feel. For example, if children are learning the letter shape <S>, then, as well as practising writing the shape, they need to see the shapes on display in the classroom and in their books. They might cut out examples of the letter S from newspapers and magazines and make a collage of them. They might paint, trace, colour in, join the dots, use modelling clay to make the shape; they can draw the shape in a tray of sand, or make the shape with glue on a card and sprinkle sand over to make a 'feely-S'. They can be asked to visualise the shape in their minds and to imagine drawing the shape. They can make the sound /sss/, long and short, with different emotions: a happy /sss/ and a sad /sss/. If sight words are being learnt, the same range of possibilities for multi-sensory practice exists.

Coloured chalks or pens are helpful to highlight key features of texts, sentences or words.

Attention to detail

Children spend the first years of their lives learning about 'conservation': they learn as babies that when their mothers leave the room, they do not need to panic because she will come back. They learn that a 'cup' is still a 'cup' even when it is upside down or used to hold flowers rather than liquid. However, when they meet written text, they have to focus on a finer level of detail as to what matters and does not matter: a letter M upside down is not an M, but a different letter, W; that both <d> and <D> are called 'dee', but if the upright stroke is too short, it is no longer 'dee', but 'ai'; that <saw> has a quite different meaning from <was>.

In a letter shape, attention must be paid to the length of each stroke, relative to the others in the letter, and to the roundness or straightness of shapes. In addition to multi-sensory experience of these, teachers can play an important role in directing attention to what matters, showing children the easiest way to make shapes and giving feedback to children on their individual efforts. Over time, children's attempts will get closer and closer to conventional shapes.

Fun with literacy skills

There is a lot to learn about written English and the more fun that can be had in the process the better. Learning the alphabet can be made more exciting by singing or chanting it rhythmically. It can be recited backwards or starting somewhere other than A.

Simple games may help interest and motivation: e.g. the teacher says a letter at random from the alphabet and children shout out the next letter (or the next but one, or the one before). See Greenwood (1997) for more literacy games.

6.4.4 Literacy events and routines in the foreign language classroom

We can take the idea of a 'literacy event' as being some kind of social activity that involves reading and writing, and see that it can link to the idea of 'routines' and 'formats' (section 1.4). We can then find and develop opportunities in foreign language classrooms for literacy events. Figure 6.4 shows how a regular Birthday routine can incorporate various types of reading and writing. If more or less the same routine happens for each child in the class, the written text becomes part of the event and will be learnt through participation in the event.

Other classroom routines that can integrate literacy include completing weather and date charts; devising rotas for classroom duties; checking attendance; and recording reading progress, e.g. each time a child finishes a book, the title is written on a chart or picture.

6.4.5 Formal approaches to teaching literacy skills

Learning to read and write can begin from text level; from sentence level; from word level; from letter level. Each starting point has

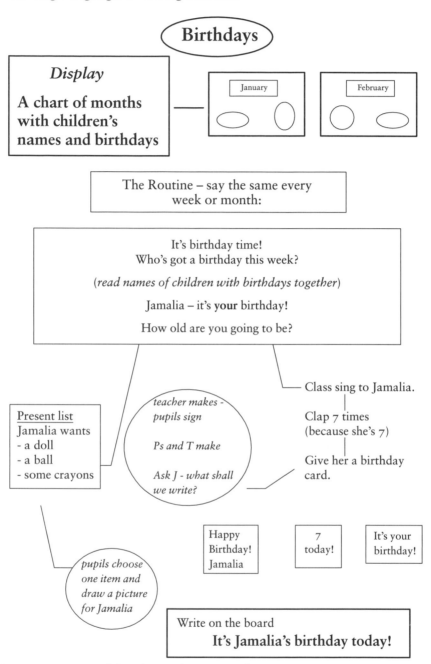

Figure 6.4 Meaningful reading and writing in classroom routines

produced approaches to teaching reading that can be used in the foreign language classroom.

Emergent literacy

'Emergent literacy' describes the (first language) phenomenon in which children seem to learn to read without any teaching, gradually, and through exposure to text and to reading (Hall 1987). When children spend lots of time being read to from interesting and appropriate books, some will begin to work out for themselves the patterns and regularities that link spoken and written text. It is this process that has been called 'emergent literacy'. If you have been involved with such a process, you will understand the sense of excitement and amazement at seeing the human mind at work. However, attempts to turn the ideas of emergent literacy into a full-scale teaching methodology, as 'real books' approach or an 'apprenticeship approach' (Waterland 1985), have floundered and have been seen, with some justification, as rather dangerous. The main problem with the notion of emergent literacy is that it works only for some children; most children need more structured help with the multiple and non-natural skills of literacy. Furthermore, in order for literacy to 'emerge', a child needs lots of time individually with a skilled adult and a plentiful supply of good quality story books; conditions that are not always available in school classrooms!

However, the emergent literacy 'movement' has had a useful impact on ideas about reading. It reminds us to put the learner first, because each child has to build up literacy skills from their own experience with texts; it has produced useful evidence about how children find 'entry points' into the complexity of reading; it reinforces the importance of children understanding what they read; and it has highlighted some of the qualities of good books for children and how school text books are often much less interesting and well-produced. As a result of the attention to the quality of children's reading books, commercial publishers have developed better quality story books that work alongside more structured and artificial texts with controlled vocabulary.

The entry points to reading found in emergent literacy are useful to note because they suggest ways into reading for young children that can be adapted for classroom contexts. Emergent readers often begin to know by heart sentences from favourite books, learning them from hearing them over and over, and will say them along with the adult reader. This 'speaking with the text' is not really 'reading', but it can be the start of learning to read. They then begin to pick out known words from text and to spot letters, linking the shapes with the sounds. With skilled adult help, this can be built into the kinds of knowledge and skills set out in Figure 6.3. The child's learning starts from having a meaning for a whole text, and moving to attend to words and letters.

Most of the work on emergent literacy has come from first language or immersion contexts, and the appropriacy of such ideas in FL contexts is not immediately clear (but see Hudelson 1994). However, a small project in a Malaysian kindergarten is demonstrating the possibilities (Cameron and Bavaharji 2000). The project has worked with parents as a key to early reading, encouraging them to read books in English with their five-year-old children, and providing activities linked to literacy, as well as a collection of interesting books that the children could choose and take home with them. While the project outcomes are still to be analysed, it was clear from seeing parents and children reading together, and from listening to children read their books, that some children have made enormous progress in literacy skills and in oral language skills over the six months of the project. The improvement in oral skills is an interesting development, and seems to have happened as children started to use the words and phrases of the books with their parents. It was not the case that these families all used English at home; some did, usually along with their first language, but others did not. They were not particularly privileged families, but the parents with the strongest motivation for their children's success seem, not surprisingly, to have produced the most benefits.

Emergent literacy ideas may then have potential for foreign language literacy, but I suggest that, as in first language, it works best for a subset of children, and that most learners will need more formal teaching alongside experiences with books. The features of emergent literacy that are most relevant for foreign language teaching are:

- children choose the books they want to hear and read;
- children are motivated by choice and by the quality of the writing they encounter;
- children often choose to read the same book many times, and this is a valuable learning experience;
- meaning comes first because the child understands the story as a whole;
- from this overall meaning, attention moves to whole words and letters, beginning with initial consonants, then final consonants, then vowels in the middle;
- the link between reading and oral skills is very strong because children adopt and play with the language of the story;
- parents can be involved with their children's language learning through reading aloud with them.

Language Experience approach

The Language Experience approach starts children reading and writing at sentence level, and its key feature is the child's use of his or her own experience as the topic of texts. It has been commercially produced as 'Breakthrough to Literacy', which has been widely used with children in Britain, for first language literacy, and with South African children in both their first and their second languages. In the commercial version, children compose sentences, with their teacher initially, from a set of word cards. The sentence is something the child wants to say: e.g. '*I went to the doctor yesterday.*' They physically move the word cards, choosing them and placing them into a plastic tray to make the sentence, placing a full stop card at the end. The sentence is then read back to the teacher, and the child copies it down in her or his book, which pushes attention to the formation of letters. Gradually, a child builds up a collection of words that are known, and moves to making several sentences. Once the sight vocabulary is established, small books are introduced.

As a way of starting reading, this method has some nice features, which can be adopted in foreign language classrooms:

– the child's ideas are used to compose the reading text;
– child and teacher together compose the sentences;
– the child's learning moves from a meaningful idea unit (the sentence as a mini-text) to whole words to letters;
– words have a physical reality, as well as meaning, for the child as they are moved and put together;
– punctuation is present from the start as part of the physical reality of sentences: spaces between words and full stops;
– the integration of writing and reading helps the child see how texts are composed and understood right from the start.

Starting from the child's experience in order to produce texts can be done in a foreign language classroom too, e.g. by constructing sentences linked to current topics and vocabulary. Children can draw a picture that is then written about, or they can illustrate a sentence that they have dictated to the teacher to 'scribe' for them.

Language Experience work can be done as a whole class, as well as individually, if the teacher asks for sentences from children and writes them on the board to build up a text. The process of joint writing presents an opportunity for talking with the children about the words, punctuation, spelling, or text organisation, which can help children's metalinguistic knowledge and push them to notice certain features of written English. If the writing is done on large sheets of paper, the product of joint writing can be made into a big book for the class, and used for further reading activities.

Sets of word cards, large ones for whole class use and small ones for individual or pair work, can be made and used for many reading activities, including making sentences. In early literacy work, children may be asked to help compose a sentence, which is written on the board, and then use small word cards to form the same sentence themselves. They can make sentences with a partner, or for a partner to read.

When we hold the Language Experience approach up against the full set of reading skills and knowledge set out in Figure 6.3 we can see that, while it starts children reading and writing through meaningful word and sentence-level work, there will also need to be, at some point, a focus on letter-sound relationships.

Whole words / key words approach

This approach was used in the globally popular Ladybird series, and in many other commercial reading series. It starts from word level, with children looking at single words on cards (called 'flash cards', because they are sometimes shown very quickly to the children, or 'flashed' in front of their eyes) to encourage rapid whole word recognition. A child will begin with five or six very common words, such as *mummy* and *likes*. The child practises saying the word when he sees the card, and once the first five or six are mastered, moves on to the next set. Once the child has about 15 words, very simple books are introduced that only use the known words. The child then reads the books at that level to the teacher, one or two pages a day, and practises alone.

The term 'key words' was used because the sight words taught were taken from the most frequently used words in English. As we saw in section 4.3.1, many of the most frequent words are function words, such as *for* or *was*, that do not have clear lexical meanings but create meanings when they are used with content words. In learning to read, these words are probably better, and more easily, learnt through multiple encounters in contexts of use, rather than separated from other words on a card. Another problem with this method is the limited interest of the texts that can be written with a small number of words.

The flashcard method for learning whole words can take a child to quite a high level as a beginner reader, but after about 50 words, it is not efficient, or even possible, to remember each word as a separate whole. To progress, the method relies on the child generalising and finding patterns and regularities in the words being learnt, i.e. the child needs to use information about letters and sounds as well. As with emergent literacy, some children do this mental work automatically, and more or less teach themselves to read. Many others though need focused help with the sounds of letters and how letters go together to make words.

The features of whole word methods that are relevant for foreign language contexts include:

- children get practice at fast recognition of whole words through use of flashcards;
- children get a good sense of achievement and motivation by being able to read a whole book quite early;
- the sight vocabulary can provide a resource that the child can use to work out how letters combine into syllables.

Phonics teaching

Phonics teaching focuses on letter-sound relations, building literacy skills from the bottom-up. The usual way involves showing children the sounds of the different letters in the alphabet, then how letters can be combined. A recent approach (McGuiness 1997) suggests children will find it more natural to start from sounds and learn which letters make them, since they are moving from experience with the spoken language to the new world of written letters and words.

Phonics teaching works if it directs children's attention to letter-sound level features of English and helps children make the mental connections between letters and sounds. It can be very dry, boring and demotivating, if done in isolation, so it is probably preferable to incorporate five or ten minutes of concentrated phonics work inside other activities. Phonics work can be integrated into story reading, class joint writing, sentence writing activities, songs and rhymes, when vocabulary is being presented or recycled, and in stages of oral tasks.

Progression in phonics teaching (based on Dechant 1991)
Consonants in English are easier to notice, and thus to learn, than vowels. They can be grouped for teaching in various ways, by the way the shape is formed in writing, by the hard / soft sounds they make, by frequency and usefulness. One suggested teaching order for English consonants is:

1. b c d g h j m n p t w
2. f l r s
3. c g (soft sounds)
4. v x y z

It is usual to start with single consonants that occur as onsets in syllables or in single syllable words, drawing children's attention to them, identifying their name and sound, playing games with them such as spotting them in books, practising writing the letter shapes so that sounds, reading and writing reinforce each other. It is important in phonics teaching to make activities meaningful for children, and to make connections with what they already know. Thus, using words the children know by sight as the context for work on letters and sounds, is likely to be more meaningful than abstract and unconnected chanting of letter names and shapes. For example, if the letter and sound {<b>, /b/} is to be taught, then children can be shown objects such as a *ball*, a *blue balloon*, and a *big basket*, and the written words for each. They then have a meaningful context for the letter and sound. They can look at the words and spot the letter shape; they can listen and hear the sound. The teaching brings the shape and sound together for the children so that they can make the mental connection. To reinforce the connection, a 'b table' might be set up in the classroom and children asked to bring in objects from home that have a /b/ sound. The teacher then labels each object as it is placed on the table.

Phonics teaching can move to consonants that occur at the ends of words, and then to vowels. The English vowel system is notoriously complicated: out of the five vowel letters, a range of different vowel sounds can be produced: long vowel sounds, short vowel sounds, and diphthongs that combine two vowel sounds, as in <boy>. The sound a vowel makes is partly determined by the letters that surround it and its position in a word and some letters are silent. In deciding what to teach explicitly, short vowel sounds are fairly consistent and thus a good place to start, e.g. the sounds in *hat / pet / sit / hop / run*. The 'Magic -e' rule can then expand these sounds: this rule says that an <-e> on the end of a single syllable word affects the vowel sound, which then (in child friendly terms) 'says its own name': e.g. *hate / pete / site / hope / June*. This rule is a good example of a useful phonics rule, because it is quite simple and true often enough to make it worth learning (although some exceptions do occur in frequently used words, such as *come*). Many other rules are so complex and have so many exceptions that they may not be worth trying to teach explicitly. Long vowel sounds in open syllables, such as *me* and *go*, can be usefully taught next, and then work on rimes can extend reading and writing skills e.g. *-ite, -eat, -ike*. This content will cover several years of work.

6.5 Continuing to learn to read

We move in this section to think about how we move children on with literacy skills once they have made a start with reading and writing in the foreign language. Similar methods and techniques may also be used with children who start learning the language from 9 or 10 years of age, and thus bring some first language literacy knowledge and skills to the process.

6.5.1 Learning a range of reading strategies

If children are to become independent readers, they need to acquire a wide range of strategies for making sense of texts. Evidence from helping children who are struggling to learn to read shows that they often stick with only one or two sources of information, which may work at the beginning stages, but which need augmenting with strategies at other scales for progression to fluent reading (Clay 1982). The child who picks up a set of words that she recognises as whole words, and uses this sight vocabulary to read simple texts, needs to also develop knowledge of grapho-phonemic relationships within words to progress to more difficult texts. On the other hand, the child who has learnt the names and sounds of the letters and can read simple, regular words by 'sounding them out', needs also to recognise morphemes by sight and to draw on grammatical information at sentence level if progression is to be made. Wherever a child starts in reading, the teacher needs to make sure development takes him or her to the other scales and that reading activities require the active integration of information across scales.

I would like, as an example, to recount my experience of reading with a little girl, who I shall call Mary. She was taking part in the Malaysian early literacy project that I described earlier in the chapter, and was one of those children making rapid progress with her reading. I asked her to choose a book to read to me; she chose one she had read many times before, and read it fast and fluently. I then gave her a different book to read, that she had not read before, so that she would be moved into her zone of proximal development and I would be able to see the strategies she used for unknown words. The book was about a girl and her pushchair, and it was this latter word that gave her the first problem. Mary's initial strategy was to look at me to tell her the new word; clearly this was what usually happened. Instead of just telling her, I showed her how she could break up <pushchair> into two 'bits' (morphemes): <push> and <chair>, and showed her the word <chair> in the first book, where she had read it with no difficulty. She was then able to work out <pushchair> for herself. I checked that she knew its meaning by asking her to point to the pushchair in the picture. By doing this, I had introduced her to the strategies of breaking down words, and using context as a support for meaning. At the same time, she was being helped to see that words can be separated from the cotext, i.e. the surrounding text, in which they first appear. As we went on with the book, I helped her to use various other strategies with new words:

– With the word <bar>, I pointed to the first letter, the sound of which she knew, and she then managed to sound out the word. She used phonics knowledge and skills to attack new words. I showed her the bar on the pushchair in a picture, because it seemed that she did not know the meaning.
– With the word <rather>, I just told her the word and did not spend any time on it, because it was not crucial to the meaning of the story and is not a particularly useful word to learn at her stage.
– With the word <meals> I told her the word and then explained the meaning as the story progressed and the heroine moved from breakfast to lunch to tea. She would probably remember this as a sight word because that was her major learning strategy to date and she had a well developed memory for sight words.
– When she came to <watching the TV>, she said 'washing'. From this 'miscue', I could see that she was making a good attempt at the word and had noticed the initial consonant and the final rime -*ing*. I pointed out the words that followed the verb, and the picture, i.e. the cotext and context, and she was then able to correct her guess to 'watching'. In our talk about reading, her strategy, of working out a word through analogy with a known word, was refined by using visual and cotextual information.

By the time we reached the end of the pushchair story, Mary had changed her expectation that I, as the adult, would tell her all the words she did not know, and was beginning to look closely at new words and try to work them out herself. As a helpful adult, I was providing, for learning to read, the types of scaffolding that are listed in Table 1.1 – not doing the work for Mary, but helping her to see how she could do it herself.

Five minutes spent listening to a child reading will reveal what knowledge and skills the child is bringing to reading, and what informational cues and strategies are being used to deal with unfamiliar words. From what is found out, the teacher can see where the child can move next in literacy development.

6.5.2 Focused teaching about written language forms

Explicit teaching about features of the written language can help move children on, as part of a broader reading skills programme. In this section, I set out a basic procedure for doing short, intensive, focused periods of teaching around lower-level literacy features within FL lessons (drawing on Dechant 1991). The procedure has five steps. It starts and finishes with meaningful discourse, focusing in the middle steps on the precise aspect of literacy writing that is the goal of the teaching. It can be used to fill gaps in children's knowledge and skills, or to highlight areas in which the FL literacy works differently from the L1.

The Steps

1. Start from a meaningful context.
2. Focus the pupils' attention on the unit and key feature being taught.
3. Give input: examples, a rule, etc.
4. Provide varied practice.
5. Give pupils opportunities to apply their new knowledge and skills in different, meaningful contexts.

These steps can be followed for any of the literacy features at word level or below:

> sight words
> initial consonants
> rimes
> final consonants
> vowels
> morphemes
> consonant clusters and blends

As an example, I describe an activity aimed at 9–10 year olds that was devised by a group of Malaysian primary teachers, around the rime <-ail>. They first created the 'meaningful context' by listing words in which the rime occurs and making up a 'jazz chant' that used as many as possible (following Graham 1979). The chant they produced went as follows:

> *THE MAIL SNAIL*
> I see a snail
> With a very long tail.
> He's crawling on the rail
> To deliver the mail.
> He's sure to fail
> Because he's stuck on a nail.

They produced a graphic drawing to illustrate the plight of the poor postman snail. The picture and oral chant were introduced as the first step. In Step 2, the written version was used, with the <-ail> rime highlighted in red at the end of the lines to draw attention to it. In Step

3, the words containing <-ail> were taken from the chant and presented in isolation on the board or on large cards. They could then be positioned to emphasise the shape and sound of the rime:

sn ail
t ail
r ail
m ail
f ail
n ail

The initial letters could be removed by rubbing out or cutting off. As Step 4, a quick game-like activity could produce words for the children to recognise, by placing initial consonants next to the rime.

Once the children have paid attention in these ways to the feature, they should have made a good start at learning it, and the last step is to move back out to a larger discourse context in which they can apply their new knowledge. In this example, it might be to say the chant again or to compose a new one, using other (known) words like *sail, pail, jail*, along with some of the original words.

6.6 Developing reading and writing as discourse skills

This chapter has stressed that literacy is about communication and that, even when the focus is on learning about the mechanics of how reading works, we can still find ways for literacy to play a role in social life, inside and beyond the classroom. When writing is used to wish a friend 'Happy Birthday' or reading used to understand a message on the class notice board, literacy skills are operating as discourse skills. On the other hand, I have also wanted to emphasise that, without informed and focused attention to the mechanics of reading and writing, children may be denied access to literacy in their first and foreign languages, and that a great deal of focused work is needed to help children make a good start in learning to read and write. The previous section showed how that focused work can continue as children move through their primary years. Alongside developing knowledge and skills at lower levels, older children can be helped to develop their written discourse skills, at sentence level and above. Developments can be seen along various interacting dimensions.

6.6.1 'Fluency' in writing and reading

'Fluency' in spoken language use has a written equivalent, although there is not a single word to label it. In reading in the foreign language, the integration of different level reading skills in tackling a text will gradually become more automatic and faster. Skilful readers can be encouraged to try to read silently; they will need reminding to keep their lips still at first, and to try to read 'through the brain rather than the mouth'. It can take several months or more to make this transition, and it may only happen for a few readers at primary level.

In writing, children who have mastered letter shapes and spelling, can be encouraged to write gradually more. To become a fluent writer, it is necessary to write often and at length. Children can be encouraged to choose and copy texts that they find interesting: items from the Internet on their favourite pop star or footballer, or the rhymes learnt in class, or sections of their reading books that they enjoyed. The element of choice is to ensure that copying is meaningful and motivating. Another way to encourage extended writing is to ask children to write a journal, giving them a regular five or ten minutes in class to write whatever they want, or about a topic from the news that they are given, perhaps without worrying about correct spellings or grammar. This kind of writing should not be 'corrected', but it might be **responded to,** by the teacher reading the entries every now and again and writing some thoughts down in response to the child's writing.

6.6.2 Complexity of written language

Much reading and writing in language classrooms happens in support of other aspects of language learning, such as writing down vocabulary to remember it or reinforcing new grammar patterns. In general, the level of the language that pupils write will lag slightly behind the level that they are comfortable with in speaking and listening. The complexity of language that they read will usually match spoken levels, but as children mature as readers so they will be able to read language that is more complex, without being worried by not recognising it all. For older children, written text can introduce new aspects of language.

6.6.3 Learning to write for an audience

Throughout the years of primary education, children gradually develop a more sophisticated understanding of how other people think and function, as they develop a 'theory of mind' that enables empathy with others (Frith 1990). This aspect of social and emotional development will impact on their ability to write (or speak) for an audience, which requires selecting and adapting language so that other people can make sense of the writer's ideas and arguments. The skills involved in expressing oneself for other people do not receive much attention in foreign language classrooms, but have been quite prominent in approaches to teaching writing at primary level in the UK; writing done by children should have a clear Audience, Purpose and Topic (i.e. it should be 'APT'). If writing in the foreign language is to have an audience and purpose then we have to think beyond writing to practise grammar or vocabulary; possible activities might include:

– letters and e-mail messages, written and sent to authors of books, pen friends overseas, magazines, schools in other countries, children in the next class;
– very simple stories, written for younger children learning the foreign language in the same school;
– articles about class events and reviews of books, new films or TV programmes, written for a class or school magazine or computer bulletin board.

Texts that are designed for an audience are worth spending more time on, and naturally promote the idea of working on several drafts, editing each in the process of producing a final version that is ready for other people to read. Editing drafts helps children develop self-direction in writing by offering them an external model of how to check their work. The experience of checking work with others can then be internalised and become a tool for individual learners. When children are learning to edit their writing, it may be helpful to focus on one or two features only at each stage. An initial draft might be read aloud to a group for comments on how well others will understand its overall idea. A later draft might be checked in pairs for verb endings or use of the definite and indefinite articles, *the / a(n)*.

6.6.4 Learning conventional formats for different types of discourse

In Chapter 3, we met the notion of 'discourse repertoires' and different types of discourse organisation; when applied to written text, we talk of 'genres' or 'text types'. As children develop as readers and writers, and cope with longer texts, they will begin to notice and use the patterns of organisation in different text types. Teachers can support this by using texts from a range of genres and by making explicit the structure of typical information texts or story texts, and showing children how the parts are put together.

To focus on text structure, short texts with clear structure and organisation can be photocopied and cut into parts. Children have to read and put the parts in order as a group, discussing what it was about the text that made them decide on a particular order. This kind of activity will get children thinking and talking about the parts of a description or narrative, and they can be helped to notice how language is used to signal the parts, e.g. through a topic sentence at the beginning of a paragraph, or through signal words or discourse markers.

When children write texts that need a particular type of organisation, they can be shown how to write a plan that shows the parts, the content and the links, and they can be encouraged to talk about their plan to the teacher or to a partner before writing the full text. Small groups might produce a longer text by sharing out the work amongst themselves. Joint writing by teacher and pupils, mentioned already, can be an occasion where the teacher can talk about the text, using helpful metalanguage; e.g. *We've introduced the people in the story; perhaps we should tell the reader what the big problem was . . .?*

More ideas for using texts will be found in the next chapter; in theme-based learning, written sources of information offer many opportunities for developing reading skills in the foreign language, and sharing what has been discovered about a topic creates possibilities for writing with a clear purpose and audience.

6.7 Summary and conclusion

6.7.1 Summary

This chapter has examined in some detail what it means to be able to read in English, as a first and as a foreign language. It has emphasised the central point that constructing the meaning of a written text requires the reader to extract and integrate various types of information from many levels of a text. In very early literacy development, combining the learning of reading and writing will help pupils to come to understand how a particular language encodes meaning in written symbols.

To fully appreciate what it means to become literate in a foreign language, we must use theory and empirical research to draw up a picture of how fluent readers operate in both the first and the foreign languages, like that shown for English in Figure 6.3. We then have some idea of which knowledge and skills can be transferred to the foreign language and which will need to be learnt from scratch.

6.7.2 Literacy beyond the primary classroom

If children leave their early foreign language learning able to read and write simple texts in the foreign language, and use a good range of reading strategies, they will have a solid foundation for future literacy development. Just as important, though, they need to feel positive about reading and writing in the foreign language, to understand why literacy is useful and to enjoy tackling a text in the foreign language, confident that they will be able to get something from it. The many colourful story and information books now available for children will motivate them to try reading in the foreign language and to enjoy the process, without needing to understand every word, and the next chapter considers how such books can be used from the earliest stages.

Apart from books in school that pupils can choose from and take home, there is now an endless source of information in English on the Internet, including sites run by teachers in different countries that show their pupils' writing. The world of cyberspace relies on literacy skills, and it already offers exciting possibilities for literacy skills development, as well as ones we cannot yet imagine.

7 Learning through stories

7.1 Stories and themes as holistic approaches to language teaching and learning

Stories and themes are placed together in this chapter and the next because they represent holistic approaches to language teaching and learning that place a high premium on children's involvement with rich, authentic uses of the foreign language. Stories offer a whole imaginary world, created by language, that children can enter and enjoy, learning language as they go. Themes begin from an overarching topic or idea that can branch out in many different directions, allowing children to pursue personal interests through the foreign language.

Exploring the use of stories and themes will allow us to re-visit the principles and approaches of earlier chapters, as we work through the possibilities and opportunities they offer. The approach in this book has been underpinned by the principle that children and their learning can guide teaching; in particular, I have tried to show how directions for teaching can emerge from the dynamic interplay between possible tasks, activities, and materials, on the one hand, and children's desire to find and construct coherence and meaning, on the other. When we have looked in previous chapters at aspects of the foreign language, task content and materials have been designed for the classroom. As we move now to stories and themes, we start from materials and content that have a more independent existence beyond the classroom. Stories bring into the classroom texts that originate in the world outside school; themes organise content and activity around ideas or topics that are broader than the organising ideas in most day-to-day classroom language learning, and that might be found structuring events outside the classroom such as television documentaries or community projects. Bringing the world into the classroom by using stories and themes creates different demands for the foreign language teacher. The teacher has to work from the theme or story to make the content accessible to learners and to construct activities that offer language learning opportunities, and in doing so needs many of the skills and language knowledge of text book writers.

In continuing to develop a learning-centred perspective to teaching foreign languages to children, I will emphasise the need for teachers to plan classroom work with clear language learning goals in mind. These more holistic, top-down methods sometimes appear to generate more than their share of fuzzy thinking about how children can learn from taking part in them. While the outcomes of activities are, perhaps, less predictable, we should still aim to think clearly about how tasks are organised and what children learn from them. A large part of the skill in designing good activities lies in recognising and exploiting opportunities that language use offers for language learning.

Stories are frequently claimed to bring many benefits to young learner classrooms, including language development (Wright 1997; Garvie 1990). The power attributed to stories, which sometimes seems to move towards the mystical and magical, is probably generated by their links into poetics and literature in one direction and to the warmth of early childhood experiences in another. Stories can serve as metaphors for society or for our deepest psyche (Bettelheim 1976), and parent–child story reading can be rich and intimate events that contrast sharply with the linear aridity of syllabuses and some course books (Garton and Pratt 1998).

However, classrooms are not family sitting rooms, teachers are not their pupils' parents, and many of the texts in books found in schools are not poetic, meaningful stories that will instantly capture children's imagination. I suggest that we can best serve young learners by adopting a critical stance to the use of stories, aiming to clarify the qualities of good stories for the language classrooms. We should also be careful that our own nostalgia does not push the use of stories beyond the reality of learners' lives in this 'information age'. Children participate in many literacy events outside school that involve texts that are not stories, and that combine text and visuals in varied and dynamic ways. They may be equally motivated by the importing of some of these other text types into classrooms, and we will look at some possibilities in the final section.

We look first at what we mean by 'stories', differentiating stories from other kinds of text in terms of what they contain and how they are composed. We examine quality in stories, and how we can discriminate 'good' stories from less good ones. We then move to what makes a story useful for foreign language learning.

7.2 The discourse organisation of stories

Story telling is an oral activity, and stories have the shape they do because they are designed to be listened to and, in many situations, participated in. The first, obvious, key organising feature of stories is that events happen at different points in time; they occur in a temporal sequence. The other key organising feature of stories is their thematic structure i.e. there is some central interest factor (theme) that changes over the timescale of the story: difficulties or evil are overcome, or a major event is survived. Very often the thematic structure of a story can be characterised as the resolution of a problem (Hoey 1983). A narrative does not need a thematic structure other than the unfolding of time, but it is then a kind of commentary rather than a story. These two central features of a story can be illustrated by considering a children's story well known in Europe and beyond, 'Little Red Riding Hood'. Fairy tales like this have existed for many years, and have spread from one culture to another, and one language to another. In this evolutionary process, they have retained and developed features that we now think of as prototypical of stories for children. In other parts of the world, there are parallels to the European fairy tale tradition: Ashanti tales in west Africa and the Caribbean; Mouse Deer stories in south-east Asia; and Nasruddin stories in Arabic countries in the Middle East, Turkey and north Africa.

In the story of Little Red Riding Hood (LRRH, for short), the main characters are a little girl, who has a red coat with a hood, hence the nickname, and who lives with her parents near a forest, and a big bad wolf, who wants to eat people, and who provides the problem. The story covers the events of one day, when Little Red Riding Hood visits her grandmother and on the way, despite her mother's warnings, leaves the path to pick flowers, and meets the wolf. She tells the wolf where she is going and he rushes ahead, eats the grandmother, dresses in her clothes, and waits for the girl to arrive. LRRH does not notice that it is the wolf in her grandmother's bed, and is about to be eaten by the wolf, when, just in time, her father arrives and kills the wolf. The grandmother jumps out of his stomach, and all ends happily. The story has two morals: that wickedness will be overcome and, at a more specific level, that children should do what their parents tell them.

The structure of typical stories was analysed by Propp (1958) and many of the same features have been found in analyses of how people tell stories in their conversations (Labov 1972). Prototypical features of stories, that will be found in most versions of LRRH, are:

– an opening: often formulaic in fairy tales e.g. '*Once upon a time . . .*';
– introduction of characters;
– description of the setting;
– introduction of a problem;
– a series of events;

– that lead to –

- the resolution of the problem
- a closing: often formulaic in fairy tales – '*They all lived happily ever after*';
- a moral: which may or may not be explicitly stated.

We should note that many texts found in course books may be called 'stories', but in fact may lack some of these prototypical features. Most often they lack a plot; instead of setting up a problem and working towards its resolution, the characters just move through a sequence of activities. Teachers should not assume that such non-stories will capture children's imagination in the same way that stories can do.

LRRH illustrates yet more features of stories, that are common, but not always all found in every story. Firstly, the way that the story is told sets up dramatic irony, in that the reader knows more than the central character. In this case, the reader knows that the 'grandmother' who LRRH finds in bed is really that wolf dressed up, and also knows that LRRH does not know. A sense of suspense is created by this knowledge gap between story characters and audience, motivating listeners to want to find out what will happen when LRRH arrives at her grandmother's house.

Secondly, there is predictability built into the narrative, through a kind of lock-step progression in which one incident seems to lead inevitably to the next:

mother warns LRRH not to leave the path or talk to the wolf
⇒ LRRH leaves the path and talks to the wolf
⇒ LRRH tells the wolf about her grandmother
⇒ the wolf goes to the grandmother's house
⇒ LRRH tells the wolf / grandmother she has big teeth
⇒ the wolf tries to eat LRRH.

Thirdly, this predictability and sense of inevitability is broken by the surprise event of the arrival of LRRH's father to save her. The pattern of a sequence of familiar and predictable events, interrupted by a surprise, echoes the one of 'security and novelty' that we met in section 1.4, and it is probably a pattern that suits human psychology: a degree of comfortable familiarity combined with just the right amount of surprise and change. In other stories, the predictability and continuity is constructed by the repetition of events, with just a small change: as when, in another familiar tale, Goldilocks tries out firstly the beds, then the chairs, and finally the porridge of the Three Bears. In each of these episodes, she first tries the Daddy Bear's bed / chair / porridge, then the Mummy Bear's, and finally the Baby Bear's. And in each instance, the first and second are unsuitable, but the third is '*just right*'.

7.3 Language use in stories

Children's stories contain uses of language that are considered typical of poetic and literary texts. Many of these devices offer opportunities for foreign language learning.

7.3.1 Parallelism

The pattern of predictability + surprise, or repetition + change, is often reflected in patterns of repetition of language. For example, when LRRH arrives at her grandmother's house and talks to the wolf wearing the old woman's clothes, their dialogue goes like this:

LRRH: Grandmother, what big eyes you've got!   BBW: All the better to see you with, my dear.

LRRH: Grandmother, what big ears you've got!   BBW: All the better to hear you with, my dear.

LRRH: Grandmother, what big teeth you've got!   BBW: All the better to EAT you with . . .

This repeated pattern, or parallelism, creates a way into the story for the active listener, as well as providing a natural support for language learning.

7.3.2 Rich vocabulary

Because stories are designed to entertain, writers and tellers choose and use words with particular care to keep the audience interested. Stories may thus include unusual words, or words that have a strong phonological content, with interesting rhythms or sounds that are onomatopoeic. The context created by the story, its predictable pattern of events and language, and pictures, all act to support listeners' understanding of unfamiliar words. Children will pick up words that they enjoy and, in this way, stories offer space for growth in vocabulary.

As an example of how a simple story can incorporate rich vocabulary, we can look at the story *On the Way Home* by Jill Murphy, which includes the following words:

- to describe familiar story book characters: *vast, huge, enormous, hairy, gigantic*;
- to describe how they moved: *zooming, lumbering, slithering, soaring, creeping, gliding, swooping*;
- to describe what the heroine did: *struggled, crammed, tickled, stamped, punched.*

Children's understanding of this lexis is very strongly supported by the repetitive story frame, in which each episode has the same format, by the use of very familiar, easy words in the narrative and in the dialogue of the real character alongside these less familiar words, e.g. *Look at my bad knee*, and by the vivid pictures.

There is some evidence that children can learn vocabulary from stories through listening, i.e. 'incidentally'. Elley (1989) carried out two studies with 7 and 8 year old first language users in New Zealand to investigate vocabulary gain from listening to stories, with and without teacher explanations of the new words. He found that word learning correlated significantly with the number of times the word was pictured, the helpfulness of cues to meaning in the texts, and the number of times number of occurrences of a word in the story (between 6 and 12 encounters with a new word are needed for L1 users to remember it). When story reading was accompanied by teacher explanations of new words, through pictures, acting out meaning or verbal explanation, the vocabulary gain doubled, and the gain was still evident three months later. Interestingly, there was variation in vocabulary gain across the stories used in the study, so that the story itself seems to make a difference. Elley suggests that learner involvement with a story may be what makes a difference, and lists the following as possible involvement factors in stories: humour, novelty, suspense, incongruity and vividness. Schouten-van Parreren (1989, 1992) suggests that letting children choose the stories they want to hear may help maximise the learning that takes place.

7.3.3 Alliteration

Alliteration is the use of words that have the same initial consonants. For example, *red riding* and *big bad*. It can offer a source for developing knowledge of letter sounds (Chapter 6).

7.3.4 Contrast

Stories for children often contain strong contrasts between characters or actions or settings. In LRRH, the innocent girl and the bad wolf are clearly contrasted characters, representing good and evil; the old woman and the young girl contrast youth and age. Placing ideas in such clear opposition may well help children's understanding of the story as a whole. For language learning, the lexical items that are used in connection with each idea will also form contrasting sets, that may help understanding and recall (Chapter 4).

7.3.5 Metaphor

In LRRH, the forest can be seen as metaphorically representing life outside the safety of the family, and the wolf as representing threats to safety and innocence. Bettelheim (1976) suggests that our early experiences with fairy stories map subconsciously on to our real world experiences, and become a kind of script for our lives. Claims of such power for these simple tales takes us far beyond the foreign language classroom, although there are gifted individuals who have used 'story making' for educational and personal development (e.g. Marshall 1963).

7.3.6 Intertextuality

This is the term used to describe making references within one text to aspects of other texts that have become part of shared cultural knowledge. For example, Red Riding Hood makes an appearance in *Each Peach, Pear, Plum* by Janet and Allan Ahlberg, and in *On the Way Home* by Jill Murphy (both Puffin Books).

When children begin to write their own stories, or little dramas, they may, just as adult writers do, involve familiar characters or pieces of language from stories they know. This appropriation of the voice of a writer is an integral part of first language development (Bakhtin 1981), and can help in foreign language learning too.

7.3.7 Narrative / dialogue

Within a story, we can distinguish two main uses of language: for narrative and for dialogue:

Narrative text concerns the series of events:

> *the little girl walked through the forest; the wolf ran to grand-mother's house.*

Dialogue is use of language as it would be spoken by the characters:

> '*all the better to eat you with*'.

Some stories are entirely narrative, e.g. *Rosie's Walk* by Pat Hutchins (Puffin Books); in others, the text is entirely dialogue, with the pictures contributing the narrative as they show something different happening on each day e.g. *Bet you Can't* by Penny Dale (Walker Books). Most stories, though, move between narrative and dialogue, and the way they intertwine in a story does much to create its particular atmosphere.

Narrative and dialogue are clearly separable to listeners and readers.

They are distinguished by their time-frame, and hence by the tense of the verbs used: narrative language recounts what happened, and verbs are typically in the Past Tense, while dialogue captures characters in their present time-frame, and uses whichever tense is appropriate to what they are talking about.

Foreign language or simplified versions of stories in English often choose the simple present tense for narrative (*the little girl walks through the forest*), probably because in EFL syllabuses it has been seen as simpler than the others and taught first.[1] If a story is told through pictures, the present continuous tense is often found (*the little girl is walking through the forest*). It seems a pity to deprive learners of opportunities to hear authentic uses of past tense forms, and the contrast with other tenses, in the meaningful contexts of stories, and I can see no intrinsic reason for supposing that use of past tense would prevent children understanding a story. In fact, if they are familiar with stories in their first language, they will probably expect to hear past tense forms and may misconstrue the verbs.

7.4 Quality in stories

The issue of what makes a good quality story is important but is clearly bound to be somewhat subjective. A good story is, at one level, simply one that listeners or readers enjoy. However, stories that appeal more than others, and that remain favourites with children and parents over many years, do demonstrate some common features that can be identified as characterising quality.

Quality stories have characters and a plot that engage children, often the art work is as important as the text in telling the story, and they create a strong feeling of satisfaction when the end is reached. A convincing and satisfying closure includes the reader in those who 'live happily ever after'.

Children need to be able to enter the imaginative world that the story creates. This means that they can understand enough about the characters and their lives to be able to empathise with them. So, a story about being lost in the desert that is to be used with children in arctic countries will need to contain lots of detail that enables them to imagine what a desert looks and feels like to be in. Many stories for children include fantastical beings or animals in imaginary worlds, but these characters and settings usually bear enough resemblance to children and

---

[1] My summary of LRRH earlier in the chapter used the Simple Present rather than the Simple Past because it was an account of the story, not a telling of the story.

their real worlds for readers to imagine them: monsters tend to live in families, tigers come to drink tea in the kitchen, frogs and ducks get jealous – all act in ways familiar to children!

Stories that have the qualities of content, organisation and language use that we have explored thus far are potentially useful tools in the foreign language classroom, since they have the potential to capture children's interest and thus motivation to learn, along with space for language growth. However, not all good stories will be automatically good for language learning, and we now move to think about what is involved in choosing and using stories not just for pleasure, but for (pleasurable) language learning.

7.5 Choosing stories to promote language learning

In this section, we use the features of stories described so far to set out questions that a language teacher might ask to evaluate the language learning opportunities offered by a story in order to choose stories for the language classroom.

'Real' books or specially written ones?

In British education in the 1980s there was a move to bring what were called 'real books' into primary schools for teaching reading (e.g. Waterland 1985). Real books were those written by 'real' authors for parents to buy for children, and there was a so-called 'golden age' of young children's literature in English in the 1970s and 1980s, as writers exploited the use of colour and pictures alongside simple story lines. Examples of writers producing quality books at and since that time would include John Burningham, Janet and Allan Ahlberg, Jill Murphy, and Pat Hutchins. A great part of what made for quality in these books was the skilful and often humorous interplay of pictures and text. Many of these books are suitable for use in teaching English, and I will show how they might be exploited in the next section.

The reading with real books movement has mostly lost momentum now in a return to more focused literacy teaching in British classrooms (Chapter 6), but there have been some lasting effects. Teachers now make much more use of story books for teaching reading. Educational publishers followed up the idea of quality stories, and commissioned specially written story books to accompany and extend structured reading schemes. While not all these books are of the quality of the original 'real' books, they are an improvement on the unimaginative books many children faced in schools. Schemes such as Cambridge

Reading and Oxford Reading Tree now offer another source of stories for teachers of English as a foreign language. The questions that follow can be applied to any story book that is being considered for use in the foreign language classroom.

Will the content engage the learners?

A good story for language learning will have interesting characters that children can empathise with, who take part in activities that the learners can make sense of. The plot will be clear, but may have a surprise or twist at the end.

The role of the pictures in combination with the text to form the story as a whole should be considered. If the pictures are indispensable, as is often the case, then somehow there will need to be enough copies or they will need to be made big enough for everyone to see.

Are the values and attitudes embodied in the story acceptable?

Stories can help children feel positive about other countries and cultures, and can broaden their knowledge of the world. However, stories should be checked for values and attitudes that may not be appropriate; for example, 'classic' stories written some time ago may carry attitudes to women and black people that are no longer acceptable.

How is the discourse organised?

Stories with a structure close to the prototypical format set out in section 7.2 are likely to be most accessible to children. The characters and setting will be described. There will be a clear plot, with an initial formulation of a problem, a series of linked events, and a resolution of the problem. An element of surprise or unpredictability will add to children's involvement with the story.

What is the balance of dialogue and narrative?

The balance of dialogue and narrative in a story may influence choice, and will certainly affect the way a story is used. Dialogue in a story may lend itself to acting out and to learning phrases for conversation. Narrative may offer repeated patterns of language that will help grammar learning through noticing of new patterns or consolidation of patterns already met (Chapter 5).

How is language used?

The built-in repetition of words and phrases is one of the features of stories that is most helpful for language learning. Careful analysis of the language of the text will reveal whether the repeated phrases and vocabulary will help a particular class. There may be some phrases used in the dialogue that children can appropriate for their own language use, such as '*look at my bad knee!*' in the book *On the Way Home* (Jill Murphy, Puffin Books). The narrative may use words that have already been learnt, offering a chance to recycle them in a new context.

What new language is used?

In planning the use of a story, the teacher can identify language use and make three rough groupings:

1. language that children have already met, and that will be recycled;
2. new language that will be useful for all children to learn from the story;
3. new language that may or may not be learnt, depending on individual children's interest.

A story can include some new language in a story, but not so much that the story becomes incomprehensible. The number of new words that listeners can cope with within one story is not clear cut; it will depend on how well the pictures and discourse organisation support the meaning of the words, how central the new words are to the plot, and the overall total of new words, which should not be too high. In preparing to use a story, new words and phrases that are crucial to understanding the story should be pre-taught, and the support offered by pictures and context for the meaning of other new language should be checked to ensure it is adequate. If necessary, further support can be provided.

Having chosen a story because it offers potential language learning opportunities, the next stage is to decide on a sequence of tasks for the classroom.

7.6 Ways of using a story

Rather than present lists of activities to use with stories, I have chosen, in the holistic spirit of this chapter, to work with a particular story, using it to illustrate how activities might be developed in line with the learning principles of the book. Further ideas can be found in Ellis and Brewster (1991), Garvie (1990), and Wright (1995, 1997).

7.6.1 Evaluating the language learning opportunities of the story

Answers to the questions from the previous section help work towards activities:

'Real' books or specially written ones?

The story is *Dinosaurs* by Michael Foreman. First published in 1972, and probably aimed at 7 or 8 year old native speaker children, it is likely to be suitable for children up to about 12 years of age.

Will the content engage the learners?

The book deals with environmental issues and has a 'message' that we should all look after the planet because it belongs to all of us. The narrative tells a simple story of a man, who builds a rocket to escape the polluted earth, lands on a distant star but finds it inhospitable. He then sets off again and lands back on Earth, without realising it. While he has been away, the dinosaurs have 'woken up' and cleaned up the pollution to create a green and pleasant land again. When the man lands back on the Earth, he thinks he is in paradise. The writer makes use of dramatic irony when readers are aware that the man is back on earth, and that the dinosaurs have cleaned it up, while he himself thinks he is on some distant star. The dinosaurs explain that he is indeed on the Earth, but that he cannot have any bit of it back, because '*the Earth belongs to everyone*'.

The narrative of the man's journey is compelling, and it works on two levels: literally, he travels from Earth to star and back; metaphorically, he moves from ignorant polluting of the Earth to a more thoughtful awareness. The re-awakening of the dinosaurs is a powerful idea.

The contrasts across the story are very strong: between man and dinosaurs, in size and in wisdom; between pollution (before) and paradise (after), emphasised by the use of colour in the pictures. There are pictures on each double page, and colour is used vividly to contrast the barren industrial wastes that man has constructed, with the paradise of flower-filled forests that he wants to own. The characters are sympathetically drawn with human-like expressions on their faces.

Figure 7.1 Pictures from 'Dinosaurs' by Michael Foreman, Penguin Books

Are the values and attitudes embodied in the story acceptable?

The message of the need to conserve the environment is even more relevant than when the book was first published. The further message is that 'paradise' can be found where we are now, if we look after it; there is no need to travel to distant stars.

How is the discourse organised?

The narrative is organised around the character of the man, with the initial problem being his desire to reach a far-off star. This dream partly causes the industrial pollution that he leaves behind him. We see the man arrive on the star and find it completely barren and empty. The story then returns to the polluted earth and the dinosaur characters are introduced. Their problem is to clean up the planet, and they are shown doing this, as the earth gradually becomes green again. The dinosaurs and the man then meet in the resolution of the narrative, and negotiate who owns the newly green earth. The closing is a kind of crescendo in the use of language and colour, and the final picture shows the man riding on a smiling dinosaur into the sunset.

What is the balance of dialogue and narrative?

There is a mix of, mostly, narrative and some dialogue. The 'dialogue' includes the man's thoughts to himself, as he flies from earth and back again; the dinosaurs talking to each other, and the final negotiation between the dinosaurs and the man as they resolve their differences and agree to share the planet.

How is language used? What new language is used?

These questions will be taken together since, in the absence of real learners to relate the language to, only informed guesses about what will be new can be made.

The *Dinosaurs* story contains a mix of simple and complex language, as these extracts show:

Examples of simple language:

1. *A man stood on a hill and looked at a star.*
2. *Just a hill, or a tree, or a flower?*

The following examples are more complex in their grammar:

3. *The rocket was ready, but there was nowhere for it to be launched.*

4. *Sadly he looked around, but the only thing of wonder was another star, far off, in the black sky.*

Because the complex forms describe ideas that are comprehensible, they should not cause too much of a problem for children who have been learning English for 2 or 3 years, and who can grasp the content. There is plenty of scope for children to extend their English through the story.

The parallelism, or repetition of grammatical patterns, that occurs across the text is likely to be helpful to language learning:

5. *Grass grew high*
   and trees grew tall.
6. *All day*
   and all night . . .
7. *a jungle – alive with beautiful plants,*
   sweet with the scent of flowers.

The following examples shows a grammatical pattern which has both repeated and contrasting parts:

8. *not a part of it*
   but all of it
   the earth belongs to everyone
   not parts of it to certain people
   but all of it to everyone.

The phrases may be learnt initially as a chunk, and will be available to be broken down later.

In terms of vocabulary, the writer uses contrasting lexical sets of words that describe the pollution and the paradise. It is in these sets that the richest vocabulary is used. Once the words are listed, we can see that the 'pollution' words are nouns and verbs, whereas the 'paradise' words are adjectives and nouns (see Table 7.1).

The discoveries about the structure of the story and the use of language that are made in an initial evaluation, such as that just carried out, can suggest ways forward in designing activities around the story.

7.6.2 Language learning tasks using the story

The examples from the text demonstrate the poetic nature of the writer's choice and use of language, and for this reason, I would want to use the story orally first. Listening to the teacher read or tell a story is a useful language learning activity at any age; using story books does not have to be about teaching reading (although it can be, as we saw in Chapter 6). Listening to a story practises the ability to hold in mind the meaning of an extended piece of spoken discourse.

Table 7.1 Contrasting vocabulary in *Dinosaurs*

pollution	paradise
NOUNS	ADJECTIVES
fires	*green*
factories	*fresh*
smoke	*new*
fumes	*alive*
waste	*beautiful*
rubbish	*sweet*
heaps	
piles	NOUNS
mess	*shoots*
telegraph poles	*blossoms*
iron pylons	*flowers*
	forest
VERBS	*jungle*
burn	*scent*
smouldered	*song*
huffed and puffed	*birds*

In the task framework of Chapter 2, the teacher telling the story would constitute the core activity of the first task, with children listening and looking at the illustrations, either sitting close enough to the teacher to see or using large versions of the pictures. The main language learning goal for the core activity of the task would be that the children understand enough of the story to enjoy it. As a preparation activity, before the story reading, it would be useful to introduce the ideas and some of the key vocabulary, and the contrasting ideas and lexis that run through the story offer a good place to start:

Preparation activity: brainstorming vocabulary

Two pictures from the story (as in Figure 7.1) are shown to the children, one of the industrial mess and one of the green paradise, and they are asked for words about the pictures that they already know. If the children can read and write in English, then the words can be written on the board in two columns as in Table 7.1, or in two semantic networks, under the key words *pollution* and *paradise*.

Children may offer words in English, or their first language, which the teacher can translate. After children have offered words, the teacher can supply a few others that will be needed to understand the story.

Core activity: reading the story

The teacher reads the story to the children, giving them plenty of time to look at the pictures.

In the first reading, the teacher should read on through the story, rather than stopping too much to talk about words or the plot. Pictures can be used to emphasise what is happening in the story.

A second reading can follow straight away. This time the teacher can pause at the end of each page to point and repeat key words or ideas, or to ask children to recall or predict what happens next.

After listening to a story, children should have the chance to respond to it. They can be encouraged to express their feelings about the story, in English if possible, using simple phrases like:

> *I liked it when . . .*
> *I thought the dinosaurs were good.*

Follow-up activity: vocabulary learning

A simple immediate follow up would be to get the children to draw a picture as a further response to the story, and to choose and write down some of the vocabulary from the Preparation list next to the picture. They might be asked to choose five new words that they like and are going to learn, and take the picture home to show parents and practise their words. At the beginning of the next lesson, they can be asked to tell the words to a friend to motivate their self-directed learning.

The language learning goal of the follow-up activity is much more specific: to learn the meaning of five new words and recall the words in the next lesson.

This three stage task would probably take about half an hour and, in doing it, learners have only dipped a toe into the ocean of possibilities that any story offers. In the next section, I again use *Dinosaurs* to illustrate ideas, but also discuss possibilities more generally.

7.7 Developing tasks around a story

7.7.1 Listening skills

The first encounter with a story is only the beginning of language learning work that can be done around it. If a story appeals to children, they will want to hear it again and again. Once a story has been used, it can be added to the collection in the classroom, and looked at by the children in spare moments, borrowed to take home, or read again by the teacher in future lessons. The five or ten minutes spent listening to a familiar story will re-activate vocabulary and grammatical patterns, and offer opportunities for children to notice aspects of the language use that passed them by on previous readings or that they have partly learnt.

In listening to a story, children are practising listening for 'gist', i.e. the overall meaning. They can also be helped to focus on detail when the text is met on further occasions. If the teacher records the story on to cassette during one of the tellings, the recording can be used for further listening practice, at home or in class.

7.7.2 Discourse skills

A story creates a world of characters who talk to each other and this discourse world presents opportunities for communicative activities and work on discourse skills.

Acting roles

The dialogue in a story can be separated out from the narrative, if necessary in a version simplified by the teacher, and spoken by the children who take on roles of characters. If the teacher reads the narrative and children dress up and act out the dialogue, the story becomes a performance that might entertain another class, providing useful repeated practice in the process.

Rather than using all the dialogue, sections of it might be extracted for a closer focus. For example, the story contains a stretch of 'negotiation' between the man and the dinosaurs over who owns the earth. This could be practised between children taking the roles, or using puppets.

Retelling the story

As mentioned earlier in the book, asking children to retell a story in a foreign language is a very demanding task, much more demanding than in the first language. After all, one of the advantages of stories is that they can be slightly beyond the children's receptive level because of the support they offer to understanding. If children are to retell the story, they are asked to work at this level in production. They are unlikely to be able to do this and the experience will be difficult and perhaps de-motivating.

If children are to reproduce the whole story in some way, with its temporal sequencing, then the language demands will need to be reduced. For example, learners could be given (or draw) a set of pictures of the story (the collection of pictures produced in the follow-up to the first hearing could be used) and arrange them in order. They might then also get a set of simple sentences written on strips of card to match the pictures. The pictures and sentences could be stuck into the children's books and used for reading. If they are not writing in English, pairs of children could work on composing a sentence orally for each picture and, after they have practised several times, can tell the whole class their 'story', using the pictures as prompts. They might reconstruct the story, orally or in writing, using much simpler text. For example:

> *the man wanted paradise*
> *he went in a rocket*
> *he went to a star*
> *the star was empty*

Using the discourse of the story in other contexts

Short phrases from the story may be usable in other contexts, and children may well use them spontaneously when they have heard them in the story several times. The discourse of the story may also contain sections of language use that can be extracted and focused on to develop discourse skills for other situations. For example, the story has two instances in which characters arrive and comment on what they find:

1. The dinosaurs arrive on the polluted earth, look around and comment on the mess they find:

   Pooh! There is nothing on this planet but mess. If we are going to live here, we'll have to get busy.

2. The man lands in a beautiful jungle and admires it:

   At last I have found my paradise.

These evaluative comments are rather similar to the sorts of messages that people write on postcards from their holidays. To extend their repertoire of this type of discourse, children could be given a set of postcards from various places with suitable comments on to read. They then choose comments for other places, perhaps moving into the imagination: to write on postcards from Mars, from the bottom of the sea, from London or New York.

A writing task linked back to the story might be to make and write a postcard that the dinosaurs and the man would send, that includes their evaluative comments.

Using situations from the story as starting point

The story can act as a starting point for further events, that in turn generate activities that practise oral or literacy skills, such as pretend interviews on cassette or video, articles for a school magazine, contributions to Internet discussion sites. Here are some ways in which a story can serve as a starting point, illustrated from *Dinosaurs*:

– Characters can be transplanted to other situations,
　　e.g. *if the dinosaurs came to our school, what would they say, and what would they do?*
– The 'problem' of the story might be transferred,
　　e.g. *what are the pollution issues in our neighbourhood? what should be done about them?*
– Characters can take part in events beyond the story,
　　e.g. *the man writes a diary of his trips; the story is retold from the man's point of view; a spokesperson for the dinosaurs is interviewed for TV about what happened.*

7.7.3 Focused reading skills practice

Some of the activities already mentioned involve reading and writing, but the development of literacy skills might not be central language learning goals in the activity. In this section, we see how stories might contribute to focused literacy skills practice.

When we looked at emergent literacy in Chapter 6 we saw how regular routinised reading of stories can be used to promote early literacy development. Large versions of stories, or 'big books', are very helpful to practise both top–down and bottom–up skills in reading (as per Figure 6.3). With beginning readers, big books can be used to show the direction in which books and sentences are read, to point out repeated words and syllables, or initial consonants. More advanced readers can read along with the teacher: listening and following silently the first time, joining in the next time and eventually reading aloud individually. Just as it is useful language practice to hear a familiar story many times, so it is useful literacy skills practice to read a familiar story many times. The finding and integration of information about letters, words and sentences can become more automatic each time, and children will be motivated by feeling like fluent readers.

Comprehension skills can be practised through guided prediction during the telling of the story, e.g. the teacher asks *What do you think he will find when he lands?*

Knowledge and skills at letter–sound level can be practised by choosing from the story repeated patterns to focus on, using the procedure in Chapter 6. The *Dinosaurs* story does not have many options, apart from a number of words that contain the short vowel sound made by <u>:

> *cut rumble huff puff rubbish up jungle*

Some of the new words might also be taught as sight words, once their meaning is well established.

7.8 Summary

We have seen in this chapter some of the considerations facing teachers in choosing and using stories for language learning. I have suggested that teachers should critically evaluate the quality and the language learning potential of stories before using them in the classroom. This requires close attention to the discourse organisation, the use of language, and the quality of the story. A writer's use of language is central to the quality of a book, and so it is no coincidence that good quality children's stories also offer language learning opportunities.

We have examined various ways of using children's stories in the foreign language classroom to help the development of vocabulary and grammar, and of oral and literacy skills. To turn a children's story book into a tool for language learning requires a teacher to deploy a range of skills and knowledge. As we move, in the next chapter, to look at theme-based learning, we will find many of these skills required again.

In language teaching and learning, stories and themes overlap at the macro-level of providing holistic learning experiences, but they also overlap at a more micro-level, where a story can provide a theme to be explored (as in some of the activities in the previous section), or where a theme can be developed through the use of stories.

8 Theme-based teaching and learning

8.1 Issues around theme-based teaching

The essential notion of theme-based teaching is that many different activities are linked together by their content; the theme or topic runs through everything that happens in the classroom and acts as a connecting thread for pupils and teacher. Good theme-based teaching has produced some of the most inspiring teaching that I have ever seen; done less well, it leads quickly to chaotic and ineffective classrooms. Because it can lead to such extremes of learning experiences for children, it is worth taking a long, hard look at what makes for good theme-based teaching.

Effective theme-based teaching is extremely demanding on teachers in both planning and in implementation; knowledge of a wide repertoire of activity types and resources is needed to plan for children of all abilities to be stretched and learning all the time, and to avoid children spending too long on cognitively less demanding activities, such as drawing pictures. Skilled management of class, group and pair work is needed to keep all children actively learning, even when good activities have been planned. An equality issue also can arise if teachers choose themes that they hope will keep the interest of the most demanding pupils, but then neglect the interests of quieter pupils. Knowledge of patterns of cognitive, language and motor skills development is needed to plan, ensure and evaluate progression in all areas of the curriculum through theme-based teaching over the school year. Organisational and technical skills are needed to find or create a wide range of resources. To the knowledge and skills required for good theme-based teaching, we must then add the language-using demands that will be made on the foreign language teacher to carry out theme-based work in the foreign language.

Difficulties with maintaining progression, motivation and control, as well as a range of more politically motivated concerns about standards, have led to the demise of theme-based teaching in many schools in England, where it was a major methodology from the late 1960s on (see next section). At the same time, theme-based teaching is being espoused by Ministries of Education elsewhere around the world who are dissatisfied with the outcomes of other types of primary or elementary school curriculum.

In this chapter, the origins of theme-based teaching are briefly described, as a starting point for using the ideas in foreign language teaching. We then look at the various stages in the process of planning teaching around a theme and investigate how to maximise language use and language learning. Examples of themes are used to show how the language learning potential of theme-based teaching can be identified and offered to pupils.

8.2 Theme-based teaching of a foreign language

8.2.1 Origins and transfer to foreign language classrooms

Theme-based, or topic-based, teaching has been practised since the 1960s in UK primary classrooms, where children typically spend all day with the same teacher. In this setting, different areas of the curriculum can be taught in an integrated way, without being separated into subject areas that have to be taught at specific times by separate teachers. Teaching that is integrated around a theme is claimed to better suit the way that young children naturally learn. In its original (first language) uses, theme-based teaching required teachers to choose a theme or topic, such as 'People who help us', and then to plan a range of teaching and learning activities related to the theme, that incorporated aspects of mathematics, science, art, language, history, geography, music and so on. For example, children of five or six years might work with the teacher to make a list of people who help them on the way to school: parents who make the breakfast, a friend who walks with them to school, the lollipop man who helps them cross the road, the playground helper who looks after them before school begins. They could then draw pictures of each person and write their names underneath. They could then put the pictures in order on a frieze of 'People who help us each day'. In this activity, the children would have worked on their language, literacy and art skills, and on the concept of temporal sequencing which will be needed in maths and in history. Another day they might visit the fire station to learn about how fire engines work. In the process of this activity they might cover aspects of geography (drawing a map of where the fire station is in the town); some science (about fires, oxygen, water and chemical extinguishers); some maths (counting the engines and the personnel, working out how many go on each engine); some language work in writing a letter of thanks after-wards, and so on. With creative thinking and skilled organisation, a theme can generate a long list of activities relating to all areas of the curriculum under one theme.

Theme-based teaching has been transferred across from general primary education to the teaching of English as a foreign language (Garvie 1991; Holderness 1991; Scott and Ytreberg 1990). It offers one way of solving the problem of what to teach in primary FL classrooms, where a focus on the language itself might not be appropriate (Tongue 1991), and meshes with ideas about communicative language teaching, in that children will have opportunities to learn the foreign language through its use to carry the thematic content. The potential of theme-based teaching to provide realistic and motivating uses of the language with meaning and purpose for children is clear; the realisation of that potential requires, as in first language teaching, high levels of knowledge and expertise from teachers.

8.2.2 Variations on a theme

In the simplest version of theme-based foreign language teaching, a topic provides content for a range of language learning activities. Halliwell (1992) goes beyond this and suggests that the links between the foreign language classroom and other lessons at primary level can work in several directions:

– other subject areas, such as maths or art, can offer teaching techniques and activities, as well as content, that can be used in the foreign language classroom;
– foreign language lessons can provide content for other subject areas;
– whole subject lessons can be taught in the foreign language.

This last variation edges foreign language teaching towards a partial version of immersion education, found increasingly in European schools, sometimes under the banner of 'plurilingual' education; for example, German pupils learning geography in English (Wode 1999) or Scottish pupils learning Maths in French (Hurrell 1999).

A further variation on theme-based teaching is an 'activity-based' approach, for example that developed by Vale and Feunteun (1995). In this approach, an overarching theme links the content of a lesson, and learning of language takes place as children participate in a range of activities on the theme, such as sorting, measuring and playing games. Again, many of these activities come from other curriculum areas. Figure 8.1 shows some of the many activities that can be transferred from other subject areas for use in the foreign language classroom (drawing on Halliwell 1992; Vale and Feunteun 1995).

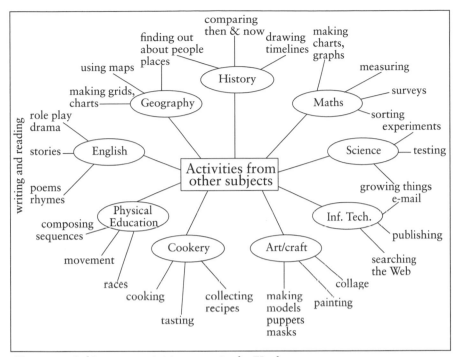

*Figure 8.1 Subject area activities to use in the FL classroom
(drawing on Halliwell 1992, Vale and Feunteun 1995)*

Examples of lessons using very simple language to carry out activities can be found in Halliwell (1992).

Vale and Feunteun suggest that activity-based approaches offer 'whole learning / whole language experience' in which the activities 'are of value to the overall educational and social development of the child, and not merely to develop English language skills' (Vale and Feunteun 1995: 28).

Whole language approaches to teaching ethnic minority children have been popular in American elementary schools (e.g. Genesee 1994). Theme-based and whole language work can successfully construct meaningful learning opportunities for children, but so too can many other tasks and activities, including those discussed elsewhere in this book. The notion of 'whole-ness' does not only apply at the macro level of a theme across a lesson or series of lessons, but can apply to the smallest activity in which meaning, form and use are combined in social interaction: a child who needs a pencil and asks successfully for it in the foreign language has used the language in a 'whole' discourse event (section 3.2). Furthermore, as we have seen with the teaching of discourse skills, vocabulary, grammar, and literacy skills, there are some aspects of language that cannot fully develop without focused attention. It is a paradox that we need to work with: that focused and partial practising may be needed for the development of macro-level holistic language skills (Widdowson 1998).

8.2.3 Choosing theme-based teaching for the foreign language classroom

Theme-based teaching can be used in large or small amounts, and in varying concentrations. In concentrated form, and in skilled hands, it could replace course book and syllabus altogether. More realistically, it can be adopted for one or two lessons in a week, or for several weeks in a term, to supplement other work, and to help teachers build up the skills and knowledge that are demanded. Even when the course book is used fairly closely, theme-based ideas can provide extra activities. Many course books use topics or themes to structure their units, although this is often a superficial covering for a grammatical or functional sequencing. The title of a unit, such as 'Pets' or 'My Family', can be treated like a theme, and adopting a theme-based approach can extend teaching and learning beyond the confines of the text book.

Foreign language teaching, in adapting ideas for theme-based teaching, should try to avoid as far as possible the kinds of problems faced by its use in first language education, mentioned in section 8.1. It is clear, although again somewhat paradoxical at first sight, that good holistic learning experiences are constructed through rigorous attention to detail in planning and teaching. As with using stories, there is no magic that can replace informed and detailed analysis and planning by the teacher. In the next section, we see how planning can move from content to language learning goals.

8.3 Planning theme-based teaching

The language learning opportunities offered by theme-based teaching in the foreign language classroom arise from the content and the activities that pupils undertake. Together, the content and activities produce language-using situations and discourse types. In this section, we see how planning can move from content /activity to language use, and produce language learning goals for theme-based lessons.

8.3.1 Advance versus 'on-line' planning

Theme-based teaching can be tightly planned in advance, or it can be allowed to evolve 'on-line' through dynamic teaching and learning, that changes direction in the light of task outcomes, developing and evolving with the emerging interests of children and teacher. Like the effortless movement of skilled dancers, it would be a mistake to think that this type of teaching can take place without years of painful practice and experience. Even the expert teacher will usually need to carry out careful planning of a theme in advance, to prepare sub-themes, tasks and materials, and to identify the language learning goals of each activity.

The dynamic nature of theme-based teaching can be enhanced by building in 'choice points', where pupils and teacher have choice over direction, activity or timing. As a theme proceeds, there may be points at which the class can decide which of two or more possible directions the theme-based work will take. In a theme-based lesson, children can be allowed to choose a fixed number of activities from a small set of activities. They can also be encouraged to take some responsibility for their own learning by being required to organise their time. After a plenary session in which the tasks for the lesson are explained and understood, children can decide in what order to do the activities; the only constraint is that they must complete all activities within the given time, which could be the lesson or the week. To help with time management, children can copy a list of activities from the board, number them in their chosen sequence and tick them off as completed. The use of choice points contributes to children's capacities for self-directed learning by giving them supported practice in making decisions as learning proceeds, so that later they will be able to identify these points themselves.

8.3.2 Finding a theme

Finding a theme or topic is the easiest part! A theme can come from the children's current interests, from topics being studied in other classes, from a story (e.g. dinosaurs or conservation of the environment from *Dinosaurs* – Chapter 7), or from a local or international festival or event. A list from Vale and Feunteun (1995) of possible themes shows something of the range of sources:

- Spiders and mini-creatures
- Circus

- Potatoes / vegetables
- Islands
- Bridges
- Jack and the Beanstalk
- Halloween / festivals
- The House that Jack Built.

Children might be given a stake in the process from the start by asking them to suggest themes, or to select a theme for the term from a list. It is necessary for staff across a school to liaise over themes, so that children do not find themselves studying the same theme more than once with different teachers.

8.3.3 Planning content

Two basic planning tools for theme-based teaching are brainstorming and webs. Both techniques allow the connection of ideas in non-linear ways, reflecting the learning processes that we are aiming to produce. Brainstorming is a mental process that starts with one idea and then sparks off others through random and spontaneous links. All possibilities are noted down and are then used to select from. A 'web' is a way of writing down ideas and connections without forcing them into linear form as in a list or in text. The main idea or topic is put in the centre of the paper or board, and connecting ideas written around it, with lines showing connections. A web can be used in brainstorming, and / or can be used after brainstorming to put some order into the random collection of ideas. In section 4.4.4, we saw that a theme can be considered as including:

people + objects + actions + processes + typical events + places

This notion helps start the brainstorming process. When applied to Vale and Feunteun's theme of Potatoes, the theme spreads from farming and eating potatoes into areas of concern such as the scientific manipulation of crops and whether international businesses threaten local traditions. Figure 8.2 shows how a brainstorming around the theme might develop. Notice that the ideas relate mostly to non-school life and that they are still just content, not yet foreign language learning activities.

Potatoes
and

People
farmers
gardeners
eaters
cooks
customers
Walter Raleigh (brought the potato to England from America)

Objects
types of potatoes
farming implements e.g. hoes
cooking implements
   e.g. peelers, chip pans

Actions
digging
planting
harvesting
peeling
chopping
chipping
eating

Processes
growing
cooking
making crisps
buying and selling
staple foods in diets
exploration of the New World
how food and cooking can spread
internationally genetic modification

Typical events
the potato harvest
a visit to a fast food restaurant

Places
fields, restaurants

Figure 8.2 Brainstorming around the theme of potatoes

To this list, we can add types of discourse typically associated with any of the above, since that will take us, via language in use, towards language learning. Potato-related examples of discourse would include:

– menus, ordering
– instructions on seed packets
– recipes
– historical information
– newspaper reports on genetic modification and international businesses.

The availability of texts like these in the foreign language will influence the theme planning. It is useful to build up a collection of authentic materials on trips and from magazines; the Internet provides a rich source of information in English.

The ideas can now be grouped into sub-themes, such as Growing Potatoes; Using Potatoes; The History of Potatoes, and drawn as a web (Figure 8.3). From these sub-themes, planning can move to identifying activities and language goals.

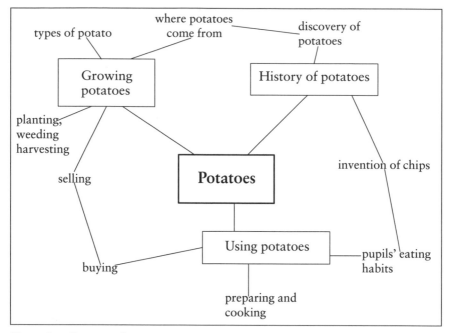

types of potato

where potatoes come from

discovery of potatoes

Growing potatoes

History of potatoes

planting, weeding harvesting

selling

Potatoes

invention of chips

Using potatoes

buying

pupils' eating habits

preparing and cooking

Figure 8.3 Potato web

An alternative planning procedure is to build up web linking activities to areas of the school curriculum: maths, technology, etc. Figure 8.4 shows the topic web for Potatoes from Vale and Feunteun (1995: 236). The rectangular boxes linked to each curriculum area contain school-based activities, and the outermost layer shows the language learning goals of each activity.

Activities and content have, of course, to be selected to suit the age of the children.

The brainstorming and webbing processes can be carried out with the children, rather than by the teacher alone. A good way to start is by asking the children for words connected to the theme, and writing these on the board, constructing a web as words are suggested. This can be done in the foreign language, or bilingually, with the teacher translating words that children suggest in their first language. The advantage of doing this work with the children is that it also provides a quick assessment of their knowledge and interest around the topic, through the words that they suggest and through areas that they do not mention. The words that need to be translated provide a starting point for vocabulary learning goals for the theme-based teaching, since they reflect meanings that the children can and want to express, but for which they do not have the language.

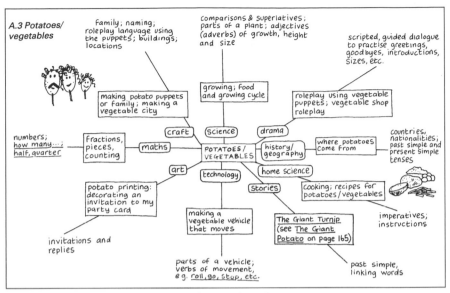

Figure 8.4 Topic web for Potatoes (from Vale and Feunteun 1995, p. 236)

An initial brainstorm can also be used to produce **guiding questions** for the theme work as a whole. Children and teachers can draw up a set of questions they want to find answers to. For example, they might want to find out:

- how many types of potato are there?
- what do sweet potatoes taste like?
- where do the potatoes we eat come from?
- how many kilos of chips does the class eat in a year?

These (genuine) questions can guide the sequencing and content of activities.

8.3.4 Planning language learning tasks

Having identified sub-themes and guiding questions by taking a 'content perspective' on the theme, planning now has to bring a 'language-learning perspective' to it, so that planning moves from content to FL classroom activities, with discourse types and aspects of language use guiding the construction of language learning tasks with clear goals and stages (as in Chapter 3). For example, finding out what sweet potatoes taste like could involve a sequence of tasks such as those shown in Figure 8.5, each using the foreign language in activities and in discourse. In this example, we continue to use activities largely drawn from the

Theme: POTATOES
Sub-Theme: WHAT DO SWEET POTATOES TASTE LIKE?
Tasks, Activities, and Discourse Types

TASK 1
Finding a recipe to cook the potatoes
searching on the Internet for possible recipes
choosing which recipe to try
compiling a shopping list

TASK 2
Going to the supermarket to buy ingredients
planning the trip
noting where things come from to put on a map
making a record of the trip with photographs or video, and
a spoken commentary

TASK 3
Cooking the recipe
preparing ingredients
doing the cooking
recording and evaluating the process

TASK 4
Tasting the results
inviting other classes to taste, writing invitations
conducting a taste survey and posting results on the Internet
writing out the recipe for home, school magazine

TASK 5
Producing a book, or video, or photo and tape record of the whole
series of events

Figure 8.5 Tasks, activities and discourse types around the potato theme

world outside the classroom, rather than from other subject areas in the school curriculum. The activities to be carried out by pupils sometimes generate particular types of discourse, either as sources or as outcomes in teaching and learning; these are underlined in Figure 8.5.

The tasks can then be organised into stages, each with language and content goals, and fitted to the timing of lessons. Doing the whole series of tasks might take half a term, but it might be decided just to do a reduced version of Tasks 3 and 4: Cooking and Tasting, that could be fitted into one or two lessons.

8.4 Learning language through theme-based teaching

8.4.1 The language learning potential of theme-based teaching

The previous section shows that adopting a theme to guide planning can open up limitless opportunities. It is necessary to select from the possibilities to match the interests of a particular class, and then to construct classroom tasks that will build on what pupils already know of the foreign language and extend their language learning. In this section, we look more specifically at the potential for language learning through themes.

The use of the foreign language in theme-based teaching, and thus the learning potential, is largely determined by the content and activities. The language is not, as in course-book lessons, selected in advance as a set of language items to be taught. As the previous section emphasised, careful planning can predict and help maximise some possibilities, but there will still be a degree of unpredictability about the language that will arise in theme-based activities such as understanding recipes found on the Internet or preparing and cooking food. The teacher is required to be very sensitive to the language, both to predict language use in advance and to make the most of the unpredictable uses of the language. Children may need support to understand content, and, when useful language items do occur unexpectedly, the teacher needs to be able to seize the opportunity and help children to notice and use the language.

As we have progressed chapter by chapter through the book, we have seen that the language learning of children is likely to revolve around chunks of discourse learnt from talk, stories and songs, vocabulary development, and some aspects of (mostly implicit) grammatical knowledge, together with elementary literacy skills. Early foreign language learning can be much more 'organic' in its development than the linear syllabuses of many secondary course books, graded by grammar or function. Theme based teaching can contribute to this organic develop ment from partial to more complete knowledge by building links and connections in the networks of children's language resources.

8.4.2 Learning vocabulary

Theme-based work is likely to introduce new vocabulary items, with the theme providing support for understanding and recall. Vocabulary items that have already been introduced in the course book may be met again in the new context of a theme, and the encounter will reinforce the words or phrases while also adding new meaning aspects to them.

Some recent evidence for the benefits of this type of teaching for vocabulary learning comes from the use of a foreign language as a medium of instruction in German schools (Wode 1999). Twelve-year-old pupils taught geography through English, after two years of learning EFL as a subject, were tested on the vocabulary through oral production tasks. In comparison with students who had not had English-medium teaching, the 'partial immersion' students used larger vocabularies with a wider range of items and more synonyms. Their vocabularies also contained more words that could not be traced back to their English course book or to the task instructions; these words probably came from the teacher talk during subject learning. Wode claims that teaching content through the foreign language offers more opportunities for incidental vocabulary learning than teaching the foreign language as a subject.

8.4.3 Language learning through 'communicative stretching'

Theme-based teaching can produce moments when pupils' (and sometimes teachers') language resources are stretched to their limit. Supported by meaningful content, children may be able to work out the meaning of new or unfamiliar language, or, motivated by real interest in a topic, they may struggle to communicate their knowledge to someone else, as we saw the Norwegian pupil doing when talking about his budgie in Chapter 3. Stretching resources in this way pushes the child into the ZPD (Chapter 1) and can be very productive of learning.

One particular process that occurs in communicative stretching is the grammaticisation of language learnt earlier as formulaic phrases or chunks (section 5.3.1). In situations where language resources are stretched, children may need to break down chunks of language, previously learnt as wholes, into their elements, recombining the parts to create new phrases that convey the child's meaning.

8.4.4 Learning discourse skills

Working with an increased range of discourse types

A real benefit of theme-based learning is that it offers a natural use for a wider range of discourse types, both spoken and written, than is usually found in a course book. Themes can include different aspects of the same topic that each require different types of discourse. Potatoes in the above example (Figure 8.4) will be talked and written about as science, as history and as cookery, using and producing informational discourse, the discourse of scientific reports, recipes and a range of spoken language across the different activities. Even at a very simple level of language, children can begin to experience these different types of discourse.

School-based activities, such as those in Figure 8.1, also produce a range of discourse types, such as graphs, charts, reports, and commentaries. Some of these are pre-cursors and foundations of subject-specific discourses that children will become familiar with at secondary level, and for those situations where children will study some or all of their subjects through the foreign language, early experiences with these types of discourse will support their later studies.

Using information texts, on paper and on computer

Texts that can be used in theme-based teaching will include relevant songs, rhymes, video, stories, and non-fiction informational texts, including sources accessed through the Internet or on CD-ROM, catalogues, leaflets and magazines, and educational materials written for native speaker children. Informational text types provide language learning opportunities that go beyond those of the narrative or story. For example, an information book contains organisational features such as a contents page, an index, headings and sub-headings. The text itself is likely to include short self-contained chunks of information, often around pictures or diagrams. The different types of writing – introduction, description, narrative, argument, summary – will use grammar and vocabulary in different ways from stories. Information books can be used as resources for finding out specific information or as starting points for a theme. They offer opportunities to see the language used for these purposes and to develop reading skills at text level. They also provide a model for writing information texts in the foreign language.

Using the computer to access information practises the use of key words and skimming techniques in 'surfing the net'. On each screen, a choice must be made about where to go next and this is done by reading what is available and comparing the possibilities to the user's current goal. Once chunks of text are reached, then the user needs to read the first few sentences and scan the rest in order to decide whether it is worth more intensive study. Children are likely to pay more attention to images than to text, using the information provided by the images to support understanding of the text. We need to know much more about how children 'read' information on computer, but it would seem helpful to surf for specific information, having discussed in advance and agreed on 'guiding questions'. The computer search then becomes a task with specified outcomes, such as a verbal report back on what was found in answer to the questions.

Instead of children surfing the net, teachers can find useful sites in advance that they direct children to or can download information into computer files that children can then access without needing to be on line. Pages from the computer can be printed out and used as paper-based text.

8.4.5 *Motivation to precision in language use*

When communicating with others about a theme, it can become more important to communicate precisely and accurately. Precision in language use involves learners selecting and adapting their language resources to say or write exactly what they mean; accuracy, the term more often used in the literature, refers to using the language correctly relative to the target form. Precision is thus user-oriented, whereas accuracy is language-oriented. Often, of course, precision requires accuracy, but it always requires more than that; it requires learners to access and use the language that will best express their personal meanings, and may further require negotiation with others to ensure that they understand the meanings as intended.

8.4.6 *Outcomes and products from theme-based learning*

Theme-based work lends itself to the production of displays and performances of various sorts that, because they will have an audience, motivate children to re-write, practise or rehearse towards a polished language performance or text.

As a theme proceeds, children will produce pieces of work – poems, pictures and sentences, reports, graphs and so on. These can be saved by each child in a personal folder for the theme. As a final stage in the theme, the pieces of work are gathered together to make a record of what has been covered for the children and for other people. Various modes and media are possible:

- Big books produced by the class or by groups of children.
- A magazine or newspaper, with articles and pictures around sub-themes, compiled by the class and photocopied for parents and other classes.
- Visual display on the classroom walls or school notice board: a frieze, sets of pictures and headings, pieces of writing, posters.
- Video, with spoken commentary.
- Performance: acting out a story or presenting a documentary-type report.
- Computer record: web pages constructed around the theme and put on the school web site; CD-ROM with video and text.

Possible audiences for these products will include parents, other classes and teachers in the school, and children in other schools who are communicated with by post or through the Internet.

8.5 Increasing target language use in theme-based teaching

When children spend time 'making and doing' – drawing, colouring, sticking, modelling and so on – language use may grind to a halt, or, quite naturally, first language may be used. When activities become exciting and interesting, children will want to talk about what's happening and switch to first language. This is a serious potential drawback to theme-based foreign language teaching, that parallels the realisation that older learners working on communicative tasks may automatically switch to first language when the task becomes difficult or particularly interesting (Skehan 1996). When we design tasks and lessons to be interesting and challenging, we create conditions in which people want to communicate with each other; using the foreign language to communicate will always be more difficult than using first language and this creates conflicting forces in the dynamics of communication. However, some very simple adjustments can increase the use of the foreign language in this type of classroom activity.

Inserting choices or decision-making

Each step in the making and doing process offers opportunities for use of the foreign language. If children are, for example, making a potato puppet (Figure 8.4), they will need materials. It is possible for the teacher just to hand out the materials, but it is also possible to turn this into an opportunity for using the foreign language meaningfully. Pupils can be shown the materials available and told their words in the foreign language: *potatoes, straws, string, sticks.* Then, as a group, they are asked to decide which materials they want, using simple phrases in the group decision-making: *do we need string? how many potatoes do we need?* The group then prepares a representative who is sent to the teacher to ask for those things: *please can we have four potatoes and some string?.* The teacher can support the representatives in their language use, and may send them back to the group to check more precisely what is needed. Each stage in this decision-making process will generate repetition of the vocabulary about the materials, as well as other simple but useful phrases, which the teacher will need to model before and during the choosing. Written language could be practised if children are given a list of materials that they choose from, or if they have to write a list for the teacher, perhaps to request materials for the next lesson that will be gathered in advance.

It is by noticing and exploiting such opportunities that the teacher uses theme-based work for language learning, and not just for content learning.

Giving feedback to each other

Pupils can plan an activity together before starting, and can be brought together in the middle of the process to show their 'work-in-progress' to others. They can be helped to point out what they are pleased with so far, or what they are having problems with. If planning and giving feedback are carried out with the teacher at the beginning of the year, pupils can gradually take over the processes themselves, using the language modelled by the teacher. This language might include simple ways of offering advice to others:

> *Why don't you . . .?*
> *You could . . .,*

and of giving positive feedback:

> *That's nice.*
> *I like the . . .*

At the end of an activity, time is usefully spent evaluating product and process.

Teacher intervention

While the children are busy on making and doing activities, the teacher can move around the classroom using key language items in talk with the children, commenting on what they are making and suggesting alternatives.

Encouraging private speech in the foreign language

Vygotsky emphasised the importance of private speech in children, the 'talking to oneself' that leads developmentally from social speech with others to inner speech and thinking (McCafferty 1994). In first language research, a link has been found between children's use of private speech when working on tasks and academic achievement (Bivens and Berk 1990). Talking to oneself when making or doing something can help even adults to focus and concentrate. We do not know whether private speech occurs in a foreign language, or whether private speech in either first or foreign language can help language learning, but it may be helpful to model for children the types of talk that they might say to themselves. Certainly the link between inner speech and thinking suggests that encouraging foreign language inner speech might have long term learning benefits. If children do use the foreign language to mutter to themselves while they are working on activities, they will get extra practice in selecting and adapting language. The type of talk that would be used in private speech will be useful in other, more interactional, discourse.

Preparation for an activity can include the teacher modelling language that children might use to talk to themselves as they do the activity, such as self-evaluating language:

> *How does that look?*
> *A little more red? A little more black?*

or self-directing language:

> *first the head, then the body, then the tail.*

Rhythmic and repetitive patterns of language will be more likely to be recalled.

Background language exposure

Children might be encouraged to say rhymes or to sing as they work. Playing tapes of songs as children work will give them further exposure to the language. Very undemanding tasks, such as colouring, can have more demanding background language, such as the teacher reading a story.

8.6 Summary

Stories, in the previous chapter, and theme-based teaching, in this one, both offer exciting possibilities for young learners and their teachers. They open up the language classroom by bringing in the world outside and linking into children's real interests and enthusiasms, not just those that materials writers suppose them to have. There is real potential for effective language learning to take place, and for participation in a range of discourse events in the foreign language. However, theme-based teaching if it is done well is very demanding. Alongside knowledge and skills in the foreign language, excellent classroom management skills are needed to keep everyone on task and learning; each of the possible activities mentioned in the chapter has potential for time-wasting and noise! I am reminded of physical education lessons when I was at school; as a change from the usual drills and carefully regulated movement, we sometimes played a game called 'Pirates'. All the gymnastic equipment was set up and we had to run around from piece to piece, making sure we were not on the floor when the teacher blew her whistle. Some pupils had a wonderful time, using the apparatus in imaginative ways and getting far more exercise than usual. I was one of those children who hated gym, and this kind of lesson also suited me fine – I could skulk away in a corner, linger on the same piece of apparatus for as long as possible and choose the least demanding piece to climb on: a low bench was as valid in this activity as the highest rope or wall bar. The freedom of the activity not only did not increase my physical fitness but enabled me to do even less than usual without being noticed!

The chapter has highlighted the following processes that can help ensure that theme-based teaching results in well-structured and exciting learning, rather than noisy activity for some and opting-out for others:

- careful choice of theme to involve all children;
- detailed planning, using brainstorming and webs;
- linking content with activities and discourse types;
- pre-planned organisation of materials and activities;
- teacher and class together deciding on 'guiding questions' that structure activities;
- building in 'choice points' where children are guided in making decisions over direction, activity or timing;
- management of classroom activity and use of resources;
- attention to amount and type of language use during activities;
- regular monitoring of each child's involvement and success in activities and language use, by teacher and children themselves;
- use of final products to motivate and involve all children.

9 Language choice and language learning

9.1 Introduction

9.1.1 Language choice and language learning

This chapter considers issues around the uses of the foreign and first languages in the classroom. It looks at evidence from real classrooms and how we might interpret what has been found. In many situations, teachers are required to use only the foreign language in their language lessons, or they feel that they ought to. In practice, research and anecdotal evidence suggests that most teachers who share their pupils' mother tongue, use a mixture of the foreign language and the mother tongue. We will examine this evidence in some detail to look for patterns in the types of activities that each language is used for, and to see how teachers and pupils switch between languages in the course of activities. When we have a clearer picture of patterns of language choice, we can then develop the principle of 'deliberate language choice', in which choice is guided by the overarching goal of fostering the children's foreign language learning. This enables us to move away from the simple but impractical guideline 'use only the target language' to more subtle and helpful principles for language choice: 'use as much of the target language as possible, and ensure that use of first language supports the children's language learning'.

The rest of the chapter will be devoted to exploring how those principles translate into action. Choosing to use more of the foreign language may mean that extra work is required to support children's understanding. If pupils are required to use the foreign language, then we know that this makes a greater demand on them than just understanding and that, again, appropriate support will be needed.

9.1.2 Target language only?

Policies that insist on 'target language only', i.e. that all foreign language lessons should be conducted in the foreign language, are usually justified in terms of maximising learners' exposure to the language and thus their learning opportunities. The underlying assumption here is that the more language the pupils hear, the more they will learn. Where the foreign language is not heard outside the classroom, then it does indeed matter that children hear as much as possible when they are in class. However, to assume a simple linear relationship between exposure to language and learning – that more of one always results in more of the other – irons out much of the complexity of teaching and learning, and ignores the possibility that certain uses of a common mother tongue might also contribute to foreign language learning.

Why does a gap appear between policy and practice around using the target language? One important reason may be that teachers do not feel sufficiently confident or competent to use the foreign language for the full range of functions that are created by activities and tasks in lessons. Using only the foreign language requires that teachers have a repertoire of language for classroom management and organisation, for discipline, for giving feedback, for talking about language, and for chatting with children more informally. To be confident in using the foreign language, teachers need initial and in-service training that broadens their range of language skills and keeps them up-to-date and fluent.

A further reason may be that, in asking for foreign language use only, policy makers place teachers in a continual struggle against the natural forces of communication between people. If teacher and class share a common mother tongue, then not to use that first language is very unnatural. The age of young learners may make use of the foreign language feel even more unnatural. As we will see in the next section, when we review evidence from studies of language use in classrooms, language choice is often motivated by interpersonal factors. Again, this does not mean that the foreign language cannot be used as the main communicative means, but it does mean that it needs to be done consciously and deliberately.

9.2 Patterns of first language use in foreign language classrooms

9.2.1 Evidence about first language use

Empirical studies of language use in young learner classrooms are fairly thin on the ground. Martin (1999) and Merrit *et al.* (1992) report on primary classrooms, but on content, rather than FL lessons. Pennington (1995) has useful data from secondary English classrooms in Hong Kong, in which some of the children would fall into our 5–12 year age range. Hancock (1997) reports on Spanish learners of English who are just beyond that, at 14 years of age. I also draw on some studies carried out by Malaysian teachers as part of their final BA dissertations, and anecdotal evidence from in-service training of teachers. From these sources, a fairly consistent picture emerges of language choice: although the amount of mother tongue / foreign language varies, when mother tongue is used in lessons, it is more likely to be used to manage classroom activity and behaviour. Furthermore, although there is variation in the patterns of language choice from one situation to another, we can see that the motivation of any particular choice is partly contingent i.e. made in the light of what is happening in the moment, and partly a result of conventions or habits that the teacher and class have developed over time. We can only understand those choices by considering classroom action as taking place in a wider social and institutional context.

Pennington's study of eight teachers showed that their use of mother tongue varied from almost none to almost the whole lesson (Pennington 1995). The amount used was not dependent on the teachers' proficiency, since they could all use English fluently and confidently. Rather, the difference seemed to come from the teachers' perceptions of their pupils' ability, and the status of the school. In high prestige schools with academically able pupils, less first language was used. With less able children, who may also be less motivated and well-behaved, there was more 'compensatory' use of the first language.

Even when most of a lesson was carried out in the first language, the core of language content – vocabulary and sentence patterns – remained in the foreign language. The teacher in Pennington's study who used most first language still managed greetings and farewells to the pupils in the foreign language. Functions of the use of first language that were found in the researched classrooms are listed below:

Teachers' use of the first language

- explaining aspects of the foreign language;
- translating words or sentences;
- giving instructions;
- checking understanding of concept, talk, text, instructions;
- eliciting language;
- focusing pupils' attention;
- testing;
- talking about learning;
- giving feedback;
- disciplining and control;
- informal, friendly talk with pupils.

Pupils' use

– asking for help from teacher or peers;
– responding to teacher questions.

9.2.2 Interpreting patterns of first language use

The previous section has set out some answers to the question, *When do teachers and pupils use their first language in lessons?* In this section, we move on to ask: *How can we explain these patterns of first language use?* Three possible ways of interpreting the patterns of language choice are presented, two from Pennington's work (1995, 1998) that focus on functions and a further interpretation that focuses on the interpersonal functions. Having set out possible interpretations, we can then proceed to draw out implications for classroom practice.

Choice of language as compensatory or strategic

In her 1995 paper, Pennington makes a distinction between compensatory and strategic uses of the two languages available to teachers. In choosing to use a shared first language, teachers may compensate for problems that they perceive with their pupils' language level or ability, or with discipline and motivation. First language use may also compensate for teacher-related factors such as lack of confidence, preparation or language proficiency. The 'strategic' motivations that Pennington suggests are linked to creating and maintaining levels of formality and informality in classroom discourse, and to structuring and controlling lessons and behaviour.

We should note that the so-called compensatory uses of L_1 are based on perceived problems: in other words, they may or may not be *real* problems, and they may be more or less serious than they are perceived to be. It is important that we continually unearth and evaluate our perceptions; if they remain unquestioned, there is a risk that teachers' decisions are inappropriate.

Interpersonal factors in language choice

An alternative interpretation of the patterns of language choice in classrooms arises if we examine the interpersonal motivations that may lie behind any instance of language choice. In doing this, we move to focus on how a particular choice of first or foreign language affects the particular group of teachers and pupils. The choice of which language to use will be influenced by previous choices and by the wider context.

At the same time, the choice of language adds to and creates a context in which language is to be learnt. This learning context includes the attitudes and values that pupils are encouraged to take to learning the foreign language.

One way to think of interpersonal factors is as a combination of three sub-factors: alignment, emphasis, and evaluation (Graumann 1990). Each of these three sub-factors can operate in any particular instance of language use:

Alignment: The choice of first or foreign language for particular functions can convey to pupils a sense of how much their teacher 'is on their side' or, alternatively, wishes to distance him or herself from the pupils' concerns. If the teacher uses the first language in the foreign language classroom, she or he may thereby create a feeling of being aligned with the pupils. The alignment of teacher and pupils through their shared language may then emphasise the 'foreign-ness' of the target language. More positively, use of the shared language can reassure pupils that the teacher understands their language learning problems; it can emphasise shared language learning goals and values.

If the teacher uses the foreign language, this may emphasise the distance between pupils, as novices in the FL, and the teacher, as more competent. A positive, aligning use of the foreign language would be its use as a shared means of communication and enjoyment of new skills.

My study of native speaker primary classrooms (Cameron 2001) showed that teachers aligned themselves with pupils when they had to do something potentially negative for the children, such as telling them off or showing them where they had made mistakes. In the native language, this threat to pupils' self-esteem was mitigated through the use of metaphorical language. In a foreign language classroom, it is likely that a teacher might turn to first language to have a similar effect. Teachers in different cultures will, of course, have differing views as to what might be a negative act.

Emphasis: The choice of first or foreign language may serve to emphasise the importance of what is being said. The use of first language to control and discipline may underline the seriousness of the offence, while using the foreign language may de-emphasise the importance, and thus work only for less serious problems.

Evaluation: The choice of language also carries attitudes and values to foreign language learning. A teacher who uses the foreign language only for content of a lesson, and not for other purposes, reinforces the idea that the foreign language is a 'subject of study' rather than a means of communication.

Summary

We can combine these different interpretations of language choice to better understand what is going on in classrooms. Together, they remind us that interpretations of content cannot be separated from the inter-personal, and that the interpersonal is embedded in institutional and social settings. Teachers make decisions as instructors, and as real people interacting with other real people – their pupils, and as members of a profession and the school as an institution. Any instance of language choice is situated at the end of a long chain of socio-cultural history: professional training, school policy and conventions that have become established over years. And if we look forwards, rather than backwards in time, any instance of choice will play a role in building up the language learning context for the pupils.

Action and convention on any one level influence and are influenced by action and convention at other levels of scale. Changes made to action or convention at one level can affect any other level. In the next section, we look in more detail at the most fine-grained level of classroom interaction: how teachers and pupils respond to each other. First, though, I pull together some implications from the consideration of patterns of language choice in this section.

9.2.3 Interim implications

- In interpreting and changing patterns of language choice, we have to consider individuals as acting within layers and scales of action and history.
- When teaching children with very low levels of the foreign language, as will often be the case with young learners, use of the first language may seem unavoidable. However, there are several reasons why we should question this conclusion:
    (i) Convention and accepted values in an education system may mean that language choice is no longer questioned or challenged, and the possibility that low level pupils could use more foreign language is not considered.
    (ii) So-called 'low level' learners may struggle with the *written* foreign language that they were taught through and assessed on, but their *spoken* foreign language might not be so 'low'. For younger learners, we have the opportunity to keep the oral language as the major focus for several years, and pupils who will struggle with the written forms are not so swiftly disadvantaged and demotivated.
    (iii) Before adolescence, learners are less inhibited about using the

foreign language in lessons, and so, although they do not know much of the foreign language, they may be willing to use what they have and try to communicate. A 'low level' young learner and a 'low level' secondary pupil may know similar amounts of the language but they are likely to be very different in personality and attitude.

9.3 Dynamics of language choice and use

9.3.1 A dynamic view of language choice

A dynamic view considers movement between languages in classroom interaction, rather than just which language is used. To see the dynamics of language choice, we have to look at quite a fine level of detail, within and across turns of talk. At this scale, we will see how teachers talk and respond to pupils and, *vice versa*, how pupils talk and respond to teachers. In this talk, both teachers and pupils make choices about which language to use. They may also change, or *switch*, languages during their talk. Switches and choices made at this micro-level build up the patterns that we observe at the larger scales of the lesson and school practice. Furthermore, if we want to change practice, the changes will need to be made at this level.

9.3.2 Examples of language switching in the foreign language classroom

In this section, examples from classroom talk are used to describe movement between languages and to discuss why they might occur and what they might build up to over longer timescales. The classroom data used to illustrate language switching patterns that occur in FL classrooms was collected by a Malaysian teacher. In this classroom, the pupils are 10–11 years old and share a common language, Bahasa Melayu (BM), with their teacher. They are working with a short text from their course book. Talk in first language is in bold, with a translation following in *italics*. The lesson is used only for illustration, since one lesson does not give enough data to draw conclusions about the teacher's practice.

Dynamic 1: Helping pupils understand by translating

The first extract shows a switching pattern used by the teacher throughout the lesson. He regularly moved from the foreign language to the first language when he gave instructions to the pupils. He would first give instructions in English, the target language, and then repeat all or part of the instruction in the shared first language.

T: OK (.) now group one (.) say a word that you do not understand (.) **perkataan yang kamu tak faham** [*a word that you do not understand*]

. . .

T: now (.) when I point to the word I want you to put up your hand and say the word (.) OK? **sebut perkatataannya** [*say the word*]

There is no problem here with the teacher having enough of the foreign language; his instructions in English are clear and accurate. The teacher seems to feel that the pupils need more help to understand the instructions; this would be a compensatory use of BM, which occurred in giving instructions, and also sometimes, in asking questions. Repeated switching from English to BM to translate information builds up a dynamic in the talk that may have knock-on effects over time.

In interpersonal terms, this FL → L1 dynamic, or switching strategy, aligns the teacher with the pupils and emphasises key aspects of the instruction. However, although the strategy is helpful to the pupils in the short term, it may be less helpful in the longer term. If a first language translation regularly follows an instruction or command in the foreign language, the children may come to recognise the pattern and stop trying to understand the initial version in the foreign language.

Can the dynamic be adjusted to be more helpful to language learning? One alternative strategy for helping the understanding of instructions, would be to ask a pupil to give an L1 version after the teacher's FL instructions. The pupil who replies is doing some useful language work, and pupils who did not understand have a further chance. If this is a regular pattern in classroom talk, pupils will listen more carefully to the teacher's instructions, not only to know what to do, but also to get a turn at translating. This small change in the dynamics of micro-level talk could have an impact on learning in the longer term; further research would be needed to measure this impact.

Dynamic 2: Keeping to the same language

In the next extract, there is more complicated movement between first and foreign languages as the teacher and pupils talk about strategies for finding the meaning of new words.

1	T:	**baik apa patut lita buat untuk mencari makna perkataan?**
2		[*what must we do to find the meaning of words?*]
3	P:	**cari dalam kamus** [*find in the dictionary*]
4	T:	good (.)
5		**cari dalam kamus** [*find in the dictionary*] (.)
6		you must use the (.) dictionary (.)
7		now take out your dictionaries and try to find the word <u>communities</u> (.)
8		**cepat! cari!** [*quick! find!*]

The teacher's first question, in first language, is answered by a pupil in first language (line 3), and this response is received with an English word, *good* (line 4), and then the pupil's first language phrase is repeated by the teacher (line 5). It is then repeated in English in line 6. The next instruction (line 7) is then given by the teacher in English, with a first language re-emphasis in the last line.

The dynamic at work in this extract seems to be the natural tendency in talk to respond in the same language used by the previous participant; when the teacher uses first language, the pupil naturally responds in first language. Something similar seems to happen in the teacher's second turn when he repeats the pupil's first language answer in a positive feedback move. Although the first part of the feedback uses the English word *good*, the pupil's use of first language seems to have a strong influence, leading the teacher to switch back to the first language, even though the choice to stay in English was open to him. When we investigate choice of language, we need to consider the implications of both what does happen and what does not happen.

The participants in the talk are not equal partners in terms of their 'power' to make choices. The teacher, as the adult and the person with more power in the classroom discourse, can shift the language more easily than a pupil can, and his choices thus have more impact on the overall uses of the two languages. After he repeats the pupil's sentence (line 5), the teacher moves the language to English by translating it and then giving the next instruction. This move is an example of the teacher invoking his rights to choose which language to use. We can note how his choice here, as elsewhere, results in particular language learning opportunities for the pupils. The teacher's conversational 'power' and rights imply that the teacher also has a large part of the responsibility; he can shift the language being used and should use that to maximise foreign language learning.

Notice how in the last line, the previous dynamic of translating a foreign language instruction into L1 recurs when the teacher repeats part of his English instruction in first language. When combined with the second dynamic we have observed, we see a very strong force for more and more use of the first language: if the teacher translates an instruction or questions, the turn will finish in Lɪ, and it is likely that the next (pupil's) turn will continue to use the Lɪ.

Dynamic 3: Giving meaning through a first language equivalent

In the final extract, we see how the conceptualisation of vocabulary learning as learning first language equivalents of new words provides an underlying dynamic to the lesson. Something of the teacher's view of what it means to learn new words can be inferred from the process of the lesson (although further information, such as interview data, would be needed to confirm this). The pupils are first asked to underline new words in the text, then they say the words to the teacher who writes them on the board. The whole class then practises pronouncing the words (before any work is done on the word meanings). The pupils then turn to their dictionaries to find out the meanings. These are bilingual dictionaries, i.e. they give first language translations of the words. The extract shows talk around one of the new words and its meaning.

1	T:	what is community in the dictionary?
2		**apa maksudnya?** [*what is the meaning?*]
3	P:	community **maskarakat** [*community*]
4	T:	**ya (.) hidup berkumpulan** [*yes (.) living in a group*]
5		now what is colonies?

Here we see two familiar dynamics at work: in lines 1 and 2, the teacher gives a first language translation of his English question; in lines 3 and 4, the pupil's use of the first language is replied to in the same language. I suggest that the third dynamic at work here is caused by the teacher's perception of learning vocabulary as finding an equivalent in the first language. Through this dynamic, once again the language in use moves back from the foreign language to the first language. Although we can only describe what happened in this lesson, the teacher who recorded it, and other teachers, who have read the transcript, affirm that this understanding of vocabulary learning is not unusual. As we have said before, teachers' understandings of what they are doing in lessons are influenced by various factors in their histories and their working situations.

The order of languages could again be reversed, so that pupils might suggest words in first language that may occur in the reading text. They would then find, or be given, the foreign language equivalents to look for in the passage. This strategy would put the focus of the cognitive activity on to the foreign language, increasing learning opportunities.

Summary

These classroom extracts have shown how the choice of which language to use may be affected by:

- which language was used in the immediately preceding turn
- who is speaking and their conversational rights to shift the language
- the norms and patterns of language choice that have built up over time between the teacher and class. These conventions become a further factor affecting future language choice.

9.4 Taking responsibility, making choices

9.4.1 Starting small

When we see that small-scale instances of language choice have their roots in the larger social and historical context of foreign language teaching, we may feel somewhat pessimistic about changing anything. However, we should be reassured by current thinking about complex systems, of which classroom language use would be an example. This theory shows that very small changes at one level of action may well generate large changes to the system. An individual teacher can adopt a slightly different attitude to use of the foreign language, and this can make a big difference to the language learning opportunities of pupils.

In this spirit, I want to suggest that helpful principles about which language to use might be phrased as follows:

- use as much of the target language as possible
- ensure that use of first language supports the children's language learning

The next sections consider what these might mean in practice.

9.4.2 Teacher-led choice

It has become clear that the teacher, unavoidably, has ultimate responsibility for the movement between languages that happens in a lesson, and that teacher's repeated patterns of choice contribute to constructing the overall attitudes of the class towards the foreign language.

A teacher who adopts the above principles will consciously switch back to the foreign language each time the discourse switches to L1; if a pupil uses first language, the teacher can answer in the foreign language, as happens in North American immersion classes with children new to the language of education. In this respect, teachers who speak the language of their pupils are at an advantage over native speakers of the foreign language, who cannot offer pupils their ideas back in the new language. The teacher will find ways to carry out classroom activities that do not rely on first language use.

Explaining new language

When new words or sentence patterns are encountered, pupils need support to work out their meaning and, as with the teacher whose lesson we looked at above, many teachers may feel that they can help in this process by giving a translation into first language. In some countries, text books may present new words in lists with their first language equivalents, and we do know that this is a relatively efficient way to learn vocabulary, at least for older learners who can read (Nation and Waring 1997).

There are, however, many other ways to support a child's search for the meaning of new words and sentences, as we have seen in earlier chapters. Many language items that children will meet can be understood through pictures, video, actions or gestures, and, once past the initial stages, new items can be explained through previously learnt language. We should remember how helpful it is to repeat talk in the foreign language, in exactly the same form, as well as in slightly different ways.

Translation into first language can be used in ways that support foreign language learning, as when a pupil translates from the foreign language used by the teacher, as a check of understanding. A further idea is for the teacher to translate all of a sentence *except* the new word; this provides the pupils with a linguistic context that can support their working-out of the meaning of the new word.

If first language equivalents of words are given on first meeting, then it is possible to give further information in the foreign language, such as sentences with the word in use or frequent collocates. In the third extract, the teacher added '*living in a group*' in first language, but this would probably be understood in the foreign language. He might also have added: *communities look after each other. Monks live in religious communities.*

Giving instructions

When a lesson involves a change of activity, such as children moving into groups or starting a new task, use of first language may be motivated by efficiency or by helping particular pupils who do not understand. Often the instructions to an activity may be more complex than the activity itself: a simple board game may require complicated instructions about taking turns or penalties for landing in certain spaces. In this case, it may be justified to give beginners instructions in the first language, with a parallel foreign language version that is simple and repeated in the same form each time the game is played, so that it becomes familiar and gradually understood.

Instructions can be supported with pictures relevant to key stages, left on the board or the wall in the right order to act as a reminder. For example, if children are to talk in a group, then write their own story and then tell their story to the group, the first picture would show a group of children talking, the second a lone child writing and the third a child telling a story to the group. Times could be added too.

Checking understanding

Checking that children have understood explanations and instructions is important for class management and for learning; too often, children come back after an activity has started and ask what they were to do. Teachers can use a range of strategies other than just asking '*did you understand?*' which will usually get the reply '*yes*', even if this is not the case.

Pupils can be asked to explain what they have just heard to a partner to cross-check their understanding. Individuals or pairs might draw a picture to show their understanding. If pictures have been used to support explanations or instructions, understanding can be checked by asking pupils to select the correct picture or to arrange pictures in the right order.

As mentioned above, one pupil can be asked to explain the teacher's talk to everyone else, in first language if necessary.

Talk about learning

Talk about learning would seem to be a clear example of where use of the first language might actively support the foreign language learning. First language might well be supportively used in discussing how children like to learn, good study habits, why the foreign language should be used as much as possible, why sometimes making mistakes does not matter, and so on.

Talk about language

In metatalk, i.e. talk about language, foreign language terms can be gradually introduced, but there will be times when an explanation in first language can have an immediate impact on foreign language learning, for example, in describing the structure of a particular type of text.

Children can enjoy making comparisons between first and foreign languages, pointing out words that are similar or very different, showing how the two languages work differently, e.g. to create plurals.

When any explanatory talk is done in the first language, it can be summarised in simple, clear sentences in the foreign language. The next time round, the foreign language explanation might be given first. In this way, each experience with the foreign language is contributing to a gradual building up of language for classroom management and for metalanguage in the foreign language.

Feedback

As we saw in the section on alignment, above, first language may be chosen for correcting children as a way of 'softening' the negative statements. However, in such situations, tone of voice and expression convey the teacher's attitude and so foreign language feedback can be effective. It is also useful for children to learn phrases that they can use with each other in group and pair work.

Discipline

While non-serious instances of misbehaviour such as noisiness can be dealt with in the foreign language through phrases learnt over time, there may be more serious breaches of discipline that require use of first language. It is in these situations, that the 'pretend' nature of the foreign language lesson stands out most clearly. When teacher and pupils use the foreign language, they are in some sense out of character. When discipline is called for, it is as if teacher and pupil have to leave the pretend climate of the lesson and be real people in their real world for the seriousness. On the other hand, a colleague of mine reports being very effectively told off in the foreign language by a particularly ferocious teacher – we should note that the effect of this was strong demotivation!

Informal talk

In the literature, use of first language was frequently noted as occurring between teacher and pupils when they were talking informally at the end of lessons, or 'off record' (Hancock 1997). Again, it would be possible for the teacher to use the foreign language to respond to pupils' first language, at least sometimes.

Making language choice conscious

The last two contexts of use emphasise the 'pretend' nature of using the foreign language in a school classroom. Rather than trying to ignore this, we might use it to make pupils more aware of their language use. A teacher in Malta told of how she asked the children to pretend to be like robots with a switch that they could toggle between English and Maltese. Once she had set this up in the children's imagination, she could just remind them by saying, '*Switch to English!*'.

A class mascot who 'only' understands the foreign language (Scott and Ytreberg 1990) has been successfully used in classes in Malta and Norway. The class may have a teddy bear who comes out each lesson and sits on the teacher's table. Children are told that they should use the foreign language so that the teddy can understand them, and young children up to about 9 years old are usually happy to go along with this idea. The mascot can even become a useful talking partner for the teacher in demonstrating dialogues and new language!

9.5 Summary

In this chapter on language choice and use, we have seen that a range of types of pressure may lead participants in foreign language lessons to use the first language, but that it is possible to counterbalance these forces with deliberate tactics. The teacher has the power and responsibility to ensure that such tactics are led by learning principles, and it has been suggested that whichever language is used should be deliberately chosen to maximise language learning opportunities. We have seen that, with this principle in place, the first language can sometimes have a positive role to play in foreign language lessons.

10 Assessment and language learning

10.1 Issues in assessing children's language learning

10.1.1 Introduction

The nature of children's foreign language learning might be expected to generate a range of assessment issues in need of attention. Factors such as the following might make the business of assessing young learners different from assessment practices in other FL situations:

- **Age**: children's motor, linguistic, social and conceptual development must be taken into account in designing and implementing assessment.
- **Content of language learning**: a focus on oral skills, vocabulary development and language use at discourse level.
- **Methods of teaching**: interactive use of games, songs, rhymes, stories to carry language content and practice.
- **Aims**: programmes for young learners often cite social and cross-cultural aims, as well as language learning aims.
- **Learning theories**: e.g. zone of proximal development; learning through social interaction, able to do more with helpful other.

A survey of the sparse information that is available on young learner assessment (but see Rea-Dickins 2000) suggests that assessment practices, far from taking careful account of the above factors, may find themselves in conflict with them. In this first section, macro-level and then more micro-level conflicts are identified. Section 10.2 sets out principles for assessment that emerge from our learning-centred perspective. Key concepts in assessment are explained in section 10.3. In section 10.4, we consider techniques other than testing that teachers can use to assess children's language learning. Section 10.5 discusses self-assessment in the young learner classroom. Section 10.6 considers how the outcomes of assessment can be used to support learning through feedback to children. The chapter concludes with some thoughts on the impact of assessment practices on children's motivation and future learning.

10.1.2 The social realities of assessment

Social realities, in the form of political, commercial and cultural dynamics underlie several conflicts around the role of assessment in language teaching and learning, particularly when we are concerned with assessing children.

It would seem reasonable to require assessment to *serve* teaching, by providing feedback on pupils' learning that would make the next teaching event more effective, in a positive, upwards direction. Teaching and learning needs should dictate the form and timing of assessment. In practice, the scenario is quite different: assessment seems to *drive* teaching by forcing teachers to teach what is going to be assessed. And this happens around the world, with young learners as well as older students. Three examples will illustrate the power of assessment over teaching and over learning.

In England, after decades without any national testing requirement at primary level, the government introduced a national curriculum and assessment at age 7, 11 and 14, with baseline assessment on entry to school at age 5. Initially, assessment tasks were designed to involve the children in familiar activities and enable the teacher to assess each child, but these were soon reduced to paper and pencil tests taken in exam conditions. Practice books are bought in newsagents by anxious parents, and, increasingly, classroom work in Year 6 (age 10–11 years) is preparation for the attainment tests. As I write this, parents and teachers have begun to protest at the 'stress' being felt by seven year old children, and to ask for a review of assessment procedures.

In Malaysia, the communicative English language syllabus becomes in practice a formal, grammar-based syllabus, because the examination at Year 6 is grammar-based, and parents and headteachers demand that pupils are prepared for the examination. From the age of 7, pupils are tested every month, every term and every year. The marks are used in some schools to place children in different classes and different groups within a class. The test results do not impact on teaching, because the next stage of the syllabus (or course book) will be tested in the next examination. The testing practices and the syllabus together determine what a child will experience in lessons, with little room for taking account of his or her individual needs.

On a global scale, a relatively new test for young learners developed by UCLES has taken off rapidly, mostly through private language schools. One hundred and fifty thousand children world-wide are expected to take the test in the year 2000, with particularly large numbers in China and in South America, but also in Pakistan, Bangladesh and European countries. Although the test assesses a child's progress rather than awarding a pass / fail, parents often want to know whether their child has 'passed'. The Examination Syndicate produces a list of words and topics that will be tested. Books of past papers are being published and will no doubt be worked through by anxious children preparing for the tests. It will be increasingly difficult for a teacher or language school to teach topics or vocabulary that are not on that list because they may reduce their pupils' chances of success in the test. Changing an international test is a long process, because new items must be validated against old ones so that scores are comparable. Inevitably and inexorably, the test, however well intentioned and planned, concretises language teaching by diminishing the opportunity for creativity in the classroom.

In the world of foreign language teaching, assessment, usually in the form of 'testing', has become a multi-million dollar global business, in which the need for internationally recognised certification of language proficiency works with learners' or their parents' understandable demands to see proof of the outcomes of their struggle to learn and the money they have invested in it. In turn, the market-driven development of quality tests relies on and supports the development of research and theory around language testing. As a result, the academic field is peopled with intellectuals who progressively complexify the concepts and techniques to such an extent that the language teacher or teacher trainer finds it difficult to make sense of what is written, let alone to ask critical questions. It is an irony that testing experts can increasingly only talk to and understand each other, when, around the world, on a daily and weekly basis, teachers who are largely untrained in testing write and mark tests that determine the learning opportunities of millions of children.

The dynamics of the interacting worlds of learners, academia and commerce combine to produce effects of testing on language learning that are felt throughout the system. This 'washback' from assessment to learning has an impact on individual learners, teachers and the wider system:

- stress is placed on children by the demands of assessment;
- individual children's learning needs are downgraded in the push to cover the syllabus or course book before the next assessment;
- classroom activity is restricted to test preparation;
- educational change is limited by the power of the assessment machinery.

Not all washback effects are negative. We might argue that children will encounter stress anyway in their educational lives, and that well-designed assessment may help them learn how to cope with more stressful examinations later in life. We know, too, that some ideas for educational change may be over-optimistic or just plain silly; good assessment may prevent damage to children's learning opportunities from irresponsible change. The power of assessment to change practice can be used positively and innovative testing can increase attention to neglected aspects of learning, as happened when oral skills were assessed for the first time in English schools. Test results provide useful feedback to stake-holders – governments and parents – about how well children are being taught, and about the effectiveness of policy and schools. Comparison of school results can highlight where pupils are underachieving that might otherwise not be noticed, and thus lead to improvements in learning opportunities.

The various realities of assessment in education create an uncomfortable scenario for advocates of learning-centred teaching. We have to recognise that these assessment realities derive from cultural and commercial factors that cannot be ignored, and that will change only slowly, if at all. Given this background, our concern must be to understand the impact of assessment on teaching, and its variations in different cultures, so that we can try to maximise its benefits for learning.

10.1.3 Classroom realities

When we move from macro-level scenarios to what actually happens in schools and classrooms, we find evidence of further conflicts in assessing children's language learning.

A survey by Rea-Dickins and Rixon (1999) of 120 teachers and teacher trainers, mostly from Europe, revealed that the vast majority (93%) of the teachers do assess children, with the stated purpose of helping their teaching (87%). Most of this assessment is prepared by classroom teachers, who are also mostly responsible for marking and record-keeping. However, when they investigated *what* was being assessed and *how*, Rea-Dickins and Rixon found 'a mismatch . . . between curricular aims, pedagogy, and test content' (1999: 96). The focus for most of the assessment was on children's achievements in language learning, rather than on other curricular aims such as increased language awareness or social awareness. Moreover, by far the most frequently used method of assessment was the paper-and-pencil test, testing single items of vocabulary and grammar through single sentences. The content and method of this type of assessment contrasts vividly with the classroom experience of children who have learnt language through participation in discourse-level stories and songs. Rea-Dickins and Rixon note the mismatch in level of text, but we should also note the disjuncture between the interactive learning environment and the non-interactive, solo experience of doing a test.

A further contrast that emerges from the survey is between the attention to oral skills in the classroom and in assessment. Very few of the tests that were reported focused on spontaneous speaking; it seemed that what was assessed was what was relatively 'easy' to assess. It is much easier to develop written tests than assessments of spoken language. Since the rise of communicative language teaching in the 1980s, testers have been struggling with how to assess oral skills, and spoken tests are now becoming available over the telephone and computer. On the ground, in schools and classrooms, because it is much more difficult to devise and mark oral assessments fairly, most assessment is still carried out on paper. It is possible that a requirement for grades and marks to show progress forces teachers into using written tests, perhaps with the unfortunate consequence of concentrating teaching on the written forms before children are able to cope with the demands that would make.

Elsewhere, Rea-Dickins and Rixon draw attention to the more advanced assessment practices that can be found in use with English as a Second Language (ESL) and first language children, and suggest that assessment of children's foreign language learning can draw on this work to improve methodology (Rea-Dickins and Rixon 1997). We return to the possibilities offered by these neighbouring fields later in the chapter.

Before that, the issues that have been identified in this section are used to generate some guiding principles for the assessment of children's foreign language learning.

10.2 Principles for assessing children's language learning

10.2.1 Assessment should be seen from a learning-centred perspective

We should at this point restate the learning-centred perspective of the book so that it can be applied to assessment. We have been building up a picture of foreign language teaching that has children's learning in the centre, trying to understand how classroom activities and talk will be experienced by children. We have emphasised children's willingness to participate in social interaction and their drive to make sense of the activities and talk they engage in. A Vygotskyan perspective on learning emphasises that learning occurs in social contexts and through interaction with helpful adults or other children. As we have examined the development of different aspects of foreign language knowledge and skills, the approach has been to examine how children's participation and engagement can provide opportunities for changes in these language resources that we would call 'learning', including the internalisation (Vygotsky 1962) or appropriation (Wertsch 1998) by the individual child of language used first with other people. Vygotsky turned ideas of assessment around by insisting that we do not get a true assessment of a child's ability by measuring what she or he can do alone and without help; instead, he suggested that what a child can do with helpful others both predicts the next stage in learning and gives a better assessment of learning. This kind of 'scaffolded assessment' (Gipps 1994) is far removed from the child seated in silent isolation to take a test.

10.2.2 Assessment should support learning and teaching

If learning is our central concern, then, in an ideal world, assessment should contribute to the learning process, for both an individual child and for the class. From the three examples in the first section of the impact of assessment, we can see that, even when a supportive relationship between assessment and teaching / learning is intended, social realities can rapidly push the relationship into something quite different.

In order to be more in control of the relationship between assessment and learning, teachers need to have a clear understanding of language learning processes and of the socio-cultural context in which they operate. They can then predict the impact of assessment on their teaching and plan accordingly. If the picture of language learning can be communicated to learners and their parents, then it may also help parents to understand what assessment can tell them and what its limits are.

Metaphors help us in constructing and communicating ideas and concepts, and I want to suggest a possible metaphor for language learning. In second language acquisition research over the last decades, the metaphoric view of language learning as the building of a higher and higher tower of bricks, through the accumulation of bits of grammar and vocabulary, has shifted to a more organic view of language learning as growth and development. At several points in the book a metaphor of plant growth has been applied to foreign language learning. We extend it now to assessment, visualising roots of language knowledge spreading out to support increasing use of the language. The plant develops through the nutrients it absorbs from its environment and different types of growth occur at different points in its life cycle. Assessment asks how well the plant is growing. However, growth is not just about the height of the plant, but concerns the strength of its root system, the quality of its leaves, the number and richness of the flowers. We would want to avoid the kind of assessment that involves pulling up the seedling to see how far the roots have grown and that, in doing so, slows down the very growth we want to happen. This might be a parallel with grammar-based tests that prevent more communicative approaches to teaching. Instead, we would want to find some 'non-invasive' methods of assessment that indicate learning; it is unlikely that a single measure will suffice to describe overall growth.

Thinking through the metaphor suggests a basic principle that assessment should not disrupt learning. We can go further than this negative requirement and ask that it positively support learning. There are various ways in which assessment can have positive effects:

- the process and outcomes of assessment can motivate learners;
- an assessment activity can provide a helpful model of language use;
- an assessment activity, and feedback from it, can support further learning;
- the outcomes of assessment can help teachers plan more effective lessons;
- the outcomes of assessment can inform the evaluation and improvement of courses and programs.

The principle of support will force us to look carefully at what opportunities an assessment activity offers for learning.

10.2.3 Assessment is more than testing

A gardener continuously assesses how well various plants are growing, noticing changes and judging what they mean by bringing past experience and knowledge to what is seen. Similarly, a skilled teacher continuously assesses pupils' learning through what s/he notices and how s/he interprets these observations in the light of experience and knowledge. It is not necessary to test children to understand how much they have learnt – or at least it is not necessary to do it too often. There are other, supportive, ways to assess language learning that go beyond testing, either the simple classroom test or the more stringent national or international test. Such 'alternative assessment' techniques include observation, portfolios, and self-assessment (O'Malley and Valdez Pierce 1996), and we will look at some in more detail later in the chapter.

Once again though, we should note that such skilled assessment of learning is not a trivial matter, but needs training and refining over several years.

10.2.4 Assessment should be congruent with learning

By 'congruent' I mean that assessment should fit comfortably with children's learning experience. On the whole, it is fairer to assess children on the basis of what they have been taught and *how*, using assessment activities that are familiar to children from their classroom experience.

This principle suggests that assessment should, like teaching and learning, be interactional rather than an isolated, solo experience.

McNamara (1996) discusses the neglect of social interaction within testing of older learners; working with children highlights the issue even more strongly. We also need to ensure adequate oral assessment of discourse skills.

10.2.5 Children and parents should understand assessment issues

Even if individual teachers want to convert their understandings of learning into new assessment practices, nothing can change without the support and involvement of key players: the learners themselves and their parents. In current terminology, they are prime 'stakeholders' in the educational process. As we examine techniques for assessment, we will emphasise the need for children to understand the purposes of activities and to play a role in them. Self-assessment can be a part of learning from the beginning, and can contribute to the development of self-motivated and self-directed learners at later stages.

Teachers are restricted in the individual decisions they can take on assessment; often, in fact, they can take no decisions because there are national regulations that must be followed. In some situations, though, decisions are left to schools, perhaps about how to prepare children for national examinations or how often to assess in between national tests. Then teachers can be involved in constructing school policy that is built on learning-centred principles. School policy on assessment must of course take account of parents' demands, but also has a responsibility to inform and educate parents about the theories of learning that underpin a school's teaching. Parents around the world want the best for their children, but this often manifests itself as wanting the same as happened in their own schooling. Parents need to know what teachers are doing and why; the effort it takes to explain will be repaid by parental support for teachers. Even stronger support can be had if teachers explain and model what parents can do to help their children. For example, the Malaysian parents involved in the literacy project mentioned in Chapter 6 came to understand that reading story books to their children could help develop literacy skills more effectively than testing spellings at the early stages, and so started buying story books for them instead of the activity books they used to buy. At the very least, parents can see how they can most effectively help children cope with examinations, and teachers can explain how assessment activities other than tests provide information on children's learning.

Having set up in the first two sections the background for the assessment of children's language learning, in terms of issues and principles, this section will clarify some of the important concepts and terms needed for deeper discussion of assessment.

10.3 Key concepts in assessment

10.3.1 Assessment – testing – evaluation

We have already seen that tests are just one technique or method of assessment. The other term that needs differentiating is evaluation. Evaluation refers to a broader notion than assessment, and refers to a process of systematically collecting information in order to make a judgement (Rea-Dickins and Germaine 1982: 22). Evaluation can thus concern a whole range of issues in and beyond language education: lessons, courses, programs, and skills can all be evaluated. If we were to evaluate a course, we would need to collect many different types of information: course documentation, observation of lessons, interviews with pupils and teachers, course feedback questionnaires, examination results. Analysing and combining the different types of information would enable a judgement to be made about the success, or viability, or cost-effectiveness, of the course.

Assessment is concerned with pupils' learning or performance, and thus provides one type of information that might be used in evaluation. Testing is a particular form of assessment, that is concerned with measuring learning through performance.

10.3.2 Formative and summative assessment

A useful distinction in assessment is made in terms of the *purpose* and *use* of assessment information. Formative assessment aims to inform on-going teaching and learning by providing immediate feedback. A teacher who assesses pupils' understanding of a listening text and uses the outcomes to change her plan and give more practice before moving on to a speaking activity, is carrying out formative assessment. Ideally, formative assessment should influence both teaching and learning by giving feedback to both teacher and learners (Gipps 1994).

Summative assessment, on the other hand, aims to assess learning at the end of a unit, term, year, or course, and does not feed back into the next round of teaching.

The formative / summative distinction is hardly visible in the current state of child language learning assessment (Rea-Dickins and Rixon 1997). In order to become better defined they suggest that a wider repertoire of techniques is needed and attention to closing the gap between pedagogy and assessment practices is highlighted in section 10.1.3 above.

10.3.3 Diagnostic and achievement assessment

Many assessment activities provide both formative and summative information, but it is helpful to be clear as to the primary purpose and use of an assessment because this can affect what kind of information the activity needs to produce. An assessment of pronunciation skills that is formative will need to tell us where pupils are having difficulty so that the teacher can decide how to give extra practice; a test that gives a list of marks will not help the teacher make such decisions, but an activity that produces a description of each child's performance will. This example highlights the distinction between assessing achievement, i.e. what a learner can do, and diagnostic assessment that aims to establish what a child can and cannot yet do, so that further learning opportunities can be provided.

10.3.4 Criterion-referenced and norm-referenced assessment

If we assess learners' achievement, we can produce a ranking of learners which says that child X has learnt more than child Y and less than child Z; this would be norm-referenced. Alternatively, we can compare a learner's performance, not to other learners, but to a set of criteria of expected performance or learning targets. Criterion-referenced assessment can match the child's performance against an expected response on an item, or it may make use of a set of descriptors along a scale, on which a learner is placed. ESL assessment in Australia makes use of a set of 'bandscales' on which a learner is placed through performance on classroom tasks (McKay 1995).

Examples of a statement about expected response and a descriptive scale are given in respect of speaking skills. In the first example, taken from the Cambridge Test for Young Learners (UCLES 1999), the learner is asked simple questions by an examiner. The criterion used to assess the child's speaking skills is the production of answers in single words or short phrases, and is rated on 'interactive listening ability, pronunciation and production of words and phrases' (UCLES 1999: 12).

In the second example, teachers assessing the oral skills of second language learners are given a six-level scale on which they can place each learner (O'Malley and Valdez Pierce 1996). The sub-scale for fluency has the following descriptor statements:

1. repeats words and phrases;
2. speaks in single word utterances and short patterns;
3. speaks hesitantly because of rephrasing and searching for words;
4. speaks with occasional hesitation;

5. speaks with near-native fluency; any hesitations do not interfere with communication;
6. speaks fluently.

(O'Malley and Valdez Pierce 1996: 68)

Criterion-referencing of learners' performance relies, of course, on expected norms, but the distinction is useful and is important for our principle of wanting assessment to support learning. While norm-referencing may motivate some children to do better than their peers and move up the ranking, it may have a negative effect on a much larger proportion of the children. Giving feedback on assessment in terms of how well you are doing relative to others does not help you know how to do better. A band scale like the second example is potentially much more helpful because it gives a picture of the process of learning that each learner will move through and thus lets a learner see where they are compared to more expert performance. However, to be useful in this way means that such scales must be very well researched and it is likely that, while a very specific description will be more useful, an increase in precision also makes the scale less reliably applicable to individuals.

10.3.5 Validity

The concepts of reliability (see below) and validity are used to describe the technical quality of assessment practices. They are more often applied to testing, although are also important in alternative assessment. Validity is the more important, particularly in alternative assessment, and concerns how far an assessment assesses what it claims to. If a test does not measure what it claims to, then there are clearly dangers in using it (Gipps 1994). In order to evaluate the validity of an assessment, we must compare the skills or knowledge that we want to assess with what is actually assessed, and also examine the claims made about pupils' ability from their performance in the assessment. Consider a simple test that showed children various pictures of objects to name in the foreign language as a test of vocabulary. Suppose the pupils being tested had learnt the word '*milk*' and linked it to the cartons of milk that they regularly buy from their supermarket. If the test picture for *milk* showed a glass bottle on a doorstep (as milk is experienced by a child in the UK, although increasingly infrequently!), then the testee may well not be able to answer. Rather than testing knowledge of the vocabulary item, the test was testing knowledge of another culture. It would thus not be valid as a test of the word *milk*.

If an assessment omits some aspects of what is being assessed, its validity can also be reduced. For example, if we claim to have assessed a child's *writing skills* but only give a mark for spelling and neatness, and omit discourse level skills of organisation and sequencing, this would not be a valid assessment.

It will be clear that the assessment of young children's, mostly oral, language learning is not validly done through pencil and paper tests that require written responses (see section 10.1.3).

To make sure an assessment is as valid as possible, we need to think very carefully about what exactly we want to assess, what exactly the proposed assessment will assess, and what can be claimed from the outcomes of the assessment.

Validity has also been extended to include considerations of the social consequences of assessment (Messick 1989), in asking whether the uses to which results of assessment are put are justified by the nature of the assessment. For example, assessment can be used to select pupils, to stream pupils by grouping together those with similar results, or to take some pupils out of the mainstream and into special educational units. Tests or assessments should not be used for purposes they were not designed for without checking on their validity in the new circumstances.

10.3.6 Reliability

Reliability measures how well a test or assessment assesses what it claims to: would the assessment produce the same results if it were taken by the same pupils on different occasions, or if the same test or assessment was scored by different people? (Gipps and Stobart 1993).

When applied to tests that produce numerical marks, reliability can be checked by statistical comparison of performances on two similar tests a few days apart. However, this method would not work for criterion-referenced assessments because individuals may not be widely spaced across the results.

It should be clear that reliability can be affected by the conditions under which pupils are assessed, and thus by what teachers do when they explain assessment activities to pupils (Gipps 1994). Reliability is increased by being very explicit about instructions to pupils and, in scoring, by moderation, i.e. having markers score the same scripts until they mark consistently in the same way.

Validity and reliability can be conflicting needs for assessment techniques and procedures. The most reliable assessments will be pencil and paper tests in which each item measures only a single aspect of a skill and which give each testee a numerical mark. But the most valid assessments will be those that collect a lot of information about performance on several aspects of a skill. When validity is increased, reliability decreases. The validity / reliability conflict echoes that described in section 10.1.2, and creates a real dilemma for education, that is being felt across America and Europe, between political movements to use assessment to increase the quality of education by monitoring national standards via tests, and new approaches to assessment in which teachers and pupils use a range of techniques to feed back into setting targets and motivating learners (Gipps 1994). Gipps suggests that the way through this conflict lies in careful identification of the purposes and uses of assessment, so that a suitable balance of validity and reliability can be found for each instance.

10.3.7 Fairness

Fairness, or 'equity' (Gipps 1994), needs to be considered in the design and use of assessment. In the first section, we saw something of the power of assessment:

- in shaping the curriculum and pedagogy;
- in affecting pupils' motivations and sense of themselves as learners;
- in awarding certificates, setting and streaming;
- and, in some situations, controlling access to the next stage of education.

(based on Gipps 1994: 144)

Furthermore, assessment in children's language learning, as part of their early experience, can influence whether or not pupils choose to continue learning the foreign language or whether they lose interest and motivation. Because assessment potentially has such a powerful 'washback' effect on children's lives, issues of fairness must be taken seriously.

Equity principles require that children are given plenty of chances to show what they can do, and that their language learning is assessed through multiple methods. It is important in planning and designing assessments that the content is scrutinised to make sure that culturally unfamiliar pictures or concepts do not reduce children's chances to demonstrate their language learning. The types of questions, test items, or assessment tasks should also be familiar to pupils, if they are to show their ability to best advantage. Children who have not played games in their classrooms would be at a severe disadvantage if tested through game-like activities (Dossena 1997). Where assessment requires oral production, we need to be aware of how children's willingness to talk to adults can vary, and how different children may come to interview-type assessments with very different previous experience of talking to adults on a 1–1 basis. Instructions to children also need to be carefully planned and given, if they are to have equal chances to achieve on the assessment.

Scoring and recording the outcomes of assessment also need to be carried out with attention to fairness, so that, for example, observing children in activities to assess their oral skills is not biased by their behaviour, or appearance, or gender.

10.3.8 Planning the assessment of children's language learning

The concepts discussed in this section matter for classroom assessment as well as for large-scale testing. Points of importance from this section can be summarised as a checklist of questions around assessment that teachers can use when planning assessment and to help decide what types of assessment are appropriate.

Questions to guide assessment planning

Purposes and objectives of assessment

Which aspect(s) of language learning do I want to assess?

How does this relate to the learning experience of the children?

What do I want to use the assessment outcomes for?

Who else will use the outcomes? and for what purposes?

Methods of assessment

How will information be gathered to assess the aspect(s) of language?

How will the information that is collected be interpreted?

How will pupils be involved in gathering the information?

Quality management in assessment

How can I make sure the assessment is valid?

How can I make sure the assessment is reliable?

How can I make sure the assessment is fair?

Feedback

Who will I share the assessment outcomes with?

How will I communicate the outcomes of assessment?

Uses of assessment

How will the outcomes of assessment inform future teaching, planning and learning opportunities?

Impact of the assessment

What washback effects from assessment to teaching may occur?

What will the impact be on pupils' motivation?

The next section will focus on methods and content of assessment, and on the kind of inferences that can be made from information collected during assessment.

10.4 Teacher assessment of language learning

At this point in the chapter, we leave testing to one side (see Rea-Dickins 2000) and focus on teacher assessment of language knowledge and skills in classroom situations. Earlier chapters of the book are reflected upon in assessment terms.

10.4.1 Assessing in relation to goals

In Chapter 2, I emphasised the importance of having clear language learning goals for classroom activities, and the emphasis was reiterated in connection with stories and themes as holistic, integrative methods for language teaching. By making goals explicit, it was argued, we have a check on the potential value of each lesson to the pupils. These same goals will make assessment a much more straightforward process because they can act as a target or focus against which we can measure what was actually learnt. We may decide to assess all goals together, or each separately.

There are some simple, informal ways of assessing learning that will work with very young children. For example, if goals include learning the names of animals (as in Chapter 3), assessment might be done during teaching using simple techniques such as:

understanding	The child listens to a word and points to the picture.
	The child listens to 3 animal words and chooses 3 pictures in the same sequence.
production	Teacher points, child says the animal word.
	Pairs 'test' each other with picture cards, teacher observes.

For children, informal assessment like this will not feel threatening. For the teacher, learning activities become assessment activities when there is a clear assessment focus, i.e. some specific aspect of language learning is attended. Assessment requires the focused use of skills that are also essential to teaching: finely tuned observation and systematic, detailed record-keeping. We consider each in turn.

10.4.2 Selecting an assessment focus

The focus of assessment is the precise aspect of language that is being attended to and assessed or measured. For example, in attending to how well a child recalls a word and its meaning, the teacher may also decide to attend to pronunciation. When the focus is discourse rather than words, as in the task analysed in Chapter 3, the focus may be on interactional skills, such as turn-taking or answering questions, on discourse organisation of extended talk or writing, or on the grammatical complexity or accuracy of the language produced by a child (Skehan 1996).

There may be more than one focus; in the assessment of writing, both word-level accuracy and discourse organisation may be considered. Knowing that each focus is to be attended to will help ensure that assessment is fair and valid, because each can be assessed separately and the effect of one on assessment of the other can be minimised. When oral language is assessed, however, it can be difficult to observe or attend to more than one assessment focus. One solution is to make a recording of children's talk to assess later.

An important consideration in assessing language learning is whether the language is to be assessed in or out of the original learning context. For example, a child will learn *here, there, everywhere* in the context of 'Old McDonald had a farm' – the song is the original learning context of those adverbs. But knowing them and being able to produce them in that context is only a first step in the learning. If we observe whether or not the child sings them in the song, we have assessed his or her learning of the words in the original learning context. Eventually we want the child to be able to use those words out of the context of the song, to talk about things other than animal noises, and in other structures than *here a . . ., there a . . .* (which is actually rather archaic and hardly heard in everyday spoken English). Different words and phrases in a learner's repertoire will move beyond their original context and into wider use at different rates, and depending on the teaching. We cannot therefore generalise about when to assess. We should note, however, that the teacher needs to be aware of whether the words should be assessed only in their original learning context, or whether the child can be expected to use them in other contexts and they should therefore be assessed in other language contexts.

Possible assessment focuses for children's language learning are set out in the table below. To be effective in assessment, each focus would need to specify the actual items: words, discourse units, grammatical forms, learning skills.

	Vocabulary	Discourse	Grammar
Oral skills	understanding meaning of words and chunks recall of words and chunks knowledge of thematic word sets appropriate choice of words and chunks in discourse pronunciation of words and chunks	precision in talk fluency in talk response or initiation in conversational exchanges understanding of sentence-level discourse e.g. instructions understanding of oral texts – stories, songs, rhymes, chants, dialogues – overall meanings production of extended discourse – retold and original	complexity of clauses and phrases understood and produced accuracy of morphology and syntax – used in understanding, in production creative use of whole-learnt chunks metalanguage – understanding, use
Reading skills	sight vocabulary letter-sound links	understanding of stories and other whole texts sentence and text level reading strategies e.g. prediction	working out accurate meanings
Writing skills	spelling letter formation	organisation of texts at sentence level and above precision and accuracy in conveying ideas	accuracy in use of grammar
Learning skills	guessing words from context organising own work on tasks setting targets for learning using targets for learning work with a partner work in a group self-assessment skills dictionary use		

10.4.3 Assessment by observation

Observation is one of the most useful assessment techniques to use with children because it does not disturb the children and allows them to be assessed in the process of ordinary classroom activities. Skilful teachers are probably constantly observing their pupils and adjusting their talk or the lesson activities to take account of the feedback they get from their observation: they may pause in singing a song to explain some of the key words again because they notice that several children do not seem to understand the meaning of what they are singing, or to practise the pronunciation of a particularly tricky word on its own. They may repeat instructions for an activity one more time than planned because they observe that not all the pupils have understood. They may stop as they walk round the classroom and help one child who is observed to be struggling with making the shape of one of the alphabet letters in their writing.

In addition to this continuous process of *observe – notice – adjust teaching*, observation can be pre-planned for assessment purposes. The teacher selects the focus of assessment and decides in advance that she or he will observe the children during the next lesson to assess how well they have learnt that particular aspect of the language. 'Observation', as a metaphor to describe how we collect this type of assessment information, builds on the idea of having a 'focus' and emphasises that we have to do much more than just 'look' at what pupils say or do. Rather, we need to look very carefully at the particular aspect of language that we are concentrating on, and use our experience and knowledge about language and learning to guide us in what we look for and how we interpret what we see.

Here is an example. A teacher of a class of seven year olds was eager to show me, as a visitor, some of the theme-based work that her class had done. The children performed a short play on the topic and sang some songs. If I had just looked at what the children did, I would have seen a bunch of happy children having a good time using English. By *observing* the children, I could see a more complex picture: some knew all the words and carried the performance along, but some children clearly did not know what to say and got by in the noise and excitement by moving their lips or by just staying quiet. And, as in every class, there were one or two children who took advantage of such a situation to get on with their own business: kicking the person next to them or talking in the first language. Of course, it is not valid, reliable or fair to assess children's learning from a public performance like this, without knowing individuals and their learning histories. The point I want to make is that the observation was 'finely tuned' by the focus; it was a very specific and goal-directed way of looking and seeing. The example can be summarised as follows:

> My **assessment focus** was something like *Do all the children understand the meaning of what is happening?*
> The **information** that would give me some evidence of their understanding was in their participation, what they actually did and said, and in something much less tangible about how they participated, trying to assess from their expressions whether they seemed to understand what they said.
> My **assessment technique** was observation, i.e. close and purposeful noticing of children's talk and actions.

10.4.4 Creating opportunities for assessment during classroom activities

When observation, or other technique, is used for assessment, there are several factors to take account of in planning:

Who will be assessed? It may not be realistic to assess each child on the same occasion, in which case a group of children can be selected for observation. By focusing on six or seven children during one lesson, the information collected is likely to be of better quality. Over three or four lessons, the whole class can be assessed. Larger classes will need other techniques: perhaps observation of groups. Sometimes, the teacher may choose to observe just one child – perhaps one who seems to be struggling or one who seems to be bored with lessons. We need to be aware that children who have picked up the language from home, TV, or their computers, may find lessons too easy and misbehaviour can result from boredom as well as from difficulties.

When in the lesson will I assess? By matching the assessment focus against the lesson plan, the teacher should be able to spot a point where assessment is particularly appropriate. If oral language is the focus, the best time may be when children are working in pairs rather than a whole class. Alternatively, during a writing or making-and-doing activity, the teacher can talk quietly to individual children and assess their learning of certain phrases and words through their ability to use them in conversation.

Task-based assessment is a more formalised version of spotting opportunities for assessment that has been developed in Australia for use with second language learners of English (McKay 1995). Teachers and teacher educators worked together to develop a set of tasks that have a clear assessment stage. Teachers' notes show exactly what is to be assessed and how. Across all the tasks, the full range of language skills and knowledge can be assessed, and enable teachers to describe a child's proficiency by placing him or her on a bandscale. As Rea-Dickins and Rixon (1997) suggest, this type of assessment methodology may have potential for children's foreign language learning, not just in providing coverage of assessment through classroom activities, but in the teacher development that occurs in the preparation of assessment activities.

10.4.5 Record-keeping

The most common way of recording observations of children's performance is through a checklist on which the teacher simply ticks when a pupil has achieved a goal. Figure 10.1 shows an Assessment Chart from Playway to English 1 (Gerngross and Puchta 1998). Such a chart could be designed for a unit of work by identifying the language learning goals and converting them into assessment foci or statements of performance, as in the left-hand column. I would suggest, however, that 'recognise and use of language' be separated, since, as we saw in Chapter 3, the very different demands of understanding and speaking can lead to them appearing in performance at different times.

Although these checklists are easily managed and convenient, they do limit the amount of information that can be recorded about each child. An alternative is to have a loose-leaf record book with a section for each learner. The section can contain formal records of assessment, such as results of a miscue analysis (Chapter 6) or rating of oral language assessment. At regular intervals, say, every two weeks, the child can be observed during a lesson, and notes jotted down about their participation, language use, confidence, social skills and anything else that is of interest. Over the year, the formal records and informal notes will give a useful picture of the overall development of the child as a language learner.

10.5 Self-assessment and learner autonomy

In this section we look at how far young learners are able to assess their own language learning. Self-assessment can help learners to understand more about the language learning process and to become more independent.

10.5.1 Self-assessment

The benefits of self-assessment are easily stated, but need some thought as to their applicability for young learners of foreign languages.

Photocopiable master

Assessment chart of pupils' progress Units 4 – 6

By the end of Unit 6 pupils can ...

Pupils' names

Linguistic skills

- recognise and use language related to pets
- guess animals and answer questions *(Is it a mouse? Yes, it is. No, it isn't.)*
- answer and ask simple questions *(What's this?)*
- make suggestions *(Let's play)*
- understand dialogues
- answer questions concerning quantity
- answer questions concerning colour
- ask each other questions concerning the colour of toys
- form the plural of nouns (singular + s)
- recognise and use language related to toys
- recognise and use language related to colours
- ask about the colour of toys
- understand narrative texts
- reconstruct narrative texts

Cognitive, motor and social skills

- complete logical sequences
- play a memory game with a partner
- play a coloured spinning top
- match sounds with toys
- make a coloured spinning top
- play vocabulary games with a partner
- recite a rhyme in front of the class
- understand and carry out a set of instructions
- discover and correct mistakes in the content of a story
- understand the time sequences of a story
- match animals with their tracks
- create their own logical sequences
- play Bingo

Class: _____ Teacher: _____ Date: _____

meaning of symbols: ✓✓✓ = well achieved ✓✓ = about average ✓ = needs more practice

Figure 10.1 Example of an Assessment Profile (from Playway 1998, p. 325)

Through self-assessment:

- learners can understand more about the learning process;
- learners can be motivated towards more involvement in their learning;
- teachers can understand more about individual pupils;
- learners will be better prepared to carry on learning, beyond the classroom;
- a more equal relationship is created between teachers and learners.

In Vygotskyan terms, a pupil who learns to assess his or her own work moves from being 'other-regulated' to being 'self-regulated' or autonomous. Using the analogy from Chapter 1, of the child learning to feed him or herself, the other-regulated child depends on the other (parent or other adult) to organise and control the feeding situation, by presenting the food, holding the spoon, moving food from bowl to mouth; the self-regulated child will hold the spoon, load the spoon and manipulate the moving of the spoon into the mouth. Some years later, the other stages of the process will come under the child's control when she or he learns to shop, prepare and cook food. The other-regulated language learner depends on the teacher to decide what is to be learnt, to present the language, to decide on activities, to control activities and to evaluate how well the language has been learnt through the activities. The self-regulated learner will take over parts of this process, and be able to adjust them to suit meaning styles and preferences.

It is commonly recognised in today's world that autonomous and self-regulated learners will be at an advantage in continuing to learn and adjust throughout their lives as technology and information develop rapidly and continuously. Learner autonomy then is 'a good thing' and to be encouraged, but how realistic is this in classes of five year olds? My own view is that we tend to underestimate the potential for self-regulation in our children, seeing them too often as blank sheets to be written on, empty vessels to be filled, or wild and in need of taming. Young children can, within the limits of their cognitive development, be helped to organise their resources, both internal and material. It is not unusual to see classes of five year olds who know where to keep their books and papers, how to tidy the classroom, how to organise their work and how to decide in what order they will complete their classroom activities (see Ellis 1991; Brewster, Ellis and Girard 1992).

In the foreign language classroom, the language used to organise such training will probably need to be the mother tongue, and so further decisions must be made about the value of the time required, and balancing between spending the time on developing learner autonomy or on language learning. In deciding how to develop learner autonomy, it will be useful to tie increased responsibility to the language content: for example, the phrases *I like / don't like* often appear very early in a syllabus. With these simple phrases, learners can evaluate how much they enjoy different types of activity or to pick out the good points of a story. Similarly, learners can easily cope with *I learnt* and use this to recall what was learnt in order to reflect on it.

Children of seven and eight years of age can begin to understand criteria for good performance or production, and if these are simply phrased may be able to use the foreign language. Once, when working with native speaker seven year olds, I helped them to reflect on their interactional skills by recording them talking and getting them to listen to the talk; they identified problems such as not listening to each other, interrupting, or talking too long and off the point, which were then turned into a list of 'Our rules for talking'. Making the list also involved teaching the children a new word: *relevant*.

Our rules for talking

(1) Don't all talk at the same time
(2) Talk one after the other round the circle
(3) Wait until somebody has finished
(4) Don't tell stories that aren't useful or relevant

After each further discussion session, they gave themselves marks out of 10 for how well they had obeyed their own rules. This is an example of helping children not only understand someone else's assessment criteria, but also to set their own. In foreign language classrooms, parallel opportunities may arise when children are giving a public performance such as a short play or presentation around a theme (Chapter 7). After listening to each other, the class can be asked what was good and what could be better, and the ideas they suggest written up as criteria for a good performance.

When children reach the stage of writing, samples of good work can act as benchmarks against which they can compare their own writing. Reading other children's work extends reading skills as well as demonstrating target levels of achievement. Peer-assessment is a good half-way stage towards self-assessment. Pairs of children can swap pieces of writing and be asked to tell each other good points and things to improve on a next draft. Again, this process will need to be modelled by the teacher first, and should if possible be done through the foreign language.

10.5.2 Goal setting

Being able to set realistic and useful goals for one's own language learning is one of the skills of autonomous learners and is part of the cycle that links self-assessment to learning. Even very young children can be helped to set goals for themselves by, for example, choosing five words out of eight to learn at home, and then testing each other. As they get older, so the length of the time for which the goals are set can be increased from a few days to a term at a time. At the beginning of the term, the teacher may explain the goals that she or he has set for everyone, and then ask the children to select a further set of goals for themselves from a list of possibilities; children who need to practise writing can choose writing goals; those who want to read more may decide they will try to read four books in the term. At the end of term, or other time period, it is important to evaluate how much progress has been made towards the goals, and to discuss why some have been achieved but others have not.

10.5.3 Portfolio assessment

A portfolio is a collection of examples of work that, as a collection, reveal both the capability and the progress of a learner. Artists, photographers and architects typically build up portfolios, in which they put together pictures they feel best represents their style and skills. They then use the portfolios to demonstrate what they have to offer to potential customers or employers. Applied to language learning, a portfolio would include such things as samples of writing and lists of books read (O'Malley and Valdez Pierce 1996). Portfolios can link assessment with teaching and with metacognitive development through including pupils in the evaluation of performance, thereby developing skills in pupils' self-assessment. Pupils are involved in deciding what to include in their portfolios and in assessing or evaluating the pieces of work according to clear and explicit criteria.

A limitation of portfolio assessment is its application to oral skills development. Being paper-based, it is more suited to collecting written texts. Children can include their self-assessments of oral language activities and progress, but it is more complicated to include samples of talk. Perhaps as computers with CD ROMs become more accessible, children will be able to build up computer-based portfolios with recorded samples of speech as well as scanned-in or digitally photographed texts.

Meanwhile, portfolios around literacy skills development seem to offer interesting possibilities (see O'Malley and Valdez Pierce 1996, Chapter 3 for details on how to build up portfolios with children). We can also note how portfolio assessment allows for much greater child involvement in the process of recording progress and achievement, and try to find such techniques in oral assessment.

10.6 Use of assessment information

Earlier in the chapter we established the principle that assessment should support learning and teaching. In order to make it do this effectively, we need to consider how the outcomes of assessment are used to generate various forms of feedback that can change teaching and learning.

10.6.1 Outcomes of assessment and uses

Summative assessment techniques, such as tests, produce outcomes in the form of grades, marks and rankings of students, but little more qualitative information that can be used diagnostically. Summative outcomes can be used to evaluate the effectiveness of a course or programme, along with other information such as student and teacher evaluations, and course documentation (Rea-Dickins and Germaine 1982). Rankings of students are used for placement purposes: deciding which schools, classes, sets or groups students will be placed in.

Leaving this type of assessment purpose aside, we can move to formative assessment that is intended to make a difference to teaching and learning. Observations, portfolios, checklists, rating scales each offer information that can be converted into feedback for parents, pupils, and other teachers, and that influence how the next lesson or unit is planned by the language teacher.

10.6.2 Making feedback helpful to learners

If assessment feedback is to be helpful to learners and improve their learning, it needs to be specific and detailed enough to make a difference and, equally importantly, it needs to be related to a target performance or understanding towards which the learner can move. The target performance, which may be presented as a list of criteria, a rating scale, or as examples of exemplary performance, offers learners the opportunity to see what they are aiming at. Feedback should also help learners to compare their current performance against the target performance, and to close the gap between them (Gipps 1994). The process in which assessment and feedback can scaffold the learner to better learning is summarised below:

> learner understands the target performance
> ↓
> learner compares target and current performance
> ↓
> learner closes the gap between target and current performance

The target performance could be modelled by the teacher, or on video or audio cassette, or by pupils who are at a higher level. Murphey (2000) suggests that 'near peer role modelling' will help move children through their zone of proximal development, not just in relation to assessment but more generally in learning language, and not just in terms of the language but also in learning strategies and metacognitive development.

The teacher of young learners can intervene to help the learner 'close the gap' in several ways:

Corrective feedback aims to help pupils correct their language use towards the target language. It will explain why correct responses are correct and incorrect ones are wrong; pupils will be shown a model of the correct responses. In language learning, corrective feedback will be primarily concerned with accuracy. With children, and probably older learners too, it is not necessary always to point out errors; often, repeating what a child says with the correct form stressed will work as corrective feedback. The pupil should be allowed to repeat the correct form, and should receive some signal that this is now correct.

Example

Pupil:	*I come to school at eight o'clock.*
Teacher:	*I **came** to school at eight o'clock.*
Pupil:	*I came to school at eight o'clock.*
Teacher:	*Well done!*

Evaluative feedback includes a judgement on the pupils' performance.

Examples

1. Quoted from a primary school lesson (L1):
   That one was quite easy. Quite a few got that one right. Now the next one was very hard. You had to think.
2. *That was very good – I liked the way you said the sentences clearly.*

Notice that in the first example the teacher did not help the pupils to do better next time; she just gave an evaluative comment on their performance. In the second example, the teacher pointed out something specific that was good.

Strategic feedback offers advice on what to do to improve performance.

Examples

1. to help a child say <the> / ðe /
    look at my tongue – put your tongue on your teeth – the
2. to increase fluency in speaking in a dialogue, pupils might be advised to say the phrases to themselves 'in their heads' during the preparation stage, or just before they speak. (This is called *mental rehearsal*.)

In the early stages, some of this feedback will need to be done through the mother tongue, although a rating scale or strategies for improving performance can be introduced to the children in the foreign language. If the same phrases are always used, they can work as feedback.

10.7 Messages from assessment

To conclude this chapter, I want to highlight the idea that assessment practices not only determine children's futures and how their time is spent, but also carry messages for children about what parents and teachers consider important in language learning and in life.

Feedback practices show pupils directly what is valued in the work that they do. If spelling and neatness are what the teacher attends to, then the child will get the message that this is what matters in writing; if a teacher always praises the children, even when they are not making an effort, they quickly learn that the praise is hollow. If on the other hand the teacher knows a child's capabilities, recognises when she or he is trying especially hard and offers praise and supportive feedback, the child learns that his or her learning matters to the teacher and that it is worth struggling. If all other subjects count for selection but the foreign language exam does not, then language classes are not likely to be highly motivated.

Educational research demonstrated long ago that children live up to the expectations of their teachers, whether those are low or high. Expectations are perhaps more clearly revealed through assessment practices than anywhere else. The negative washback from assessment to teaching and learning which I described in the opening section can be made to work positively by giving weight to what matters in language learning. For young children, what matters is a solid base in spoken language, confidence and enjoyment in working with the spoken and written forms of the language, and a good foundation in learning skills. We should be searching out assessment practices that will reinforce the value of these to learners and to their parents.

11 Issues around teaching children a foreign language

11.1 Review of ideas

The book has aimed to put learning in the centre of the frame, and to use what we know about learning as a key to more effective language teaching. Frameworks for thinking about the language and about classroom activities have been constructed and used in analysis and application. This final chapter begins with a review of these constructs that pulls together the central ideas of the book.

Learning

At the root of learning is the process of making meaning out of participation in the social world. As children's minds stretch to find meanings in new experiences, so learning occurs.

Meaning and learning can be seen as both social and conceptual. In making sense of their experiences, minds stretch to make accumulating and conflicting information coherent by re-organising internal categories and the informal theories that hold them together. In making sense of other people and what they do, minds stretch to understand intentions and other people's minds.

Language and learning are interdependent – language leads to learning through enabling participation in the social world and the expressing and sharing of meanings; learning increases the power of an individual's language resources.

A foreign language

Learning a foreign language is different from learning the first language, even for children at the young end of our age range. It is different because the first language is already a huge system that a child has in place; because, in comparison, the child will encounter such a small amount of the foreign language; and because it is 'foreign' – often the language 'belongs' to people in a distant and strange culture.

The foreign language that children will learn has been mapped out by starting from vocabulary and discourse, as two aspects of language that offer most opportunities for seeking and finding meanings to children: vocabulary, because words serve to label concepts and lead into the explanatory theories, scripts and schemata that make sense in the inner mental world of the child's experiences of the 'real' world; discourse, because discourse events are the site of social interaction. Grammar was seen as emerging from the use of words in discourse, and literacy skills as building on oral skills by introducing a symbolic representation of talk.

Learning the foreign language

Developing foreign language resources and skills occurs through the building of vocabulary and supporting the development of discourse abilities. I have argued that developing discourse skills requires both participation in discourse events and practice with the foreign language at word and phrase level. Participation in discourse should be the starting point and the target of language learning – it is where new language items and their meanings are encountered, and where part-skills can be integrated.

Learners need to notice the details of how the foreign language works, from the inside of words up to the large units of stories or descriptions. They need to incorporate this knowledge through use, and to be able to use the knowledge in their own communication.

Teaching

I have separated the processes of teaching and learning to emphasise that teaching can never guarantee learning; all it can do is to construct opportunities for learning and to help learners take advantage of them.

A learning-centred perspective should help to see how any activity can be adjusted to provide opportunities that are accessible to learners but will stretch minds beyond their current capability. Through a theorising of practice, the book has provided tools and concepts for planning, teaching, and assessment in learning-centred language classrooms. In this last chapter, I want to look forward to what needs to be done to continue the development of an 'applied linguistics' for the teaching of foreign languages to children.

11.2 The need for research

The job of describing, through theory and through empirical research, what happens when children learn a foreign language is far from complete. The theoretical frameworks developed in this book have had to rely sometimes on work from neighbouring fields. Research in the field is beginning, but much more is required in order to make syllabuses and teaching effective. Areas in need of investigation on a young learner research agenda would include:

- How much foreign language knowledge do children have at the end of their primary or elementary school experience?
- How does this vary with syllabus, methods, first language, age of starting, inclusion of literacy, etc.?
- Is there an optimum amount of time, e.g. in lessons per week, that children should spend on foreign language learning?
- What map of the language system (i.e. grammatical knowledge) do young learners develop after 2 / 4 /6 years of teaching?
- How much of their foreign language learning do children forget as they move on?
- What is the effect of different first languages on foreign language oral and literacy skills development?
- How do children make sense of the activities they encounter in foreign language lessons?
- How do children use their vocabulary knowledge in participating in discourse?
- What do they learn from different types of activities?
- How can holistic activities like theme-based teaching and stories be best combined with part-skills practice?
- How does the development of foreign language oral skills affect learning to read and write in the foreign language?
- How do children use their first language in foreign language lessons, e.g. in talk with peers, in silent translation?
- How effective is self-assessment in improving learning?

11.3 The need to develop pedagogy

Answers to these research questions would help develop effective classroom practice and theory to underpin pedagogy. In this section, I present a selection of pedagogic issues that I consider to be in need of attention.

11.3.1 Aims of teaching foreign languages to children

Children are taught foreign languages in state education systems and in growing private sector organisations. Governmental reasons for lowering the age of starting to learn a foreign language usually include the desire to improve national standards in foreign language use; parents likewise often believe that children will benefit. There is as yet no very convincing evidence that expenditure on language teaching will make this happen (and, indeed, evidence to the contrary in some situations, e.g. Williams 1998). As the outcomes of young learner programs are evaluated, we may find a need to reconsider the aims and objectives of starting young.

11.3.2 Developing methodology

Early children's courses often drew heavily on secondary level language teaching or on mainstream primary education. As experience and empirical data on learning outcomes related to different methods accumulate, we may well need to reconsider methodological assumptions that derive from these sources. I have questioned some assumptions already in this book, but I suspect many more will need to be held up to the light in the future.

Computers and the Internet are changing the possibilities for language learning. As yet, little impact has been made on classroom practice, but outside school, students' lives are more and more likely to involve the use of information technology. If students are not to feel that they walk back through time when they enter the classroom, we must be open to new ways of using computers, videos, and tools not yet invented, so that what and how we teach in school meshes into their lives.

Schools in Europe are increasingly trying out a version of immersion education that exposes children to the foreign language through subject area lessons, e.g. history in a French school is taught in Spanish. As we saw in Chapter 8, the boundaries between this 'plurilingual education' and theme-based foreign language teaching can become blurred. It seems important that these variations on teaching foreign languages to children be brought closer together through exchange of experiences and through theory. By examining the similarities and differences in methods and in outcomes, each may find new techniques to develop pedagogy.

11.3.3 Continuity in language learning

One of the key issues to be dealt with in language teaching is how, as more and more children learn foreign languages at ever younger ages, their language education is to continue into and through secondary schooling.

For the theory of children's language learning, this issue presents itself as a need to think through how early language learning will evolve into later learning, and how to continue to motivate children to enjoy language learning. Children who learn a language for several years will enter the secondary phase of education with a reasonable vocabulary, a repertoire of phrases that can work in conversation, abilities in understanding and participating in discourse, and with basic literacy skills. Furthermore, a first year secondary foreign language class will contain pupils at a range of levels of proficiency in the language.

I would suggest that both motivational and learning needs could be helped by a change of approach at this point. The spoken language that children have learnt can be used as a resource for exploring the language system more explicitly, developing metalanguage and skills of analysis, and building the language by consolidating previous knowledge, filling gaps and adding new items and structures. This is not to advocate formal and difficult grammar-based approaches. Meaning and discourse should still be central, but a more analytical approach can be taken to how the language is used. For example, vocabulary that has been learnt mainly through topic-related sets could be revised through activities with sense-relations or through computer analysis of how words are used in texts. Grammar that has been learnt through use but not explicitly described can be mapped out with learners, and examined at work in different types of discourse, such as newspaper reports or children's books. The differing language resources amongst students becomes a help in such activities, rather than a problem for the teacher, as students can share their language knowledge. Similar methodology has been developed in 'language awareness' for both first and second language learning (e.g. Bolitho and Tomlinson 1980; Kowal and Swain 1994), helping children reflect on language that they already use so that they come to see, understand and name patterns, and to use them to generate new language.

The content of language lessons will also need attention – many secondary books contain topics that will be all too familiar to students who have learnt the foreign language from a young age. The international and global uses of the major foreign languages might become a content-focus at secondary level. If topics, such as 'The Family', are revisited, then more demanding aspects will have to feature, e.g. different types of family structure in different cultures.

In terms of literacy skills, an early start will produce a greater range of skills at later stages; this would suggest that there will need to be more emphasis both on remedial reading and writing in the foreign language and, for those who are succeeding, on extending their skills to reading and writing in more genres.

Schools will also need to keep and pass on accurate and detailed records of each child's language learning, if the best use is to be made of early lessons. Cross-phase planning at local level by teachers from schools will be helpful.

11.4 Teaching foreign languages to children

What colour are the stars?
（child overheard on a train, questioning her mother）

Do we live one big life, or do we all live separate lives?
（7 year old）

Aiming to theorise children's foreign language learning has meant that much of this book has been analytical and conceptual. In this final section, I would like to return to my motivation for writing the book, which is continuing amazement and excitement at how children think and learn.

Children bring to language learning their curiosity and eagerness to make sense of the world. They will tackle the most demanding tasks with enthusiasm and willingness. Too often, these early gifts are turned to fear and failure. I hope that this book will remind readers of the potential that lies in every child and that, by tracing some of the connections and discontinuities between learning and teaching, it will add to the tools we have available to maximise the positive impact of what happens in classrooms.

REFERENCES

Adams, M. J. 1990. *Beginning to Read*. Cambridge, MA: M.I.T. Press.

Ahmed, M. O. 1988. Vocabulary learning strategies. In P. Meara (ed.). *Beyond Words*. London: CILT.

Anderson, A. and T. Lynch. 1988. *Listening*. Oxford: Oxford University Press.

Arnaud, P. and H. Bejoint. (eds.). 1992. *Vocabulary and Applied Linguistics*. London: Macmillan.

Asher, J. 1972. Children's first language as a model for second language learning. *Modern Language Journal* 56, 3, 133–139.

Bakhtin, M. 1981. *The Dialogic Imagination: Four Essays*. Austin, TX: University of Texas Press.

Barsalou, L. W. 1987. The instability of graded structure: Implications for the nature of concepts. In U. Neisser (ed.). *Concepts and Conceptual Development: Ecological and Intellectual Factors in Categorization*. Cambridge: Cambridge University Press.

Barton, D. 1994. *Literacy: An Introduction to the Ecology of Written Language*. Oxford: Blackwell.

Bates, E. and B. MacWhinney. 1989. Functionalism and the competition model. In B. MacWhinney and E. Bates (eds.). *The Cross-linguistic Study of Sentence Processing*. New York: Cambridge University Press.

Bates, E., B. MacWhinney, C. Caselli, A. Devescovi, F. Natale and V. Venza. 1984. A Cross-Linguistic Study of the Development of Sentence Interpretation Strategies. *Child Development* 55: 341–354.

Batstone, R. 1995. *Grammar*. Oxford: Oxford University Press.

Beard, R. (ed.). 1993. *Teaching Literacy, Balancing Perspectives*. London: Hodder and Stoughton.

Bettelheim, B. 1976. *The Uses of Enchantment: The Meaning and Importance of Fairy Tales*. New York: Knopf.

Bivens, J. A. and L. E. Berk. 1990. A longitudinal study of the development of elementary school children's private speech. *Merrill-Palmer Quarterly*, 36: 443–463.

Bolitho, R. and B. Tomlinson, 1980. *Discover English*. London: Heinemann.

Breen, M. 1984. Authenticity in the language classroom. *Applied Linguistics*. 6, 1: 60–70.

Breen, M. 1987. Contemporary paradigms in syllabus design: (Parts 1 and 2). *Language Teaching*. 20: 91–92 and 157–174.

Brewster, J., G. Ellis and D. Girard. 1992. *The Primary Teacher's Guide*. Harmondsworth: Penguin.

Brown, G. and G. Yule. 1983. *Teaching the Spoken Language*. Cambridge: Cambridge University Press.

References

Brumfit, C., J. Moon and R. Tongue (eds.). 1991. *Teaching English to Children: From Practice to Principle*. London: Nelson.

Bruner, J. 1983. *Child's Talk: Learning to Use Language*. Oxford: Oxford University Press.

Bruner, J. 1986. *Actual Minds, Possible Worlds*. Cambridge, MA: Harvard University Press.

Bruner, J. 1990. *Acts of Meaning*. Cambridge, MA: Harvard University Press.

Bryant, P. and L. Bradley. 1985. *Children's Reading Problems*. Oxford: Basil Blackwell.

Cameron, L. 1994. Organising the world: Children's concepts and categories, and implications for the teaching of English. *ELT Journal*, 48: 28–39.

Cameron, L. 1997. The task as unit for teacher development. *ELT Journal*, 51, 4: 345–351.

Cameron, L. 1999. Co-adaptation of task and language use. Paper presented at Symposium on Task-based Learning, University of Leeds, 14–15 Jan., 1999.

Cameron. L. 2001. *Metaphor in Educational Discourse*. London: Continuum.

Cameron, L. and M. Bava Harji. 2000. Using stories with young learners. Paper presented at IATEFL Conference, Dublin, 27–31 March.

Carter, R. and M. McCarthy. 1988. *Vocabulary and Language Teaching*. London: Longman

Clay, M. 1982. *Observing Young Readers*. London: Heinemann Educational.

Coady, J. and T. Huckin. (eds.). 1997. *Second Language Vocabulary Acquisition*. Cambridge: Cambridge University Press.

Cook, G. 1997. Language play, language learning. *ELT Journal*, 51, 224–231.

Coughlan, P. and P. Duff. 1994. Same task, different activities: Analysis of a SLA task from an Activity Theory perspective. In J. Lantolf and G. Appel (eds.).*Vygotskyan Approaches to Second Language Research*. New York: Ablex. pp 173–194.

Craik, F. and R. Lockhart. 1972. Levels of processing: A framework for memory research. *Journal of Verbal Learning and Verbal Behavior*, 11, 671–684.

Dechant, E. 1991. *Understanding and Teaching Reading: An Interactional Model*. Hillsdale, NJ: Erlbaum.

Doff, A. 1988. *Teach English: A Training Course for Teachers*. Cambridge: Cambridge University Press.

Donaldson, M. 1978. *Children's Minds*. London: Fontana.

Dossena, M. 1997. Testing oral production at primary level: What means for what ends? In A. C. McLean (ed.). *SIG Selections 1997: Special Interests in ELT*. Whitstable: IATEFL: 110–114.

Doughty, P. and J. Williams. (eds.). 1998. *Focus on Form in the Second Language Classroom*. Cambridge: Cambridge University Press.

Driscoll, P. and D. Frost (eds.). 1999. *The Teaching of Modern Foreign Languages in the Primary School*. London: Routledge.

Dulay, H., M. Burt and S. Krashen. 1982. *Language Two*. Oxford: Oxford University Press.

Dunn, O. 1984. *Teaching English to Children*. London: Macmillan.

Elley, W. 1989. Vocabulary acquisition from listening to stories. *Reading Research Quarterly*, XXIV, 2, 174–187.

Ellis, G. 1991. Learning to learn. In C. Brumfit, J. Moon and R. Tongue, (eds.). *Teaching English to Children*. London: Collins, 191–200.

Ellis, G. and J. Brewster, 1991. *The Story-telling Handbook*. London: Penguin Books.

Ellis, G. and B. Sinclair. 1990. *Learning to Learn English*. Cambridge: Cambridge University Press.

Ellis, R. 1994. *The Study of Second Language Acquisition*. Oxford: Oxford University Press.

Field, J. 1998. Skills and strategies: Towards a new methodology for listening. *ELT Journal*, 52, 2, 10–118.

Fotos, S. and R. Ellis. 1991. Communicating about grammar: A task-based approach. *TESOL Quarterly*, 25, 608–628.

Frith, U. 1990. *Autism: Explaining the Enigma*. Oxford: Blackwell.

Garton, A. and C. Pratt. 1998 (2nd edition). *Learning to be Literate*. Oxford: Basil Blackwell.

Garvie, E. 1990. *Story as Vehicle*. Clevedon, Avon: Multilingual Matters.

Garvie, E. 1991. An integrative approach with young learners. In C. Brumfit *et al* (eds.) *Teaching English to Children: From Practice to Principle* London: Nelson.

Genesee, F. (ed.). 1994. *Educating Second Language Children*. New York: Cambridge University Press.

Genesee, F. and J. Upshur. 1996. *Classroom-based Evaluation in Second Language Education*. New York: Cambridge University Press.

Gerngross, G. and H. Puchta. 1998. *Playway to English*. Cambridge: Cambridge University Press.

Gibson, J. J. 1979. *The Ecological Approach to Visual Perception*. Houghton Mifflin.

Gipps, C. 1994. *Beyond Testing*. Brighton: The Falmer Press.

Gipps, C. and G. Stobart. 1993. *Assessment: A Teachers' Guide to the Issues*. London: Hodder and Stoughton.

Goswami, U. 1991. Learning about spelling sequences: The role of onsets and rimes in analogies in reading. *Child Development*, 62, 1–22.

Graham, C. 1979. *Jazz Chants for Children*. New York: Oxford University Press.

Graumann, C. 1990. Perspective structure and dynamics in dialogue. In I. Markova and K. Foppa (eds.). *The Dynamics of Dialogue*. London: Harvester Wheatsheaf.

Greenwood, J. 1997. *Activity Box*. Cambridge: Cambridge University Press.

Grieve, R. and M. Hughes. 1990. *Understanding Children*. Oxford: Blackwell.

Hall, N. 1987. *The Emergence of Literacy*. Sevenoaks, Kent: Hodder and Stoughton.

Halliwell, S. 1992. *Teaching English in the Primary Classroom*. London: Longman.

Hancock, M. 1997. Behind classroom code-switching: Layering and language choice in L2 learner interaction. *TESOL Quarterly*, 31, 2: 217–235.

References

Harley, B. 1994. Appealing to consciousness in the L2 classroom. *AILA Review* 11: 57–68.

Harley, B., J. Howard and D. Hart. 1995. Second language processing at different ages: Do younger learners pay more attention to prosodic cues than sentence structure? *Language Learning 45*, 1: 43–71.

Harley, B. and M. Swain. 1984. The interlanguage of immersion students and its implications for second language teaching. In A. Davies, C. Criper and A. Howatt. (eds.). *Interlanguage*. Edinburgh: Edinburgh University Press.

Hatch, E. and C. Brown. 1995. *Vocabulary, Semantics, and Language Education*. Cambridge: Cambridge University Press.

Hoey, M. 1983. *On the Surface of Discourse*. London: Allen and Unwin.

Holderness, J. 1991. Activity-based teaching: Approaches to topic-centred work. In C. Brumfit *et al.* (eds.). *Teaching English to Children: from practice to principle*. London: Nelson.

Hsia, S., P. K. Chung and D. Wong. 1995. ESL learners' word organisation strategies: A case of Chinese learners of English words in Hong Kong. *Language and Education, 9,* 2, 81–102.

Hudelson, S. 1994. Literacy development of second language children. In F. Genesee (ed.). *Educating Second Language Children*. Cambridge: Cambridge University Press.

Hunston, S. and G. Francis. 1998. Verbs observed: A corpus-driven pedagogic grammar. *Applied Linguistics, 19,* 45–72.

Hurrell, A. 1999. The four language skills: The whole works! In P. Driscoll and D. Frost (eds.). *The Teaching of Modern Foreign Languages in the Primary School*. London: Routledge, 67–87.

Karmiloff-Smith, A. 1986. Some fundamental aspects of language development after age 5. In P. Fletcher and P. Garman (eds.). *Language Acquisition*. 2nd edition. Cambridge: Cambridge University Press.

Kennedy, C. and J. Jarvis (eds.). 1991. *Ideas and Issues in Primary ELT*. London: Nelson.

Kim, K. S., N. Relkin, K-M Lee and J. Hisch. 1997. Distinct cortical areas associated with native and second languages. *Nature, 388:* 171–174.

Kintsch, W. 1988. The role of knowledge in discourse comprehension: A construction-integration model. *Psychological Review, 95:* 163–182.

Klein, W. and C. Perdue. 1992. *Utterance Structure: Developing Grammars again*. Amsterdam: John Benjamins.

Koda, K. 1994. Second language reading research: Problems and possibilities. *Applied Psycholinguistics, 15,* 1–28.

Kowal, M. and M. Swain. 1994. Using collaborative language production tasks to promote students' language awareness. *Language Awareness 3,* 2: 73–93.

Krashen, S. 1982. *Principles and Practice in Second Language Acquisition*. Oxford: Pergamon.

Labov, W. 1972. *Language in the Inner City*. Oxford: Basil Blackwell.

Lakoff, G. 1987. *Women, Fire, and Dangerous Things*. Chicago: University of Chicago Press.

Lantolf, J. (ed.). 2000. *Sociocultural Theory and Second Language Learning*. Oxford: Oxford University Press.

Larsen-Freeman, D. 1997. Chaos / complexity science and second language acquisition. *Applied Linguistics*. 18, 141–165.

Lightbown, P. and N. Spada. 1994. An innovative program for primary ESL in Quebec. *TESOL Quarterly* 28,3, 563–579.

Lightbown, P. and N. Spada. 1999 (2nd edition). *How Languages are Learned*. Oxford: Oxford University Press.

Littlejohn, A. and D. Hicks. 1996. *Cambridge English for Schools*. Book one. Cambridge: Cambridge University Press.

Liu, H., E. Bates and P. Li. 1992. Sentence interpretation in bilingual speakers of English and Chinese. *Applied Psycholinguistics 13*: 451–484.

Locke, J. 1993. *The Child's Path to Spoken Language*. Cambridge, MA: Harvard University Press.

Lyons, J. 1995. *Linguistic Semantics: An Introduction*. Cambridge: Cambridge University Press.

MacWhinney, B. 1998: Models of the emergence of language. *Annual Review of Psychology*. 49: 199–227.

Marshall, S. 1963. *An Experiment in Education*. Cambridge: Cambridge University Press.

Martin, P. 1999. Close encounters of a bilingual kind: Interactional practices in the primary classroom in Brunei. *International Journal of Educational Development*, 19, 127–140.

McCafferty, S. 1994. The use of private speech by adult ESL learners at different levels of proficiency. In J. Lantolf and G. Appel (eds.). *Vygotskyan Approaches to Second Language Research*. New York: Ablex, 117–134.

McCarthy, M. and R. Carter. 1994. *Language as Discourse*. London: Longman.

McGuiness, D. 1997. *Why Children Can't Read*. London: Penguin Books.

McKay, P. 1995. Developing ESL proficiency descriptions for the school context: the NLLIA bandscales. In G. Brindley (ed.). *Language Assessment in Action*. Sydney: NCELTR.

McLaughlin, B. 1992. Restructuring. *Applied Linguistics*. 11, 2: 113–128.

McNamara, T. 1996. *Measuring Second Language Performance*. London: Longman.

Meadows, S. 1993. *The Child as Thinker*. London: Routledge.

Merrit, M., A. Cleghorn, J. Abagi and G. Bunyi. 1992. Socialising multi-lingualism: Determinants of code-switching in Kenyan primary classrooms. In C. Eastman (ed.), *Codeswitching*. Clevedon, Avon: Multilingual Matters, 103–121.

Messick, S. 1989. Validity. In R. L. Linn (ed.) *Educational Measurement*. Third Edition. Macmillan: New York. 13–104.

Miller, G. and P. Johnson-Laird. 1976. *Language and Perception*. Cambridge: Cambridge University Press.

Mitchell, R. and C. Martin. 1997. Rote learning, creativity and 'understanding' in classroom foreign language teaching. *Language Teaching Research*. 1, 1: 1–27.

References

Moon, J. 2000. *Children Learning English*. Oxford: Macmillan Heinemann.

Mullen, M. K. 1994. Earliest recollections of childhood – a demographic analysis. *Cognition*, 52, 55–79

Murphey, T. 2000. Negotiated second language learning micro and macro strategies for zoning in. Colloquium presentation at American Association for Applied Linguistics Conference, Vancouver, 11–14 March.

Murphy, R. 1994. *English Grammar in Use*. Cambridge: Cambridge University Press.

Myles, F., R. Mitchell and J. Hooper. 1999. Interrogative chunks in French L2: A basis for creative construction? *Studies in Second Language Acquisition*, 21, 49–80.

Nation, P. 1990. *Teaching and Learning Vocabulary*. New York: Heinle and Heinle.

Nation, P. 2001. *Learning Vocabulary in Another Language*. Cambridge: Cambridge University Press.

Nation, P. and R. Waring. 1997. Vocabulary size, text coverage and word lists. In N. Schmitt and M. McCarthy (eds.). *Vocabulary: Description, Acquisition and Pedagogy*. Cambridge: Cambridge University Press, 6–19.

Nattinger, J. and J. DeCarrico. 1992. *Lexical Phrases and Language Teaching*. Oxford: Oxford University Press.

Neisser, U. (ed.). 1987. *Concepts and Conceptual Development: Ecological and Intellectual Factors in Categorization*. Cambridge: Cambridge University Press.

Nelson, K. 1989. *Narratives from the Crib*. Cambridge, MA: Harvard University Press.

Nelson, K. 1996. *Language in Cognitive Development*. Cambridge: Cambridge University Press.

Nunan, D. 1989. *Designing Tasks for the Communicative Classroom*. Cambridge: Cambridge University Press.

Nunan, D. 1993. Task-based syllabus design: Selecting, grading and sequencing task. In S. Gass and G. Crookes (eds.). *Tasks in a Pedagogical Context*. Clevedon, Avon: Multilingual Matters.

Oakhill, J. and R. Beard (eds.). 1999. *Reading Development and the Teaching of Reading*. Oxford: Blackwell.

Oakhill J. and A. Garnham. 1988. *Becoming a Skilled Reader*. Oxford: Blackwell.

O'Malley, M. and L. Valdez Pierce. 1996. *Authentic Assessment for English Language Learners*. New York: Addison-Wesley.

Pennington, M. 1995. Pattern and variation in use of two languages in the Hong Kong secondary English class. *RELC Journal*, 26, 2, 80–105.

Pennington, M. 1998. Classroom discourse frames. Paper presented at American Association for Applied Linguistics Conference, Seattle, 17 March 1998.

Perera, K. 1984. *Children's Writing and Reading*. Oxford: Basil Blackwell.

Phillips, S. 1993. *Young Learners*. Oxford: Oxford University Press.

Prabhu, N.S. 1987. *Second Language Pedagogy*. Oxford: Oxford University Press.

Propp, V. 1958. *Morphology of the Folk Tale.* Austin, Texas: University of Texas Press.

Quirk, R. and S. Greenbaum. 1975. *A Student's Grammar of Contemporary English.* London: Longman.

Read, J. 2000. *Assessing Vocabulary.* Cambridge: Cambridge University Press.

Rea-Dickins, P. (ed.). 2000. *Language Testing. Special issue: Assessing Young Learners,* 17, 2.

Rea-Dickins, P. and K. Germaine. 1992. *Evaluation.* Oxford: Oxford University Press.

Rea-Dickins, P. and S. Rixon. 1997. The assessment of young learners of English as a foreign language. In C. Clapham and D. Corson (eds.). *Encyclopaedia of Language and Education. Volume 7: Language Testing and Assessment.* Amsterdam: Kluwer Academic Publishers, 151–161.

Rea-Dickins, P. and S. Rixon. 1999. Assessment of young learners' English: Reasons and means. In S. Rixon (ed.). *Young Learners of English: Some Research Perspectives.* London: Longman, British Council.

Reid, J. 1990. Children's Reading. In R. Grieve and M. Hughes (eds.). *Understanding Children.* Oxford: Basil Blackwell, 71–93.

Ricard, R. 1993. Conversational co-ordination. Collaboration for effective communication. *Applied Psycholinguistics 14:* 387–412.

Richards, J. 1976. The role of vocabulary teaching. *TESOL Quarterly,* 10, 1: 77–89.

Richardson, P. 1998. Literacy, learning, and teaching. *Educational Review,* 50, 2, 115–134.

Rixon, S. 1999. *Young Learners of English: Some Research Perspectives.* London: Longman, British Council.

Schmitt, N. 1997. Vocabulary learning strategies. In N. Schmitt and M. McCarthy (eds.). *Vocabulary: Description, Acquisition and Pedagogy.* Cambridge: Cambridge University Press, 199–227.

Schmitt, N. 1998. Tracking the incremental acquisition of Second Language vocabulary: A longitudinal study. *Language Learning,* 48, 281–317.

Schmitt, N. and P. Meara. 1997. Researching vocabulary through a word knowledge framework. *Studies in Second Language Acquisition.* 19, 17–36.

Schmitt, N. and M. McCarthy. (eds.). 1997. *Vocabulary: Description, Acquisition and Pedagogy.* Cambridge: Cambridge University Press.

Schmidt, R. 1990. The role of consciousness in second language learning. *Applied Linguistics.* 11, 2: 129–158.

Schouten-van Parreren, C. 1989. Vocabulary learning through reading: Which conditions should be met when presenting words in texts? *AILA Review 6:* 75–85.

Schouten-van Parreren, C. 1992. Individual differences in vocabulary acquisition: A qualitative experiment in the first phase of secondary education. In P. Arnaud and H. Bejoint (eds.). *Vocabulary and Applied Linguistics.* London: Macmillan, 94–101.

Scott, W. and L. Ytreberg. 1990. *Teaching English to Children.* London: Longman.

Sinclair, J. 1990. *Collins Cobuild English Grammar.* London: HarperCollins.

Singleton, D. 1999. *Exploring the second language mental lexicon.* Cambridge: Cambridge University Press.

Skehan, P. 1995. Second Language Acquisition Research and Task-based Instruction. In D. Willis and J. Willis (eds.). *Challenge and Change in Language Teaching.* London: Heinemann.

Skehan, P. 1996. A framework for the implementation of task-based instruction. *Applied Linguistics.* 17, 1: 38–62.

Slobin, D. 1985. *The Cross-linguistic Study of Language Acquisition.* Hillsdale, NJ: Erlbaum.

Snow, C. 1996. Change in child language and child linguists. In H. Coleman and L. J. Cameron (eds.). *Change and Language.* Clevedon: BAAL and Multilingual Matters Ltd.

Stanovich, K. 1980. Towards an interactive-compensatory model of individual differences in the development of reading fluency. *Reading Research Quarterly*, 16, 32–71.

Stanovich, K. 1988. The language code: Issues in word recognition. In S. R. Yussen and M. C. Smith (eds.). *Reading across the Life Span.* New York: Springer Verlag.

Street, B. 1996. *Social Literacies.* London: Longman.

Stubbs, M. 1980. *Language and Literacy.* London: RKP.

Swain, M. 1985. Communicative competence: Some roles of comprehensible input and comprehensible output in its development. In S. Gass and C. Madden (eds.). *Input in Second Language Acquisition.* Rowley, MA: Newbury House.

Swain, M. 1995. Three functions of output in second language learning. In G. Cook and B. Seidlhofer (eds.). *Principles and Practice in Applied Linguistics.* Oxford: Oxford University Press.

Tang, G. 1992. The effect of graphic representation of knowledge structures on ESL reading comprehension. *Studies in Second Language Acquisition.* 14: 177–195.

Tizard, B. and M. Hughes. 1984. *Young Children Learning.* London: Fontana.

Tongue, R. 1991. English as a foreign language at primary level: The search for content. In C. Brumfit *et al.* (eds.). *Teaching English to Children: From Practice to Principle.* London: Nelson: 109–114.

UCLES. 1999. *Cambridge Tests for Young Learners: Handbook.* Cambridge: University of Cambridge Local Examinations Syndicate.

Vale, D. 1990. *Early Bird 1.* Cambridge: Cambridge University Press.

Vale, D. and A. Feunteun. 1995. *Teaching Children English.* Cambridge: Cambridge University Press.

van Dijk, T. and W. Kintsch 1983. *Strategies of discourse comprehension.* New York; Academic Press.

van Geert, P. 1998. A Dynamic Systems Model of Basic Developmental Mechanisms Piaget, Vygotsky and beyond'. *Psychological Review*, 10, 4: 634–677.

van Lier, L. 1997. Observation from an ecological perspective. *TESOL Quarterly*, 31, 4: 783–786.

Van Patten, B. 1996. *Input Processing and Grammar Instruction in Second Language Acquisition*. Norwood, NJ: Ablex.

Verhallen, M. and R. Schoonen. 1993. Word definitions of monolingual and bilingual children. *Applied Linguistics*, 14, 4: 344–365.

Verhallen, M. and R. Schoonen. 1998. Lexical knowledge in L1 and L2 of third and fifth graders. *Applied Linguistics*, 19, 4: 452–470.

Verhoeven, L. 1990. Acquisition of reading in a second language. *Reading Research Quarterly*, 25, 2, 90–114.

Vygotsky, L. 1962. *Thought and Language*. New York: Wiley.

Vygotsky, L. 1978. *Mind in Society*. Cambridge, MA: Harvard University Press.

Wajnryb, R. 1990. *Grammar Dictation*. Oxford: Oxford University Press.

Waterland, L. 1985. *Read with Me: An Apprenticeship Approach to Reading*. Stroud: Thimble Press.

Weinert, R. 1994. Some Effects of a Foreign Language Classroom on the Development of German Negation. *Applied Linguistics* 15, 1: 76–101.

Wertsch, J. 1985. *Vygotsky and the Social Formation of Mind*. Cambridge, MA: Harvard University Press.

Wertsch, J. 1991. *Voices of the Mind*. Hemel Hempstead: Harvester Wheatsheaf.

Wertsch, J. 1998. *Mind as Action*. New York: Oxford University Press.

Widdowson, H. 1990. *Aspects of Language Teaching*. Oxford: Oxford University Press.

Widdowson, H. 1998. Skills, abilities and contexts of reality. *Annual Review of Applied Linguistics: Foundations of Second Language Teaching*. 18: 323–335.

Williams, E. 1998. Investigating bilingual literacy: Evidence from Malawi and Zambia. *Ed Research 24*. London: DfID.

Willis, J. 1996. *A Framework for Task-Based Learning*. London: Longman.

Wode, H. 1999. Incidental vocabulary acquisition in the foreign language classroom. *Studies in Second Language Acquisition*, 21, 243–258.

Wood, D. 1998 (2nd edition). *How Children Think and Learn*. Oxford: Blackwell.

Wood, D., J. Bruner and G. Ross 1976. The role of tutoring in problem solving. *Journal of Child Psychology and Psychiatry*. 17, 2: 89–100.

Wray, A. 1999. Formulaic language in learners and native speakers. *Language Teaching*, 32, 213–231.

Wright, A. 1995. *Storytelling with Children*. Oxford: Oxford University Press.

Wright, A. 1997. *Creating stories with Children*. Oxford: Oxford University Press.

INDEX

accommodation 3
active learners 2, 4, 6, 38
activity-based learning 182–3
affordances 5
age and FL learning 1,13–14, 16–17, 138, 243
assessment 214–240
  and evaluation 222
  and learning 218–221
  and learning goals 228
  bandscales 223
  criterion-referenced 223
  descriptors 223–224
  fairness 226–227
  feedback from 239–240
  focus 229–230, 232
  formative 222
  issues 214–218, 240
  messages from 240
  norm-referenced 223
  observation 231
  of oral skills 217
  planning 227
  portfolios 237–238
  practices 217
  record-keeping 233
  reliability 224–225
  self-assessment 233–238
  stakeholders 221
  summative 222
  testing 222
  uses 238
  validity 224–225
  washback 216
assimilation 3
attending, attention 9, 15, 20, 108, 110, 153
authenticity 30

basic level words 79–80
Bruner 8–11

choice 195, 198
chunks 50, 98, 101–2, 111, 173
classroom language 10, 112, 195, 200–209
communicative stretching 192
Competition model 14–15, 104, 134–6
computers 155, 156, 158, 193, 194, 244
content words 82, 83
context of learning 229

conversation 51, 52
core activity in a task 32
corrective feedback 113
Critical Period hypothesis 13–14
cues to meaning 14–15, 20

description task 43–51, 56, 118
dialogues 68–70
dictogloss 119
discourse skills 12, 13, 16, 18, 36 on, 245
  assessment 230
discourse skills development
  spoken 51–57
  written 154–7
  from stories 176–8
  from themes 192–195
discourse event 37
drills 117
dynamics
  of language choice 205
  of language use and learning 50
  of task demands and support 26
  of testing 216
  of vocabulary learning 84
dynamic congruence 30

extended talk 51

feedback 203, 212
  corrective 239
  evaluative 239
  from assessment 238–240
  peer 196
  strategic 240
first language
  acquisition 11–13
  and FL learning 14–15
  and grammar 104
  compensatory use 202
  strategic use 202
  use in FL classrooms 200–205
focus on form 107–110
follow-up stage of a task 32
foreign-ness of culture 12, 241
formats 9, 143–144
formulaic language 49, 50, 101–102
function words 82

genre theory 127

goals for language learning 22, 28–29
  learners setting goals 237
grammar 18, 96–122, 245
  and communicative language teaching 106, 108
  and discourse 111
  assessment 230
  development 101
  internal grammar 100
  learning-centred grammar 110
  metalanguage 106, 120–1, 245
  noticing 108–9, 114–6
  pedagogic grammars 99
  proceduralising 109, 118
  structuring 109, 116–8
  theoretical grammars 99
grammar-translation 105
graphics 23, 33

hypothesis testing 102–4

immersion 11, 17, 107
information gap 117
information processing 41
inner speech 5, 196
input 41
intelligence 6,
internalisation 7, 8, 20
interpersonal 7
intrapersonal 7

language components 17–19
language choice 199–213
  deliberate 199, 213
  discipline 212
  feedback 203, 212
  interpersonal factors 202–203
  socio-cultural context 204
  switching 205
  teacher responsibility 209, 213
learner autonomy 233–238
learning-centred perspective 1, 2, 218, 241–242
listening 40–42
  activities 60–66, 114–115, 175
  to stories 175
literacies 159
literacy skills 18, 123–158, 245
  and age 138
  and first language 134
  emergent literacy 126, 145–146
  from stories 178–179
  grapho-phonemic relationships 133, 153
  key words 148
  independent reading 151
  language experience approach 147
  literacy events 125, 143

objectives to age 7 139
  phonics reaching 149–150
  reading strategies 151–152
  skilled reading 127–134
literate environment 140–2

meaning, accessibility 36, 39
meaning, personal 48
metalanguage 106, 120–121, 211
modelling 16, 97, 156, 196
morphemes 131
motivation, long-term 240, 245
multi-sensory experience 142

narrative 12, 54–56, 161, 165, 168, 172

opportunities, for learning 4, 5, 10, 19, 20, 21, 209
output 41

paradigmatic discourse 56
paradigmatic word knowledge 78–79
past tense 33
pedagogic issues 243
Piaget 2–5, 38
plurilingual education 182, 244
precision in language use 198
preparation stage of a task 32
principles, of learning 19–20
private speech 196
puppets 114

quizzes 116

readiness 4
reading aloud 141, 157, 175
research agenda 242–243
rhymes 29, 65
routines 8, 9, 10–11, 143–144

scaffolding 8, 28, 35, 38, 152, 219
secondary school language learning 94, 244
self-assessment 233–238
self-regulation 235
sense, making 4, 19, 38
sense relations 83
social interaction 5, 18, 20, 214, 220, 242
sociocultural theory 5
songs 29, 70, 137, 140, 149
space for growth 10, 20, 27, 28
speaking 36
  and listening 40–42
  and listening activities 60–66
  and writing 66–68
spelling 127
stage theory 4

Index

stories 9–10, 40, 70, 159–179
  choosing 167–169
  contrast in 164
  dialogue in 165, 168, 172, 176
  discourse organisation of 160–162, 168, 172
  fairy tales 161
  intertextuality 165
  language use in 163–166, 169, 172
  literacy skills 178–179
  metaphor 165
  parallelism 163
  quality 166
  real books 167, 170
  using stories 169–175, 179
  vocabulary 91, 163–164, 174–175
syllables 131–2

target language use 199, 209–213
tasks 29–31
  as environment for learning 21
  as plan and task as action 35, 42–51
  demands 21, 22–28
  from stories 172–175
  in theme-based learning 189–190
  stages 31–32
  support 21, 25–28, 58–60
teaching, effect on learning 16
thematic meaning 78
theme-based teaching 29, 159, 180–198
  content 182, 186
  discourse in 187, 190, 192
  issues 180–181
  language learning 191–198
  origins 181–182
  outcomes 194
  planning 184–190
  tasks 189–190
  texts 193
  topics 181, 185
  types 182–184
  vocabulary 188, 191–2
Total Physical Response 107
translation 91, 205, 208, 210

understanding 38, 40–42, 211

vocabulary 18, 72–95, 245
  and grammar 72, 97
  assessment 230
  development 72, 73–74
  extending 90
  in theme-based teaching 188
  learning strategies 92–94
  memorising 87
  new words 85
  organisation 87–89
  progression 94–95
  recycling 84
  size 74–75
  text books 90
  translating 91, 208
Vygotsky 5–8, 38, 73, 126, 196, 218

whole language approach 183
words 7, 18, 73
  cultural content 80
  form 86
  knowing a word 75–78
  in reading 130
writing skills 155–7, 177, 194

zone of proximal development 6, 7, 10, 11, 13, 20, 26, 28, 192